Indo-Pacific Focus

The series aim to conduct in-depth and dynamic studies on the new and emerging issues and the new trends of the contemporary geo-politics of the Indo-Pacific region. It covers the key economic, political, diplomatic, security, social and cultural issues in the Indo-Pacific region, mainly including the BRI, regional integration, multilateral cooperation, physical connectivity, economic corridor, debt issue, resource exploitation, great power rivalry, political development, maritime security, terrorism/counter-terrorism, poverty reduction, ethnic and religious tensions, etc. It also predicts the possible directions of the future of the geo-politics and geo-economy in the Indo-Pacific region by incorporating the most recent developments. It tries to create a main platform for the Asian and African scholars to compete with the West-centered views on the mentioned topics by inviting experts from East Asia, South/Southeast Asia, Middle East and Africa to contribute books/chapters.

Nian Peng · Ming Yu Cheng
Editors

The Reality and Myth of BRI's Debt Trap

Evidences from Asia and Africa

Springer

Editors
Nian Peng
Research Center for Indian Ocean Island Countries
South China University of Technology
Guangzhou, China

Ming Yu Cheng
Institute of Management and Leadership Development
Universiti Tunku Abdul Rahman
Kampar, Malaysia

ISSN 2731-8869 ISSN 2731-8877 (electronic)
Indo-Pacific Focus
ISBN 978-981-97-1055-3 ISBN 978-981-97-1056-0 (eBook)
https://doi.org/10.1007/978-981-97-1056-0

This Springer imprint is published by the registered company Springer Nature Singapore Pte Ltd.
The registered company address is: 152 Beach Road, #21-01/04 Gateway East, Singapore 189721, Singapore

Contents

Editors and Contributors

About the Editors

Nian Peng is an Associate Professor and Research Fellow at the Department of Foreign Languages and Research Center for Indian Ocean Island Countries, South China University of Technology, Guangzhou, China. He is also the Director of the Hong Kong Research Center for Asian Studies (RCAS), Hong Kong. He holds a PhD in Government and International Studies at Hong Kong Baptist University. His main research interests are in the areas of China's relations with Southeast Asian/South Asian states, the Belt and Road Initiative (BRI), and maritime security of the Indo-Pacific. He authored nearly 10 books and more than 20 papers in SSCI/SCOPUS/CSSCI-indexed journals. Recent publications include *Populism, Nationalism and South China Sea Dispute: Chinese and Southeast Asian Perspectives* (Singapore: Springer Nature, 2022). His refereed articles have been notably published in *Ocean Development and International Law*, *Pacific Focus*, *Asian Affairs*, etc. He also contributes his perspectives to various local and international media outlets such as *The Diplomat* in the United States, *East Asian Forum* in Australia, *Bangkok Post* in Thailand, etc. Email: jixi2212@163.com.

Ming Yu Cheng is currently a Professor at the Faculty of Accountancy and Management, Director of the Institute of Management and Leadership Development and Chairperson of the Belt and Road Strategic Research Centre at Universiti Tunku Abdul Rahman, Malaysia. She is also a Nonresident Senior Fellow at the Hong Kong Research Center for Asian Studies (RCAS), Hong Kong. She works on a number of projects related to economic development, particularly social capital, globalization, human capital development and competitiveness studies. Her recent interests are in science & technology and industry linkages, STEM education and socio-economic aspects of the Fourth Industrial Revolution, as well as the BRI. She was a fellow of the Japan Society for the Promotion of Science Fellowship, a Fulbright Visiting Scholar at Washington State University, the United States, a Research Fellow at the Lee Kuan Yew School of Public Policy, National University of Singapore, Singapore, and a Visiting Professor at National Taiwan University, Taiwan. In 2011, she was selected to join the Young Global Leader Forum of the World Economic Forum. Email: chengmy@utar.edu.my.

Contributors

Candra Fajri Ananda Faculty of Economics and Business, Universitas Brawijaya, Malang, Indonesia

Alvin Camba Josef Korbel School of International Studies, University of Denver, Denver, CO, USA

Hari Prakash Chand Department of International Relations, Tribhuvan University, Kathmandu, Nepal

Neak Chandarith Institute for International Studies and Public Policy, Royal University of Phnom Penh, Phnom Penh, Cambodia

Sypha Chanthavong Faculty of Law and Political Science, National University of Laos, Vientiane Capital, Lao PDR

Ming Yu Cheng Faculty of Accountancy and Management, Universiti Tunku Abdul Rahman, Kampar, Malaysia

Michael Mitchell Omoruyi Ehizuelen Institute of African Studies, Zhejiang Normal University, Jinhua, China

Risyaf Fahreza Ministry of Finance, Jakarta, Indonesia

Kuk Fai Fok Faculty of Accountancy and Management, Universiti Tunku Abdul Rahman, Kampar, Malaysia

Angyu Jiang Center for International Academic Exchanges, Yunnan Academy of Social Sciences, Kunming, China

Rongchen Jiang Josef Korbel School of International Studies, University of Denver, Denver, CO, USA

Khadga Kc Department of International Relations, Tribhuvan University, Kathmandu, Nepal

Zhuo Hua Kou The Institute for Social and Cultural Research, Macau University of Science and Technology, Macau, China

Nian Peng Department of Foreign Languages and Research Center for Indian Ocean Island Countries, South China University of Technology, Guangzhou, China; Hong Kong Research Center for Asian Studies (RCAS), Hong Kong, China

Kazi Mahmudur Rahman Department of Social Sciences and Humanities, Independent University, Dhaka, Bangladesh

Myint San Dawei SEZ Management Committee, Yangon, Myanmar

Jacob Sorber Josef Korbel School of International Studies, University of Denver, Denver, CO, USA

Sok Sothearak Institute for International Studies and Public Policy, Royal University of Phnom Penh, Phnom Penh, Cambodia

Hunter Willis Josef Korbel School of International Studies, University of Denver, Denver, CO, USA

Siling Yang Institute of South Asian Studies, Yunnan Academy of Social Sciences, Kunming, China

Chapter 1
Introduction

Nian Peng and Ming Yu Cheng

Abstract This edited volume aims to advance the ongoing debate over the BRI's "debt trap" controversy within the route states by presenting compelling evidence from China, Southeast/South Asian, and African countries. This volume not only examines the origins and changes in external debt among the BRI route states before and/or after the launch of BRI, but also analyzes the outcomes stemming from the BRI projects. By doing so, a more balanced perspective on the "debt trap" narrative of the BRI projects is presented. It challenges the Western-centric notion of "Dept Trap Diplomacy", which has dominated discussions of BRI projects. The analysis also provides policy recommendations to effectively address the rising debt of the BRI route states, thereby mitigating the negative impacts of the BRI debt and fostering sustainable economic growth in these countries.

Keywords China · Asia · Africa · BRI · Debt

Since the announcement of the Belt and Road Initiative (BRI) by Chinese President Xi Jinping in 2013, the new term "debt trap/debt trap diplomacy" was created and popularized in the West to criticize the BRI projects in the underdeveloped/developing countries in Asia, Africa, Oceania and Latin America. The term "debt trap" or "debt trap diplomacy" is used to assert China's deliberate attempt to extend financial support to countries along the BRI, with the intention of increasing the debt

N. Peng (✉)
Department of Foreign Languages and Research Center for Indian Ocean Island Countries, South China University of Technology, Guangzhou, China
e-mail: jixi2212@163.com

Hong Kong Research Center for Asian Studies (RCAS), Hong Kong, China

M. Y. Cheng
Faculty of Accountancy and Management, Universiti Tunku Abdul Rahman, Kampar, Malaysia
e-mail: chengmy@utar.edu.my

N. Peng and M. Y. Cheng (eds.), *The Reality and Myth of BRI's Debt Trap*, Indo-Pacific Focus, https://doi.org/10.1007/978-981-97-1056-0_1

burden of these countries for China to achieve its political goals. The implementation of such programs is seen as a move by China to advance its strategic interests, including expanding its diplomatic influence, securing natural resources, promoting the international use of its currency, and gaining a relative advantage over other powers.

The most recent criticism of BRI's "debt trap" came from AidData, a US-based research institute at Virginia's College of William and Mary, specializing in tracking development finance. On November 6, 2023, two weeks after the Third Belt and Road Forum for International Cooperation held in Beijing in late October 2023, AidData claimed that China is owed more than a trillion US dollars (USD) through its BRI projects, making it the biggest debt collector in the world. It is estimated that China has financed almost 21,000 projects across 165 countries with 1.1 trillion USD in the past two decades, in which 80% of the loans were supporting countries in financial distress.[1]

Chinese Foreign Ministry Spokesperson, Wang Wenbin, soon refuted that "China-made debt-traps" are nothing but a narrative trap created by some forces to disrupt and jeopardize China's cooperation with other developing countries. He also elaborated on China's response to the debt issue of BRI as follows:

- First of all, this "debt trap" rhetoric goes against economic common sense. As we all know, a healthy, right amount of debt is conducive to socioeconomic development. Many countries take government debt as an important form of raising funds and lever for economic development. Anyone who talks about only the negatives of debt without mentioning its benefits or even portrays it as a poison for development is simply being ill-informed or amateurish.
- This "debt trap" rhetoric also runs counter to facts. China's investment and financing cooperation with other countries focuses on infrastructure and production sectors and has successfully helped developing countries address lack of funding, infrastructure and talents and other development bottlenecks and enhance their self-driven development capacity. A report by the US-based Boston University Global Development Policy Center noted that the investment and financing cooperation between China and fellow developing countries could help these countries to overcome bottlenecks in development, unlock growth potential and increase global real income by up to three percentage points. To describe development resources as a "debt trap" is to call whiteblack.
- This "debt trap" rhetoric wrongly pictures the will of the developing countries. Investment and financing cooperation between China and fellow developing countries is carried out in compliance with international rules, market laws and the principle of debt sustainability. Widely welcomed in the developing world, it offers a good choice for debt-laden countries to meet funding shortfalls and boost economic growth. Leaders of developing countries have noted that China shows up where and when the West will not or are reluctant to and is a true good friend. In fact, as we have seen, not a single cooperation partner has accused China of

[1] China is owed over $1tr in Belt and Road debt: report (2023).

> creating "debt traps". It is a handful of Western countries that have been spreading the fallacy of "Chinese debt traps". The multilateral financial institutions and commercial creditors these countries dominate are the major creditors of developing countries and constitute the major source of stress for them in terms of debt repayment. They are the ones that need to make substantive contributions to easing developing countries' debt burden.[2]

This is the latest and most comprehensive official position from the Chinese government on the so-called "debt trap" narrative of BRI. It sent at least four clear messages, that are, BRI brings both debt burden and socioeconomic benefits to the route states, it is unfair to overestimate the "debt trap" while ignoring the benefits as well; China aims to facilitate the economic growth of the BRI route states rather than causing "debt trap" for them; it is the West that spread the fallacy of "Chinese debt traps" rather than the BRI route states; China is not the main creditor to the BRI route states and thus should not be blamed for causing "debt trap" to these states.

We do not deny the existence of debt-related challenges in the implementation of BRI projects. However, whether China is the chief culprit of the growing debt of the BRI route states deserves further examination. In fact, rising debt, internally and externally, is a common problem the world states face together, particularly in developing and less developed nations. In general, the debt of the host country tends to rise when construction projects are financed by foreign nations, whether from China or the West. Therefore, it would be unfair to attribute heavy debt solely to projects invested by Chinese firms in the BRI route states.

Moreover, as pointed out by the AidData, China is making efforts to reduce risks associated with the BRI by aligning its lending practices more closely with international standards. This involves allowing key BRI lenders to settle principal and interest payments by "unilaterally sweeping" the foreign currency reserves held in escrow by borrowing countries.[3] In fact, China has taken various measures to address the debt issues associated with the mega projects under the BRI. For instance, China agreed to the third country's participation in BRI projects, such as Saudi Arabia's investment in the China-Pakistan Economic Corridor (CPEC). Indeed, the main focus on BRI should go beyond mere criticism of the "debt trap". Instead, the emphasis should be on finding solutions to address the debt challenges, thereby fostering the economic growth of the BRI route states. Addressing the debt issue should be the top priority for both China and the BRI route states, as well as the Western countries.

Given this, this edited volume has not only examined the origins and the evolution of the external debt of the BRI route states before and/or after the launch of BRI, but also revealed the benefits brought by BRI projects. In doing so, it aims to present a balanced view on the "debt trap" (rather than to challenge the Western-centric "debt-trap" narrative of BRI projects) and BRI projects. This book also offers policy recommendations to effectively address the rising debt of the BRI route states, thereby

[2] Foreign Ministry Spokesperson Wang Wenbin's Regular Press Conference on November 7, 2023 (2023).

[3] China is owed over $1tr in Belt and Road debt: report (2023).

minimizing the negative effects of BRI debt and promoting economic development in these countries.

Although there are other studies examining the "debt trap" phenomenon associated with the BRI, this study makes a significant contribution by incorporating local viewpoints and evidence from Asian and African perspectives. Government officials, university scholars, researchers and think tank experts from China, South and Southeast Asia as well as Africa were invited to share their insights and engage in discussions on this emerging issue. The broad approach and extensive coverage of all relevant countries makes this book a valuable resource not just for a specific academic community. It is appealing to a diverse readership, including academics, policymakers, journalists, and general readers.

The main content of the book is divided into 12 parts. In Chap. 1, *Nian Peng* and *Ming Yu Cheng* provide an overview of the book. In Chap. 2, *Zhuo Hua Kou* and *Nian Peng* seek to clarify the misunderstandings of BRI's "debt trap" from the West and probably some BRI route states by investigating the debt situation in the route states which received most of the BRI investments and analyzing China's solutions to solve the debt issue on BRI projects. While they acknowledge that debt concerns pose a significant challenge for several large BRI projects, they reject the notion of a Chinese-engineered "debt trap" or "debt trap diplomacy". To provide a better understanding of the implications of BRI projects, this chapter meticulously examines the debt situation of some of the BRI route states and shed lights on the mutual benefits generated by BRI projects. It also analyzes China's efforts to solve the debt issue associated with the BRI and provides an update on its progress. The Chapter concludes that the adverse impacts of the debt issues associated with BRI projects are likely to diminish substantially in the near future.

In Chap. 3, *Si Ling Yang* and *Ang Yu Jiang* reveal that India is actually the first country that proposed the "debt trap theory" about BRI and analyze India's hype on the "debt trap theory" in Sri Lanka, Pakistan, Nepal and the Maldives. They argue that India's "debt trap theory" presents the characteristics and trend of "internal and external interaction" and "Indo-Western linkage". On the one hand, the "debt trap theory" is effective if state solidarity did not exist; on the other hand, India and the West can form a power political tradition based on realism. Although the "debt trap theory" was hyped by Indian scholars and the Indian media, it has been internalized into India's power political strategy. This has been verified in the change of power in Maldives. In India's "debt trap theory", the island country Maldives has unparalleled typical significance in the Indian Ocean. It is hard to tell whether the signal releasers and the actors of the "debt trap theory" believe in the "debt trap", but for Indians, who believe in the power tradition, the truth is secondary. What is important is that in the change of state power in Maldives, India has made full use of the "debt trap theory" as the starting point to exert the power and political influence among countries.

In Chap. 4, *Myint San* investigates the debt issue of Myanmar by conducting case study of the China-Myanmar Economic Corridor (CMEC). He points out that the policy-makers in Myanmar have cautioned about BRI-CMEC project activities and learned lessons from the experience of debt issues in other developing countries.

Given the complex and controversial nature of the "debt trap" concept, the responsibilities will be on both sides of the creditors and debtors. Greater debt transparency and international standards of lending are critical in addressing the risks posed by rising debt in many developing countries. Presently, because of the enduring influence of the COVID-19 pandemic and the changing global geo-politics on the national economy, Myanmar is facing difficulties in servicing its debt obligations to China. China is also trying to help Myanmar in debt restructuring, including partial debt forgiveness on a case-by-case method.

In Chap. 5, *Neak Chandarith* and *Sok Sothearak* examine the main causes and potential risks of the rising external debt of Cambodia. They conclude that Cambodia's external public debt stocks have raised concerns over debt sustainability and China's growing influence on the country, but the risk of Cambodia's external public debt is low. They find the main reasons: first, most of the debt has been used for prioritized infrastructure projects implemented under public–private partnership schemes; second, Cambodia has a well-regarded debt management framework with specific conditions, indicators, and ceilings; third, the country's external public debt has been very conservative and highly concessional; fourth, Cambodia has a large foreign exchange reserve compared to its public debt and debt obligation; fifth, Cambodia has been using a diversification strategy as its agency for bargaining. Nonetheless, they claim that there are some potential risks to Cambodia's external debt. They mainly include the private debt-which is unpredictable and for which there is no management framework in place yet; the exposure of Cambodia's GDP to export shock; and suboptimal government revenue mobilization.

In Chap. 6, *Sypha Chanthavong* examines the positive and negative impacts of the Laos-China Railway. He posits that this railway plays a significant role in the economic integration of Laos with neighboring countries and serves the passing service policy of the Lao government. Both state and local people generate income from the train. Nonetheless, the resettlement program and social and environmental concerns during the construction and operation have imposed potential risks to the smooth run of the railway project.

In Chap. 7, *Alvin Camba* and his students investigate to what extent the "debt trap" argument applies to the Philippines. They examine the BRI projects during the Duterte and Marcos eras and argue that the "debt trap" has no empirical backing in the Philippines. Instead, the "debt trap" argument has become a misnomer, a distraction to the broader issues brought about by Chinese development finance and foreign investments in the Philippines. They illustrate this argument through an analysis of international and Filipino writers about China in the Philippines, an examination of the Philippines' macroeconomic data, and a discussion of the BRI projects under the Duterte and Marcos administrations. They also propose three recommendations to increase the effectiveness of implementing BRI projects in the Philippines.

In Chap. 8, *Ming Yu Cheng* and *Kuk Fai Fok* analyze Malaysia's participation in BRI by focusing on the types of BRI projects, financing mechanisms, and economic implications for Malaysia. They deem that the impact of the BRI projects on Malaysia's debt sustainability is contingent on the commitment and approaches of both the lender and recipient. They find that Malaysia's manageable external debts, coupled with strong export earnings and economic growth prospects, create a positive outlook, and Malaysia's exposure to Chinese debt is manageable and comparatively low. However, they suggest that the governments of Malaysia and China work closely to enhance transparency in loan negotiations, mitigate potential risks, and channel financial resources towards viable projects to ensure sustainable BRI development in Malaysia.

In Chap. 9, *Candra Fajri Ananda* and *Risyaf Fahreza* discuss the "debt trap" narrative of the BRI projects in Indonesia, linked to government debt management, fiscal sustainability, and development agendas. They point out that most BRI projects in Indonesia have brought economic benefits to local communities and the whole country. More importantly, the Indonesian government is in a strong financial position, can handle different economic situations and manage debt wisely to achieve development goals. Therefore, the idea that the BRI projects will lead to a debt risk in Indonesia seems more like a myth than reality. Nevertheless, they remind that the Indonesian government still needs to remain vigilant and take several policy measures to mitigate the debt risks of the BRI projects, the Jakarta-Bandung high-speed rail project in particular.

In Chap. 10, *Kazi Mahmudur Rahman* assesses Bangladesh's worries over the goals and repercussions of the Chinese BRI projects while keeping Bangladesh's debt repayment commitments in mind by analyzing the larger economic effects and implications of the BRI projects. He claims that China is providing a substantial amount of funding for Bangladesh's numerous development projects via BRI, and the BRI provides a chance for Bangladesh to grow in financial markets and expand its infrastructure. In order to mitigate the debt risk of the BRI projects, he suggests that Bangladesh must apply more vigilance in areas of governance, foreign exchange movements, debt repayment strategy, effective execution of projects, corruption concerns, transparency and so on to avoid falling into a "debt trap"; Bangladesh should review the realities of the debt position, gauge honest projections, and estimate the expected risks before establishing debt repayment agreements.

In Chap. 11, *Khadga KC* and *Hari Prakash Chand* investigate the reality and myth of BRI's "debt trap" from a Nepali perspective. They point out that although no projects have begun under the BRI till now, some narratives of BRI's "debt trap" have emerged in Nepal. They conclude that the narrative produced in Nepal about BRI's "debt trap" is a little much myth rather than reality. Therefore, Nepal should continue with the BRI projects on the basis of Nepal's major priorities and national interests. For it, Nepal should deal with the Chinese counterpart for grants first and the rest of the amount can be managed from the soft loans.

In Chap. 12, *Ehizuelen Michael Mitchell Omoruyi* examines the potential economic benefits and challenges of BRI in the development of railway projects with an emphasis on Abuja-Kaduna and Lagos-Ibadan Standard Gauge Railway (SGR). He also investigates the emergence of a debt burden in the continent of Africa and how Africa and China would engage in the future to bolster Africa-China relations in the BRI projects. He finds that (i) the Chinese-built SGR will bring about the socioeconomic development of Nigeria, (ii) from the levy levied on containerized conveyance, the SGR will contribute revenue to the Nigerian government, and (iii) through better rail connectivity, the SGR will help bolster trade and regional integration. He recommends having more stakeholder involvement in the BRI projects and reviewing the funding mechanism to make borrowing more affordable, so as to make the BRI projects more transparent.

Finally, it should be highlighted that this book is a joint work of scholars from China, Southeast/South Asia and Africa, the anonymous reviewers, as well as the editors at Springer Nature. It also should be appreciated for Miss. Jia Yuan Yuan's editing service for all the reference. It cannot be completed without their kind cooperation and assistance. All the views in this book do not represent the affiliations of the editor and contributors, and all of the shortcomings are the responsibility of the authors.

References

China is owed over $1tr in Belt and Road debt: report", *Down*, November 8, 2023. https://www.dawn.com/news/1787406

"Foreign Ministry Spokesperson Wang Wenbin's Regular Press Conference on November 7, 2023", Chinese Ministry of Foreign Affairs, November 7, 2023. https://www.fmprc.gov.cn/eng/xwfw_665399/s2510_665401/2511_665403/202311/t20231107_11175486.html

Chapter 2
Misunderstandings of BRI's "Debt Trap": Chinese Perspectives

Zhuo Hua Kou and Nian Peng

Abstract The "debt trap/debt trap diplomacy" narrative has long been created by the West to criticize China's BRI since its inauguration in 2013. This chapter acknowledges that the debt issue is a major obstacle to several big BRI projects, but it rejects recognizing the so-called "debt trap/debt trap diplomacy" targeting China. To convince the public, this chapter carefully examines the debt situation of the BRI route states and demonstrates the mutual benefits brought by the BRI projects. It also analyzes China's efforts to solve the debt issue associated with BRI and provides an update on its progress. It concludes that the adverse impacts of the debt issue on BRI will diminish gradually in the near future.

Keywords BRI · Debt · China · Route states · Benefits

2.1 Introduction

China's Belt and Road Initiative (BRI), which was launched in 2013 by President Xi Jinping, has attached global concerns, among which the so-called "debt trap" is one of the main concerns. It was first created by an Indian scholar in 2017, criticizing China's investment in Hambantota Port, which left a high-risk debt to the Sri Lankan government.[1] Afterwards, a rising number of academic materials and media reports have stigmatized the BRI as a "debt trap."

[1] Brahma (2017).

Z. H. Kou
The Institute for Social and Cultural Research, Macau University of Science and Technology, Macau, China
e-mail: 3220006550@student.must.edu.mo

N. Peng (✉)
Department of Foreign Languages and Research Center for Indian Ocean Island Countries, South China University of Technology, Guangzhou, China
e-mail: jixi2212@163.com

Hong Kong Research Center for Asian Studies (RCAS), Hong Kong, China

N. Peng and M. Y. Cheng (eds.), *The Reality and Myth of BRI's Debt Trap*, Indo-Pacific Focus, https://doi.org/10.1007/978-981-97-1056-0_2

The "debt trap" does not address a pure economic issue but rather a political and social issue.[2] This means that Chinese government provides large mortgages to these developing countries with a high rate of debt initially. Their financial system cannot support repaying interests and principals. These countries have constant mortgages, but their unaffordable debts are growing at high rates. In this way, China is regarded as maintaining strategic and political interests in these countries. China benefits from the achievement of priority of relations with these governments. China obtains natural resources, expands diplomatic influence, collects political support in international society, etc.

Beijing, of course, has confuted this ridiculous assertion inside and outside China. In March 2019, Chinese Foreign Minister Wang Yi clarified that "the BRI" is not a "debt trap" but a "pie" benefiting the people; it is not a "geopolitical tool" but an opportunity for common development."[3] This is the first statement from the Chinese government to clarify the concerns of some non-BRI countries on the debt issue of BRI. Previously, Chinese scholars dismissed the misrepresentation of the BRI's debt issue by indicating the great benefits of BRI and opposing the Cold War mindset of some non-BRI countries that attempted to alienate China's relations with the BRI route states.[4]

In this chapter, we will first give a brief introduction to the hot debate over the BRI's "debt trap". Second, we will discuss the main creditor of the BRI route states in the past decade, make a comparison on the debt burden of the BRI route states before and/or after the implementation of BRI in 2013, and analyze the main reasons for their increasing debt burden. Third, we will examine the mutual benefits of the BRI projects for both China and the route states. Last, we will prove that China has avoided interfering with domestic politics in the BRI route states and find solutions to overcome the debt issue with the BRI route states jointly. The final part is the conclusion. Our argument is that BRI is not the main reason why some engaged countries face growing debt issues. Conversely, BRI benefits these developing countries though it also faces challenges.

2.2 Debt Burden of the BRI Route States

In the past decade, Myanmar, Sri Lanka, and other BRI route states in Asia, Africa and Latin America were alleged to have fallen into BRI's "debt trap". For Myanmar, the Public debt and Public Guaranteed External Debt (PPG) is the largest part of foreign debt, accounts for approximately 90% of Myanmar's foreign debts.[5] PPG includes

---

[2] Xu and Li (2020)

[3] *Wang Yi: "Yi Dai Yi Lu" Bu Shi "Zhai Wu Xian Jin", Er Shi Hui Min "Xian Bing"*[Wang Yi: "BRI" Is Not A "Debt Trap", But A "Pie" Benefiting the People]", *Xin Hua Wang [Xin Hua News Agency]*, March 8, 2023, http://www.xinhuanet.com/politics/2019lh/2019-03/08/c_1210076293.htm.

[4] Chu et al. (2018).

[5] World Bank (2016).

Table 2.1 Total public and publicly guaranteed debt-estimated at end-June 2020

	USD billion	In percent of total
Bilateral creditors	**8.4**	**30.3**
Paris club	5.0	18.0
Of which: Japan	3.5	12.7
Non-Paris club	3.4	12.2
Of which China	3.1	11.3
Multilateral creditors	**2.5**	**9.2**
Of which: ADB	0.6	2.2
Of which: IDA	1.5	5.6
Of which: IMF	0.4	1.3
Commercial creditors	**0.0**	**0.1**
Domestic debt	**16.7**	**60.5**
T-bills	11.4	41.2
T-bonds	5.3	19.2
Total public debt	27.6	100.0

Source https://documents1.worldbank.org/curated/en/407791611757946285/pdf/Myanmar-Joint-World-Bank-IMF-Debt-Sustainability-Analysis.pdf

"long-term external obligations of public debtors, including the national government, Public Corporations, State Owned Enterprises, Development Banks and Other Mixed Enterprises, political subdivisions (or an agency of either), autonomous public bodies, and external obligations of private debtors that are guaranteed for repayment by a public entity." From the FY2020/2021 IMF report, bilateral debt was times that of multilateral debt, which accounted for the majority of Myanmar's PPG. In such bilateral debt relations, the Paris Club holds the main creditor. In detail, Japan was the largest creditor among the Paris Club to Myanmar.[6]

Based on the model, the PPG from the Table 2.1 indicated that at the end of June 2020, the Paris club had the highest percentage. However, the lateral credits of China demonstrate the minimum percentage. Myanmar's external debt remained at a constant low level before 2013 and after joining BRI projects. The debt sustainability framework for low-income countries (LIC-DSF) created by the IMF and World Bank (WB) evaluates the capability of debt risk-taking. Two aspects are mainly referred to: PPG and public external and internal debt. PPG in Myanmar always takes the dominant part of the overall public debt.

Myanmar's short-term external debt compared to its long-term external debt has been decreasing year by year. According to the WB, "long-term external debt is defined as debt that has an original or extended maturity of more than one year and that is owed to nonresidents by residents of an economy and repayable in currency,

[6] The Executive Board of the International Monetary Fund (IMF) (2021a).

goods, or services".[7] The lower the ratio of short-term external debt is, the more reasonable the maturity structure of external debt is. Otherwise, countries that are forced to face liquidity problems are reflected by a maturity structure of external debt that is excessively heavily concentrated in short-term maturities.[8] Therefore, after engaging with China's BRI projects, the risk of debt issues, especially external debt, declined. External debt has growing space.

According to Malaysian government official data, domestic debt takes three quarters of total debt.[9] Domestic debt overwhelmingly burdens external debt. In particular, China's loan to Malaysia's total external debt is small. Thus, the main creditor to Malaysia is not China. According to International Monetary Fund (IMF) 2021 statistics,[10] Malaysia's external debt after 2007 has been increasing at a stable rate. It reached 230 billion USD in 2020. This index seems to not be related to BRI. The indexes of general government debt and federal government debt before 2013 and after 2013 both maintained a stable level of approximately 50%. Extremely large government debt appeared in the 1980s. Short-term debt is an important index to value if the debt risk is large or not. One country's debt risk will grow as the short-term debt grows. From this perspective, Malaysia's debt risk has grown because of the short-term debt growth since this century.

Even so, Malaysia's debt burden is still under control. The federal government has a fixed amount of reserves to repay external debt, and the repayment in the last 5 years is approximately 25%, which has not reached the international caution rate of 30–50%.[11] As mentioned before, China's loan to Malaysia only takes a small amount of its total external debt, not to mention the total debt. Since Malaysia joined BRI, China's fund is a necessary source for Malaysia to construct infrastructure. The Malaysian government can repay in the long future.

In the past decade, the major creditors of the Philippines were America, Japan, and other international financial institutions, such as IMF. The Philippines Finance Minister admitted that the country's projected debt to China will be only 4.5% of the total national debt by 2022, far less than that of other major creditors.[12] Sri Lanka's debt was sourced from the international financial market. Sri Lanka Central Bank showed that the main creditor at the end of 2022 was based on the international financial market, which took over one and a half parts (see Chart 2.1).[13]

Turning to Africa, the enormous public external debt dominates these countries' whole debt gross amount.[14] Compared to decades before 2013, the maturity structure

---

[7] Che (2006).

[8] Ibid.

[9] "Gross External Debt", Bank Negara Malaysia. https://www.bnm.gov.my/.

[10] The Executive Board of the International Monetary Fund (IMF) (2021b).

[11] The Executive Board of the International Monetary Fund (IMF) (2023).

[12] Federico (2019).

[13] Department of External Resources: Foreign Debt Summary from Government of Sri Lanka. https://www.erd.gov.lk/index.php?option=com_content&view=article&id=102&Itemid=308&lang=en.

[14] Merotto and Thomas (2015).

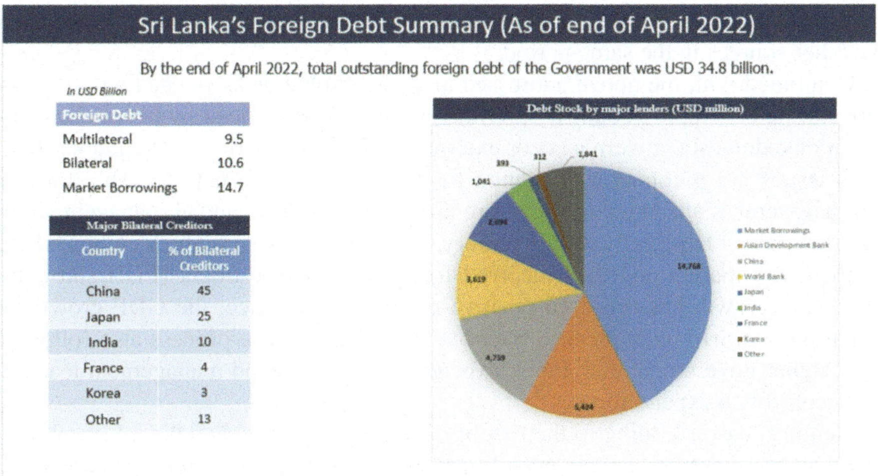

Source: *Department of External Resources*

Chart 2.1 Sri Lanka's Foreign debt summary (As of the end of April 2022)

of external debt has changed substantially. The structure became diverse rather than depending on the bilateral debt from the Paris Club. Referring to Merotto and Thomas, more than one-third of African external debt was from private commercial banks in the past decade, such as the British Barclays Bank and France Calyon Bank.[15] Additionally, international financial institutions that lent loans to Africa took more than one-third of its external debt. The latest part was loan from bilateral partners. Thus, the main creditors of Africa are commercial banks.

The African public external debt burden is always great. Since the last century, the external debt amount has increased constantly, especially in this decade, as economic growth and external debt have increased dramatically. From WB statistics, by the end of 2017, external debt as a percentage of gross national income was one and half more than the percentage in 2010. Additionally, after 2018, the growth rate of external debt in these African countries involved in BRI surpassed their GDP growth rate. Furthermore, by the end of 2021, the external debt stock as a percentage of exports compared to the last decade has more than doubled.[16] It shows that the debt burden, especially the external debt stock for African countries, has undeniably grown in the past decade. We can tell that the difference in these countries' debt burden before 2013 entering the BRI projects and after 2013 is not apparent. Referring to Ying,[17] the debt burden stock and flow should be considered for differentiation. The increased debt after 2013 takes a small amount of debt stock. The main burden is from debt

[15] Ibid.

[16] Fei and Ji (2021).

[17] Liu (2019).

stock rather than the newly generated part. The debt related to BRI is much less than the other sources in the same period.

Combined with the above addressed analysis, problems associated with debt in most of the developing countries are interconnected, influenced by historical accumulations, domestic governance, or external factors unrelated to BRI collaboration. Debt issues are a common challenge for these developing nations. The primary internal factor is attributed to immature and disorganized financial management on a larger scale.[18] Especially in this century, these developing countries embraced the international market and then received foreign direct investment (FDI) and debt. Economic growth has achieved positive results; for instance, the GDP growth of Malaysia and Sri Lanka reached over 5% in one stage. The process also followed with higher government and public expenditures. Disordered management leads to undercontrolled expenditures.

Another reason leading to the rise of debt stock and flow is political instability. Frequent presidential changes and political conflicts between different parties usually lead to ignorance of economic development and economic policies cannot be ensured. Factors such as frequent rotation of heads of state and arguments among parties prevent the new leaders of the country from concentrating on implementing the economic program. At the same time, new or upcoming policies are likely to be forced to stagnate due to government changes, and the risk of national economic fluctuations has increased unexpectedly.[19] Political stability could attract more foreign investment and (resources-seeking multinational corporations) MNC engagement. Stability needs the reassurance of national security and a lower likelihood of unrest and violence sparking. If the host country has a larger possibility of military conflicts, even during the conflicts, civilians' living requirements and security and peaceful environment are difficult to ensure and create, and any type of MNC distrusts the potential of interests.

In Malaysia, the debt problem reflects Malaysia's domestic political battle in the political game between the two parties of the "Barisan Nasional" and the "Pakatan Harapan".[20] During the two parties' election, the total national debt of Malaysia proposed by the "Pakatan Harapan" and "Barisan Nasional" is contrary based on the different estimation standards and interpretations, based on their own parties' ideas and interests. In the process, practical and helpful economic policies are barely released and implemented.[21] This harms economic development and stimulates the deterioration of debt problems.

External aspects lie in the unfriendly global trade environment, and the hegemonic position in international trade from the West, especially the US, also contributes to the debt risk of underdeveloped and developing countries. Taking African countries as an example, export goods are mainly raw materials and natural resources, such as gold and oil minerals, but imported products have high added value. In the global

[18] Li et al. (2020).

[19] Feng and Gao (1992).

[20] Zhang (2020).

[21] Zhong and Zhang (2020).

trade market, trade rules are unfair, and product values are unequal; meanwhile, the amount of imports and exports is still imbalanced, so it is a total disadvantage for African countries. In particular, after the 2008 financial crisis, FDI decreased, and the export of commodities in high prices constantly declined. Export prices decrease as import goods prices rise. The enlarged trade deficit exacerbates the challenges of economic development in Africa on a broader scale. Additionally, the consistent rise in the Fed's rate contributes to an escalation in interest rates. The exchange rate of the US dollar has increased. This leads to these developing countries' income shrunk in a further way. It was more difficult to repay debt. The increased debt burden is apparent.

2.3 Mutual Benefits of the BRI Projects for Route States and China

Since joining BRI, both China and the route states have benefited greatly from the economic and social aspects. In this part, we will take two countries, Myanmar and Sri Lanka, as examples to analyze the specific benefits they enjoy. The original intention of BRI emphasizes the meaning of equality and actively advocates that all countries, regardless of their country, size, rich or poor, should treat each other as equals and help each other at the same level.[22] Thus, it is worth discussing and measuring the equality of treating route countries and whether policies and assistance have contributed to the route countries.

According to the Conference of the first five-year progress of BRI in 2018,[23] 103 countries and international organizations have signed 118 cooperation agreements on BRI with China. In 2017, the first BRI Cooperation Summit Forum was successfully held in Beijing, with the attendance of heads of state and government from 29 countries and more than 1600 representatives from more than 140 countries and more than 80 international organizations. Among the 279 achievements of the forum, 265 have been completed or turned into normal work thus far, and the remaining 14 are under supervision, with an implementation rate of 95%.[24]

Furthermore, the cumulative trade in goods with the BRI route states has exceeded 5 trillion USD, and foreign direct investment has exceeded 70 billion USD. Overseas economic and trade cooperation zones built in the BRI route states have a total investment of more than 20 billion USD, creating hundreds of thousands of jobs and generating billions of dollars in local tax revenue. More countries express their

[22] Liu and Liu (2020).

[23] *Xin Wen Ban Jiu Gong Jian "Yi Dai Yi Lu" 5 Nian Jin Zhan Qing Kuang Ji Zhan Wang Ju Xing Xin Wen Fa Bu Hui*[Information Office Held Press Conference on the Progress and Prospects of BRI in the Past Five Years], Central Government of China, August 27, 2018, http://www.gov.cn/xinwen/2018-08/27/content_5316921.htm#1.

[24] Ibid.

intentions to join BRI institutions. The positive win–win results can be evaluated by countries.[25]

Chinese scholars have also demonstrated the mutual benefits from BRI for China and the route states through theoretical perspectives. Liu's article[26] created a multiple regression analysis to discover the correlation among BRI projects' influence, debt issue, political stability, inflation, global market and so on. The result of this qualified regression analysis is that BRI and the debt burden have a 1% negative correlation. This means that 1% of BRI applying more in these route developing countries leads to a 1% decrease in the debt burden. Additionally, when controlling for certain variables, we can clarify that compared with developing countries along the route, the debt risks of developed countries are greater, and BRI has a stronger inhibitory effect on the debt risks of developed countries along the route. Furthermore, political instability is the consequence of the barrier of economic development to these developing countries, as I discussed above, so it promotes the deeper reliability of their economic development to the BRI and loans from China due to the high rate of debt growth.

The other correlation in this research shows that differences in active participation in the construction of the BRI projects among the route countries will have a greater impact on the relationship between BRI and national debt risks. Specifically, actively participating in construction will help strengthen the BRI's inhibitory effect on the debt risks of countries along the route.[27] The level of participation on a larger scale brings about the stronger effect of BRI to restrain the growth rate of debt burden flow. The debt issue will go to a brighter way.

Another regression model uses the natural logarithm of the actual per capita GDP of the BRI route states to measure the economic growth of a country.[28] The result shows that BRI has a lagging effect on the economic development of countries engaged with it. The decline in the economic growth phenomenon rarely appears in the initial stage. In the long term, the effect becomes positive; furthermore, the effect becomes promoted such that the increase in economic growth will be better by time files.

Next, we will address the specific example of Myanmar's Kyaukpyu Port.[29] Kyaukpyu Port is a north–south long and narrow seaport formed by Langley Island and the mainland in Kyaukpyu County, Rakhine State, Myanmar. It has the natural advantage of being a deep-sea port. Its natural water depth is 24 m, and it can sail and berth 250,000 to 300,000 tons of ocean-going passenger and cargo ships. Cooperation between China and Myanmar in the development of the Kyaukpyu Deep Sea Port began in 2009. In the beginning, China International Trust and Investment Corporation (CITIC) and the Myanmar government signed the "Memorandum of Cooperation on Kyaukpyu Economic and Technological Development Zone, Deep-water Port and Railway Projects". The CITIC Consortium won the bid for the Kyaukpyu

[25] Ibid.

[26] Ibid.

[27] Qiu et al. (2021).

[28] Guo and Wang (2014).

[29] See Wei (2019).

Port and Industrial Park project. Later, President Xi met with Myanmar President U Htin Kyaw and proposed promoting the early implementation of key cooperation projects such as the Kyaukpyu Special Economic Zone in Myanmar.

According to the contract, CITIC would bundle the development and implementation of the Kyaukpyu Special Economic Zone deep-water port and industrial park project. The operation of the industrial park would bring employment and taxation. At the same time, a hinterland is provided for the logistics and management of the port, thereby promoting local economic and social development. The project document stipulates that both the deep-water port project and the industrial park project adopt the franchise model, and the franchise period is 50 years.

After the expiration of the period, an application for an extension of 25 years can be applied. The operation mode of the deep-water port adopts the design-build-finance-operate-transfer (DBFOT) method. The Myanmar government, local enterprises and the CITIC will jointly establish a joint venture company. According to the initial share ratio of "85–15%", Myanmar does not need to invest. However, Myanmar then asked to increase its shareholding ratio to 30%, which means that it needs to bear the entire 1.1 billion USD in funding for the project.

The process of the Kyaukpyu Port project is apparent and occurs during equal negotiation. First of all, the cooperation projects are what Myanmar desires. Myanmar in 2016 planned domestic economic corridors linking special economic zones and border ports to promote the connection and development of central cities, node cities, border ports and special economic zones along the route and promote cooperation between Myanmar and its neighboring countries.[30] Thus, the construction of infrastructure is most important to implement the plan. Myanmar is listed as one of the countries with the worst infrastructure investment gap, with a projected investment need of fund gap.[31] China's cooperation opportunity is a necessary domestic need.

There is another benefit for the Myanmar government. The project adopts the public–private partnership (PPP) model. 15% of the shares held by the Myanmar side are financed by local companies, and the other 15% are invested by the Myanmar government with local land. The government does not need additional capital injection, has no financing responsibility, and does not bear corresponding risks. It is expected that once the usage of Kyaukpyu Port adopts the PPP model, 0.1 million jobs will be created, and more than one million dollars in tax income will be generated.[32]

For Sri Lanka, Lankans have been discussing whether to build the Hambantota port near the main waterway of the Indian Ocean for a century. They request financial aid from their main creditors without results and then turn to China. After the port was completed, the Chinese company assisted in renting when the Sri Lankan government decided to lease out the port to relieve debt. The Hambantota Port lease is not a debt-for-equity swap. China Merchants Port paid 1.12 billion USD for a <70% stake in the Hambantota port lease compared to the global market standard. The Sri Lanka Ports Authority, on the other hand, retained more than 30% of the shares, with

[30] Zou and Wang (2020).

[31] Global Infrastructure Outlook (2016).

[32] Lu (2018).

the option to buy back an additional 20% over the next 10 years, with the option to repurchase the entire stake thereafter. Therefore, China neither owns the Hambantota Port nor is it exempted from the debt to build it. According to previous successful experience, another port rented by China also creates tons of tax income for the local government.[33]

The BRI projects benefit both sides. China companies are encouraged by a go-out strategy to participate in BRI, which involves investing, renting, building, and constructing in route states. Chinese companies contribute to local tax income and jobs, receive good income, and have more intentions to take more programs and take more responsibility in future BRI projects.

Moreover, BRI has indeed had a significant impact on the strategic decisions of Chinese enterprises to "go global". Its influence mechanism can be summarized as "push" and "pull". The "push" mainly comes from the pressure of market competition, the government's push, the public opinion's push and the stakeholder's push, while the "pull" mainly manifests itself in new market opportunities, reduction of export fixed costs, reduction of export marginal costs, and investment barriers Reductions and changes in financing costs.[34] In this respect, Chinese companies obtain strong competition in the global market compared to Western companies, so they may have a sustainable development future.

China also benefits from institutions and participates more in constructing rules and performing obligations. The establishment of BRI institutions aims to build regional institutions with cooperation, win–win, and mutual trust to take the responsibility of a reliable major country. It also means that China's rise integrates the international system and institutions, so more communication gives rise to more mutual beliefs.

2.4 China's Solutions to Solve the Debt Issue Related to BRI

The critics and arguments toward BRI are the defense of discourse from the traditional Western style. Referring to the Wendt and the "Copenhagen School" of constructivism, the discourse is controlled and constructed by the Western-built world order. The self-concepts and order constructed by China, therefore, challenge the current discourse from the West[35] and, of course, are opposed by the West. Concocting the lies of the "debt trap" is the most common one used by Western media and politicians to defame BRI.

Realizing the negative consequences of the debt issue, both China and the BRI countries have worked together to jointly solve it. First, China has avoided influencing politics in BRI route states and competing with other great powers in the region by

[33] Sha (2020).

[34] Li et al. (2019).

[35] Jin and Shen (2019), Lu and Ma (2020).

carrying out BRI projects. Thus far, no evidence shows that China has realized its critical political objectives through the BRI projects, such as building alliances or exclusive blocs targeting the third country. Actually, Chinese projects have never had any political conditions attached, while Western countries usually link aid to politics. That is why Asian and African countries prefer Chinese investments and welcome BRI. According to the most recent news from China's *Guangming Daily* on September 14, 2023, China has reached more than 200 agreements on cooperation under BRI with 152 states and 32 international organizations.[36] It is evident that BRI has been largely accepted by the route states, although there will be some problems in the implementation process.

Second, China has stated that BRI is open to any state and has tried to expand cooperation with other countries in the third market. President Xi said that BRI is an open and inclusive process rather than a "Chinese club" on August 27, 2018. He also expressed that states that are willing to participate in BRI are welcome. For instance, although China is developing the Gwadar port, many other countries have agreed to invest in Gwadar, including Russia, Saudi Arabia, UAE, Kuwait, Qatar, Japan, South Korea, Malaysia, Iran, Turkey, and some European countries.[37] In February 2019, Saudi Arabia signed a memorandum of understanding (MoU) to invest 10 billion USD in an oil refinery and petrochemical complex at Gwadar.[38] China has even pursued cooperation with Japan, a strong peer competitor of China in the areas of foreign trade and investment, under BRI. According to China's *CGTN* in May 2019, Yang Jiechi, a member of the Political Bureau of the Communist Party of China (CPC) Central Committee and director of the Office of the Foreign Affairs Commission of the CPC Central Committee, said that China welcomes Japan to play a more active role in third-party market cooperation between the two countries under BRI.[39] In this sense, China has sought cooperation rather than competition with other states in carrying out BRI projects.

Moreover, it is unlikely that China can achieve its political or strategic purposes through multilateral projects, especially when competitors participate. Actually, China's ambition of reshaping the regional or international order by initiating BRI, which is alleged by the Western media, has been challenged by both the great powers such as the US and Japan and the BRI countries. By criticizing BRI and offering alternative options, the US and Japan, together with India and Australia, have attempted to deter China from dominating the region. Some BRI countries have been keen on inviting other states to join BRI or downsize BRI projects to offset the risks of reliance on Chinese investment.

In addition, both China and the BRI countries have tried to devalue the political significance of the BRI projects and operate them in a commercial way, so as to confine the adverse effects to the economic sphere and avoid harming political ties.

---

[36] Liu and Dong (2023).

[37] Zamir (2020).

[38] Adnan (2021).

[39] "China calls on Japan to engage in BRI cooperation more actively", *CGTN*, May 17, 2019, https://news.cgtn.com/news/3d3d514e334d7a4e34457a6333566d54/index.html.

Both countries have promised to smoothly promote the BRI projects and reduce loans from China by inviting the third country or implementing the projects step by step. Thanks to these useful measures, the debt issue is currently being appropriately handled and thus does not hinder the implementation of the BRI projects.

Third, China has improved the information transparency of investment in the BRI projects and promoted the interconnection between China and the world to avoid information asymmetry. On September 5, 2023, the Chinese Center for International Knowledge on Development (CIKD) launched the *Global Development Report 2023* in Beijing, in which it pointed out that since the implementation of BRI in the past decade, nearly one trillion US dollars of investment have been generated, more than 3000 projects have been constructed, and nearly 40 million people lift themselves out of poverty.[40]

Additionally, mutual party investments are encouraged to actively participate in cooperation and reduce the proportion of Chinese investment. By rationally designing the proportion of project funding support, guiding capital injection from other countries, encouraging multilateral development institutions to carry out joint financing with the BRI states and giving full play to the role of financial leverage to promote economic development, China has tried to reduce the debt burden of the BRI route states as well as their reliance on Chinese loans. Taking Myanmar's Kyaukpyu Port as an example, it adopted the PPP mode, which involves mutual parties to control debt risks. The varieties of ownership structures not only decrease the uncertainty of risks but also increase local government trust in China. Some Chinese scholars have also suggested giving full play to the advantages of enterprises with different ownership systems, building an enterprise collaboration network, and improving the efficiency of transportation infrastructure construction[41] to reduce the debt risks of the BRI route states.

Other Chinese scholars proposed the good use of debt sustainability analysis tools and established a debt default relief mechanism.[42] For example, it uses the combination of equity investment and bank loans to provide support and then uses the debt sustainability analysis framework to obtain basic debt risk information and warn of the debt risks at some level to local government. If some countries could not repay the debt, the host government could determine the truth and adjust measures, such as decreasing the interest rate and reorganizing debt, to attend to issues in due course to avoid the larger loss between the two sides.

Finally, China has strengthened the government-to-government and nongovernment exchanges between China and the BRI route states, aiming to enhance communications with the local government and people. BRI countries have great differences in politics, culture, and economy, which makes Chinese enterprises face an extremely complex institutional environment for overseas transportation investment. On the basis of strengthening the bilateral investment agreement mechanism, state-owned enterprises with strong anti-risk capabilities can be encouraged to invest

[40] Liu and Dong (2023).

[41] Jin and Shen (2019).

[42] Ren and Zhang (2019).

in countries along the route with relatively harsh institutional environments, while nonstate-owned enterprises can be guided to invest in countries with less risks.

2.5 Conclusion

BRI, since its implementation in 2013, has achieved remarkable progress though it also faced many challenges, the debt issues in particular. This chapter uses data and examples demonstrating the BRI route states' debt structure and the main causes of their debt issue to convince that BRI has not led to a "debt trap". Conversely, it shows that the BRI projects bring mutual benefits to both China and route states. China actually put forward the ideas of equality, harmony openness, and win–win to cooperate with BRI countries.

Although the debt issue is a major obstacle to some big BRI projects, it cannot screw up BRI. To address this problem properly, China has strengthened cooperation and policy coordination with the BRI route states and made some progress on it. Given this, the adverse impacts of the debt issue on BRI would be further decreased in the near future.

References

Adnan Aamir, "Pakistan's Gwadar loses lustre as Saudis shift $10bn deal to Karachi", *Financial Times*, June 22, 2021, https://www.ft.com/content/88cfe78b-517f-41d9-97d1-9f7f540f517c.

African Economic Outlook 2021. (2021). "*From Debt Resolution to Growth Economy Africa's Way Forward*" African Development Bank 2021. https://www.afdb.org/sites/default/files/documents/afdb21-01_aeo_chinese_highlights.pdf.

Bank Negara Malaysia (2019). "*Gross External Debt*". Bank Negara Malaysia. https://www.bnm.gov.my/

Brahma, C., "China's Debt-Trap Diplomacy", *Stagecraft and Statecraft*, January 25, 2017, https://chellaney.net/2017/01/25/chinas-debt-trap-diplomacy/.

BRI in the Past Five Years]. (2018, August 27). Central Government of China, http://www.gov.cn/xinwen/2018-08/27/content_5316921.htm#1.

Che Wei Han, *Fa Zhan Jing Ji Xue [Developing Economy]* (Beijing: Tsinghua University Press, 2006), p. 317.

Wei, T. (2019). China-Myanmar Kyaukpyu port project cooperation: "debt trap" or development opportunity? Haiguo Tuji Research Institute, March 26, 2020. https://www.imf.org/en/Publications/CR/Issues/2020/03/26/Myanmar-2019-Article-IV-Consultation-Press-Release-Staff-Report-and-Statement-by-the-49292.

"China calls on Japan to engage in BRI cooperation more actively" (2019, May 17). *CGTN*. https://news.cgtn.com/news/3d3d514e334d7a4e34457a6333566d54/index.html.

Chu Yin., Qin Shuai., & Ma Tiantian. (2018, December 10). "Zhai Wu Xian Jin" Lun Zhan Bu Zhu Jiao ["Debt Trap" Is a Feeble Argument]. *QIUSHI*. http://www.qstheory.cn/dukan/hqwg/2018-12/10/c_1123830087.htm.

Department of External Resources: Foreign Debt Summary from Government of Sri Lanka. (2022, April). Summary of external debt. https://www.erd.gov.lk/index.php?option=com_content&view=article&id=102&Itemid=308&lang=en.

Federico D. Pascual Jr. (2019, March 03). "Secret loan terms fan 'debt trap' fears". *The Philippine Star.* https://www.philstar.com/opinion/2019/03/28/1905200/secret-loan-terms-fan-debt-trap-fears.

Fei Zhou Jing Ji Zhan Wang [African Economic Outlook 2021]. African Development Bank, 2021, https://www.afdb.org/sites/default/files/documents/afdb21-01_aeo_chinese_highlights.pdf.

Feng Cuncheng, Gao Xiaochuan, *Dong Ou Guo Jia Jing Ji Hua Po Zheng Ju Dong Dang* [Economic Recession in East Europe and Political Instability], *Shi Jie Jing Ji[World Economy]*, No. 4, 1992, pp. 33–38.

Global Infrastructure Outlook. (2016). Infrastructure investment needs 50 countries, 7 sectors to 2040. https://d2rpq8wtqka5kg.cloudfront.net/389138/open20170919030300.pdf?Expires=1669187188&Signature=xKTpfZHNR3vapQqrsFEIzexq~cKWM0v6rSKgnkMml7cb0BAI46pud5LXigamLTbQasPCC~6FNiHw7Ojd3BIE77jL705zVKURkQvmdgVheu0lprPj5nf1a6u87j7Q~Vwt-NhQygsXuXa3Nap6VTEh318FxmxCW537jdu7qRrYGw1Fsnmg1zhLedZ1rxlMcV-2yozYJeY9fNzjJljyob2dLp~yXYe1WEvUxU5b1cGqxUquAx0UsBBihUKW8KyJ-Zt~dhK6I2sTsXtN4J2zGboPwzX1J4kFLBVvJBRTUdFKgM~kV2WqCWUN-9JV~wZmTmNZRBbEYrBzHHpYdz51N7n4Hg__&Key-Pair-Id=APKAJVGCNMR6FQV6VYIA.

"Gross External Debt", Bank Negara Malaysia. https://www.bnm.gov.my/.

Guo Buchao, Wang Bo, *Zheng Fu Zhai Wu Yu Jing Ji Zeng Zhang: Ji Yu Zi Ben Hui Bao Lv De Men Kan Xiao Ying Fen Xi* [Government Debt and Economic Growth: An Analysis of Threshold Effects Based on Return on Capital], *Shi Jie Jing Ji [The Journal of World Economy]*, No. 9, 2014, pp. 95–118.

Jin Gang., & Shen Kunrong. (2019). *Zhong Guo Qi Ye Dui "Yi Dai Yi Lu" Yan Xian Guo Jia De Jiao Tong Tou Zi Xiao Ying: Fa Zhan Xiao Ying Hai Shi Zhai Wu Xian Jin* [The Chinese Overseas Transportation Investment Effect along the Belt and Road: Development Effect or Debt Trap], *Zhong Guo Gong Ye Jing Ji [China Industrial Economics]*, No. 9, pp. 79–97.

Jin and Shen *Zhong Guo Qi Ye Dui "Yi Dai Yi Lu" Yan Xian Guo Jia De Jiao Tong Tou Zi Xiao Ying: Fa Zhan Xiao Ying Hai Shi Zhai Wu Xian Jin* [The Chinese Overseas Transportation Investment Effect along the Belt and Road: Development Effect or Debt Trap], *Zhong Guo Gong Ye Jing Ji [China Industrial Economics]*, No. 9, 2019, pp. 79–97

Li Jun, Gan Jingyan, Yang Xueru, *"Yi Dai Yi Lu" Chang Yi Ru He Ying Xiang Zhong Guo Qi Ye Zhuan Xing Sheng Ji* [How Does the Belt and Road Initiative Affect Transformation and Upgrading of Chinese Enterprises], *Nan Fang Jing Ji [South China Journal of Economies]*, No. 4, 2019, pp. 1–22.

Li Yanfang, *Si Li Lan Ka Wai Zhai Wen Ti De Sheng Cheng Luo Ji Yu Zheng Yi Bian Xi* [Sri Lanka's External Debt: Controversy and Causes], *Guo Ji Zhan Wang [Global Review]*, No. 1, 2020, pp. 108–130.

Liu Kun., & Dong Bei. (2023, September 14). *"Cong 'Da Xie Yi' Dao 'Gong Bi Hua'-Gong Jian Yi Dai Yi Lu Xing Wen Zhi Yuan* [From 'sketching outline' to 'completing a drawing'-achieving steady and sustained development of BRI]", *Guang Ming Ri Bao [Guangming Daily].* https://news.gmw.cn/2023-09/14/content_36831384.htm.

Liu and Liu Chengkai, *Zhong Mian Jing Ji He Zuo: Shi "Zhai Wu Xian Jin" Hai Shi Fa Zhan Ji Yu?* [China-Myanmar Economic Cooperation: "Debt Trap" or Development Opportunity?], *Nan Ya Yan Jiu [South Asian Studies]*, No. 2, 2020, pp. 130–151.

Liu Ying. (2019). "Yi Dai Yi Lu" Bing Fei "Zhai Wu Xian Jin" ["Belt and Road" is not a "debt trap"], Zhong Guo Jin Rong [China Finance]. No. 6, pp. 81–82.

Lu Guangsheng, Ma Tianfang, *"Yi Dai Yi Lu" Jian She Zhong De "99 Nian Zu Qi" Feng Xian: You Lai, Ying Xiang Ji Ying Dui* [Risk of 99-Year Lease in the "Belt and Road": Origin, Effects and Responses], *Ya Tai Jing Ji [Asia-Pacific Economy]*, No. 1, 2020, pp. 5–15.

Lu Chen. (2018, December 10). Mian Dian Jiao Piao Jing Ji Te Qu Jian She Mai Chu Jian Shi Yi Bu [The Kyaukpyu Special Economic Zone in Myanmar Took A Solid Step], *Guang Ming Ri Bao [Guangming Daily].* https://epaper.gmw.cn/gmrb/html/2018-12/10/nw.D110000gmrb_20181210_1-12.htm.

Merotto, D. L., & Thomas, M. R. (2015). African debt since HIPC: how clean is the slate?. MFM Global Practice discussion paper World Bank https://openknowledge.worldbank.org/handle/10986/22399.

Qiu Yi, Pan Pan, Zhang Ling, *"Zhong Guo Fang An" Guo Zhen Bu Ju L Zhai Wu Xian Jin Ma?: Lai Zi "Yi Dai Yi Lu"Chang Yi De Jing Yan Shu Ju* [Did the China Program Create Debt Trap: Evidence from the Belt and Road Initiative], *Shi Jie Jing Ji Yan Jiu [World Economy Studies]*, No. 7, 2021, pp. 120–134.

Ren Jingru, Zhang Zongbin, *Bo Chi "Yi Dai Yi Lu" Jian She "Zhai Wu Xian Jin Lun"* [Refuting the "Debt Trap" of BRI], *Ren Min Lun Tan [People's Tribune]*, No. 16, 2019, pp. 82–83.

Sha, B. (2020). China and Myanmar sign framework agreement for Kyaukpyu deep-water port project. *HTDC research*. https://research.hktdc.com/sc/article/MzYyOTQyMDc4.

The Executive Board of the International Monetary Fund (IMF) (2021a). *Myanmar: Requests for Disbursement Under the Rapid Credit Facility and Purchase Under the Rapid Financing Instrument-Press Release; Staff Report; and Statement by the Executive Director for Myanmar*. https://www.imf.org/en/Publications/CR/Issues/2021/01/25/Myanmar-Requests-for-Disbursement-Under-the-Rapid-Credit-Facility-and-Purchase-Under-the-50036.

The Executive Board of the International Monetary Fund (IMF) (2021b). *IMF Executive Board Concludes 2021 Article IV Consultation with Malaysia*. International Monetary Fund. https://www.imf.org/en/News/Articles/2021/03/17/pr2172-malaysia-imf-executive-board-concludes-2021-article-iv-consultation-with-malaysia.

The Executive Board of the International Monetary Fund (IMF) (2023). IMF Executive Board Concludes 2023 Article IV Consultation with Malaysia. https://www.imf.org/en/News/Articles/2023/05/31/pr23191-malaysia-imf-executive-board-concludes-2023-article-iv-consultation-with-malaysia.

World Bank (2016). International Debt Statistics 2017. *World Bank Publications*. https://openknowledge.worldbank.org/bitstream/handle/10986/25697/9781464809941.pdf.

Xin Wen Ban Jiu Gong Jian "Yi Dai Yi Lu" 5 Nian Jin Zhan Qing Kuang Ji Zhan Wang Ju Xing Xin Wen Fa Bu Hui [Information Office Held Press Conference on the Progress and Prospects of BRI in the Past Five Years], Central Government of China, August 27, 2018, http://www.gov.cn/xinwen/2018-08/27/content_5316921.htm#1.

Xu, S., & Li, J. (2020). The development of the "Chinese 'debt trap' diplomacy theory" and its fallacies. *International Studies*. https://doi.org/10.3969/j.issn.0452-8832.2020.01.005.

Wang Yi. (2023, March 8). "Yi Dai Yi Lu" Bu Shi "Zhai Wu Xian Jin", Er Shi Hui Min "Xian Bing" [Wang Yi: "BRI" Is Not A "Debt Trap", But A "Pie" Benefiting the People]". *Xin Hua Wang [Xin Hua News Agency]*. http://www.xinhuanet.com/politics/2019lh/2019-03/08/c_1210076293.htm.

Zamir Ahmed Awan. (2020, October 20)."Gwadar: A Port of the Future", *People's Daily Online*. http://en.people.cn/n3/2020/1020/c90000-9770892.html.

Zhang Yingjin, *Ma Lai Xi Ya Zhai Wu Wen Ti Zheng Zhi Hua: "Zhai Wu Xian Jin Lun" Tu Xian De Gen Yuan* [Politicization of Malaysia's Debt Issue: the Root Cause of "Debt Trap Theory"], *Guo Ji Zhan Wang [Global Review]*, No. 1, 2020, pp. 131–152.

Zhong Feiteng, Zhang Shuai, *Di Qu Jing Zheng, Xuan Ju Zheng Zhi Yu "Yi Dai Yi Lu" Zhai Wu Ke Chi Xu Xing-Pou Xi Suo Wei "Zhai Wu Xian Jin Wai Jiao" Lun* [Regional Competition, Election Politics, and BRI Debt Sustainability-An Analysis of the "Debt Trap Diplomacy" Allegation], *Wai Jiao Ping Lun [Foreign Affairs Review]*, No. 1, 2020, pp. 20–64.

Zou Chunmeng, Wang Haoyuan, *Zhong Mian Jing Ji Zou Lang Jian She Shi "Zhai Wu Xian Jin" Ma?-Ji Yu Mian Dian Wai Zhai Zheng Xiang De Fen Xi* [Is China-Myanmar Economic Corridor a "Debt Trap"?: An Analysis Based on the truth of Myanmar's External Debt], *Nan Yang Wen Ti Yan Jiu[Southeast Asian Affairs]*, No. 4, 2020, pp. 77–90.

Chapter 3
"Debt Trap Theory": The Logic of Power Politics in India

Siling Yang and Angyu Jiang

Abstract In recent years, the U.S.-led officials, media, and scholars have publicly criticized China for bringing a "debt trap" to the developing countries, while the "debt trap theory" about BRI was first proposed by Indian scholars and medias. India's hype on the "debt trap theory" in Sri Lanka, Pakistan, Nepal and the Maldives presents the characteristics and trend of "internal and external interaction" and "Indo-Western linkage". On the one hand, the "debt trap theory" is effective if state solidarity did not exist; on the other hand, India and the West can form a powerful political tradition based on realism. Although the "debt trap theory" was hyped by Indian scholars and the media, it has been internalized into India's power political strategy. This has been verified in the change of power in Maldives. In India's "debt trap theory", the island country Maldives in the Indian Ocean has unparalleled typical significance. It is hard to tell whether the signal releasers and the actors of the "debt trap theory" believe in the "debt trap", but for the Indians, who believe in the power tradition, the truth is secondary. What is important is that in the change of state power in Maldives, India has made full use of the "debt trap theory" as the starting point to exert the power and political influence among countries.

Keywords Debt trap · BRI · Maldives · India · China

3.1 Introduction

Since 2018, the "Debt Trap Theory" has gradually become a way to criticize the "Belt and Road Initiative (BRI), causing a more extensive influence in the international community. Research institutions in the West, particularly in the United States (US)

S. Yang (✉)
Institute of South Asian Studies, Yunnan Academy of Social Sciences, Kunming, China
e-mail: yangsling42@163.com

A. Jiang
Center for International Academic Exchanges, Yunnan Academy of Social Sciences, Kunming, China

N. Peng and M. Y. Cheng (eds.), *The Reality and Myth of BRI's Debt Trap*, Indo-Pacific Focus, https://doi.org/10.1007/978-981-97-1056-0_3

have used the "debt trap theory" to defame China. These actions are rooted in China-US relations' transition, especially the major change in the perception of the US towards China. It makes clear that China is a geopolitical competitor of the US, and that China is challenging the international order led by the US. However, the "debt trap theory" of BRI has been spread from the regional level, especially in South Asia, where India is the "standard bearer" of the "debt trap theory". Objectively, India also promotes connectivity cooperation in South Asia, and India, US, Japan and Australia also identified connectivity as the top issue. But India not only refused to align with China's BRI, but also took the lead in launching the speculation of "debt trap". The reason is that India wants to lead connectivity cooperation. In other words, India believes that there is a power competition between China and India in South Asia. Therefore, according to the realistic power politics, the "debt trap theory" has become a new strategy for India to compete for power with China in South Asia, which has been verified in the regime change of Maldives. In a word, the emergence of the "debt trap theory" and its rise to India's strategy towards China conform to the logic of the power politics tradition, and this strategy will also affect other South Asian countries, which will have a great influence on regional security and cooperation, so high vigilance should be raised.

3.2 "Debt Trap Theory" in Realistic Power Politics

According to the Chinese dictionary, "debt" refers to the debt repayment obligation, which also refers to the debt owed; "trap" has two explanations: one refers to a pit, covered with camouflage, step on it and fall into the pit; the other is to use the metaphor of the trap of harm. "Debt trap" means using debt to trap and lure others for further gain. Such "debt traps" can indeed be seen in social life, novels and movies. With the rapid progress of the BRI, the "debt trap" has been used in China's diplomatic strategy by people with ulterior motives, that is, "debt trap diplomacy". The term "debt trap diplomacy" was proposed by Indian scholar Brama Chelani.[1] According to Wikipedia, "debt trap diplomacy" refers to diplomacy based on debt in bilateral relations between countries. It involves the intention of one creditor country to provide excessive credit to another debtor country to obtain economic or political concessions from the debtor country when the debtor country is unable to meet its debt obligations. The terms of the loan are usually not disclosed, and the loan funds are usually used to make payments to contractors in the creditor countries.[2]

"Debt trap diplomacy" is obviously the most important part of "debt trap theory". "Debt Trap" or "Debt Trap Diplomacy" gradually formed "Debt Trap Theory" through publicity and dissemination. In short, the "debt trap theory" mainly refers to all negative remarks about the debt trap against China. The "debt trap theory" is like

[1] Chellaney (2017a).

[2] Debt-trap Diplomacy. https://en.wikipedia.org/wiki/Debt-trap_diplomacy.

a system, which contains many structures and components. First, there are communication channels of "debt trap" at individual, national, regional and global levels. Second, the subjects involved in the hype include state leaders, officials, scholars and the media. Third, the object of "debt trap" speculation is mainly China and related partners.

As the Indian Foreign Secretary pointed out, India not only has many investment projects in Myanmar, Bangladesh, Maldives, Nepal and other countries but also is promoting regional interconnection with the US, Japan and Australia. The official also said that in history, solid interconnection has been a barometer of India's prosperity and well-being. At the same time, it also pointed out that if the main task of India's reform and structural adjustment in the first 20 years after the Cold War was to release economic vitality through the facilitation of domestic rules, then the current globalization stage turned to internal and external interconnection. From this point of view, India and China's interconnection should be in harmony, but India has tried to avoid contact with BRI. The official once again reiterated Modi's words insinuating China: the interconnection of the Indo-Pacific region must be based on the principles of economic feasibility and financial responsibility, and they should promote economic activities, instead of putting the country under an unbearable debt burden. Therefore, although there is not much difference between what China and India are engaged in, the key is that India wants to lead connectivity under the "Indo Pacific" framework, which has become a power struggle, that is why India promoted the "debt trap theory" initiated by China's BRI. Especially in South Asia, India cannot tolerate its regional power weakened and influenced by China.

Hans Morgenthau believes that power is always the direct goal of international politics.[3] It refers that a person controls the will and actions of others. In international relations, power refers to a country's comprehensive ability to control other countries and influence international events on the international stage. He also believes that the most stable factor is geography which a country's power depends.[4] Nicholas Sparkman put it more thoroughly, in international politics, power is that one country controls another country. He believes that the geographical factor is very important when a country formulates its foreign policy. A country's geographical location and its relationship with other power centers determine its important issues.[5]

The realistic power politics illustrates the logic of India in promoting the debt trap theory. Since its independence, India has controlled and influenced other South Asian countries through various means. Even today, India is still using blockade, economic sanctions and other means to control and influence other countries. The Indian Ocean national identity of Sri Lanka and the Maldives has also led India to see their cooperation with China as a part of the power competition. Therefore, India utilizes the "debt trap" theory to compete against China. This strategy includes four conditions: first, the non-unity of politics within the cooperative country; second, the close interaction between the agent and the signal sender; third, the interference

[3] Morgenthau (2006).

[4] Ibid, p. 148.

[5] Shixiong (2016).

of power of the signal sender (the country cooperating with China), or the signal sender has a weak ability to resist the interference of power; fourth, the tension of the alienated partner is increasing.

3.3 India Hypes the "Debt Trap" of South Asian Countries Under BRI

As someone pointed out, the "debt trap" is nothing new. As early as the 1970s and 1980s, the West put forward the "debt trap" for China's aid to Africa.[6] Today, with the continuous progress of China's BRI, the "debt trap theory" is once again rampant. But India hyped the "debt trap". On January 23rd, 2017, Brahmacelani published an article in the *World Press Syndicate* saying China's BRI is a "debt-trap diplomacy". He claimed that Chinese leaders are good at using economic tools to achieve China's geostrategic interests, supporting strategic infrastructure projects through BRI, lending huge loans to plunge them into the "debt trap" and vulnerable to China. In "China's debt-trap diplomacy," Brahmacelani believes that China-backed projects are often not designed to support the local economy, but to get access to natural resources, or markets for low-cost labor and poor Chinese goods.[7]

Moreover, he believed that China was taking measures to ensure that countries could not escape their debts.[8] He warned that by integrating its foreign, economic and security policies, China was achieving a hegemonic goal of interlinking trade, communications, transport and security. If the country bears heavy debts, their financial difficulties will only benefit China's new colonial plan. Countries that have not yet fallen into China's "debt trap" should pay attention-and take all possible measures to avoid it.[9] On December 20, 2017, Chelani once again published China's Creditor Imperialism on the *World Newspaper Syndicate*, and then published the full text on *Chelani. com*,[10] which set off a climax in the external discussion on the "debt trap theory".

3.3.1 Speculation of Sri Lanka's "Debt Trap"

The widespread spread of the "debt trap theory" is precisely due to India's speculation that Sri Lanka has fallen into China's "debt trap". At the beginning of 2017, Chelani claimed that some projects in Sri Lanka and Pakistan invested by China were in a loss and idle state, which was just what China needed, because China could achieve

---

[6] Libin (2018).

[7] Ibid.

[8] Chellaney (2017a).

[9] Chellaney (2017a).

[10] Chellaney (2018b).

military purposes by taking advantage of this, such as attacking submarines docking at Sri Lanka ports, Chinese warships entering Gwadar port to perform security tasks, etc.[11] On December 9, 2017, through legal compliance procedures, Sri Lanka officially handed over the Hambantota port to China for lease for 99 years. However, this move was interpreted by Indian scholars as "Sri Lanka formally handed over the strategic port of Hambantota to China, an Asian giant, because it was unable to pay huge debts", and sighed that China used "gunboat diplomacy" as used by European empires to make other countries surrender to China's will, and the case of Sri Lanka proved how effective China's "debt trap diplomacy" was.[12]

After entering 2018, with the changing political situation in Sri Lanka, Indian scholars and media continue to hype Sri Lanka's "debt trap".[13] Some remarks and projects of Sri Lankan President Maitripala Sirisena have been continuously publicized by Indian scholars and media, and the projects implemented may aggravate Sri Lanka's debt burden. For example, Indian media and scholars claimed that Sirisena boasted everywhere that China promised to give it 300 million dollars for any projects he wanted to build. At the same time, the kidney hospital invested by China in Sirisena's hometown was often mentioned.[14]

3.3.2 *Hype the Maldives as a "Debt Trap"*

In 2017, Indian and Western media rarely mentioned the "debt trap" of Maldives under BRI. However, the power struggle and tortuous development of Maldives in 2018 provided an opportunity for the rapid spread of the "debt trap theory" of Maldives. On October 1st, 2018, Chellaney claimed that in Maldives, China acquired several small islands by making this Indian Ocean island country bear a large amount of debts. He claimed that although he could not see the terms of the lease agreement, China acquired the islands at a very cheap price. For example, only 4 million USD was paid to get Feydoo Finolhu Island.[15]

In the same article, he used the words of Maldivian politicians to write seditiously: Without firing a single shot, China acquired more land in Maldives than the East India

[11] Chellaney (2017a).

[12] Chellaney (2018b).

[13] In February 2018, Sri Lanka held local elections seen as a bellwether for the 2020 general election, with former President Rajapaksa's Popular Front party crushing Prime Minister Wickremesinghe's United National Party and President Sirisena's Sri Lanka Freedom Party by nearly five times. At the same time, Sirisena and Wickremesinghe and their party escalated the tension, and on 26 October President Sirisena announced the dismissal of Wickremesinghe as Prime Minister and the appointment of former President Rajapaksa as Prime Minister of the new government. Wickremesinghe said he would not step down as prime minister, and the dispute between the government and the house once again caused political tensions, and Sri Lanka fell into a constitutional crisis.

[14] Chellaney (2018c).

[15] Chellaney (2018a).

Company.[16] Chellaney also believes that the "debt trap" will be the core challenge facing the Maldives led by Saleh, especially considering how China controls Sri Lanka financially to achieve its geostrategic goals.[17] Because of killing democracy, former President Abdullayamin plunged Maldives into the debt of his protector, China. Maldives' accumulated debt has more than doubled its annual income. He believes that China intends to lead Maldives into a "debt trap".[18] Because of political struggle, Saleh's Democratic Party publicly criticized China's activities in the Maldives in a statement, claiming that it was highly concerned that the Maldives was caught in the "debt trap" of China, because it would put additional pressure on the strategic assets of the Maldives, and at the same time the Indian Ocean region would be in an increasingly unstable state.[19] There is even a surprising view that India is worried that the China-Malaysia Free Trade Agreement (FTA) may put Maldives in a "debt trap" similar to Sri Lanka.[20] The Democratic Party of Maldives believes that the authorities should stop implementing the China-Malaysia FTA, because the negotiation and adoption procedures of the FTA are illegal (referring to the lack of participation of opposition parties). Former President Mohamed Nasheed believes that the China-Malaysia FTA has damaged the economy of Maldives.[21]

According to these remarks, Saleh's new government, which came to power as an opposition, is expected to re-examine these cooperation projects.[22] Scholars from the Indian Observer Foundation call it a spade: India can recover lost ground in Maldives.[23] He also said that Prime Minister Modi's participation in the inauguration ceremony of the Maldivian President showed that India supported the new Maldivian government. Moreover, Modi's trip was carried out during the interaction among the US, India, Japan and Australia, and the four-party mechanism will balance China's infrastructure loans in the region.[24] Chellaney believes that India should learn from Sri Lanka's experience, because even after authoritarian President Mahinda Rajapaksa was ousted by voters in early 2015, China still maintained its influence and advantage in Sri Lanka.[25] In Maldives, he asserted that China's influence might be weakened, but it did not quit, and it was possible to re-establish its influence through "debt trap diplomacy" like Sri Lanka.[26]

---

[16] Ibid.

[17] Chellaney (2018c).

[18] Ibid.

[19] Ramanathan (2017).

[20] Ibid.

[21] Ibid.

[22] Chaudhary and Marlow (2018).

[23] Ibid.

[24] Ibid.

[25] Chellaney (2018d).

[26] Ibid.

3.3.3 Hype Pakistan's "Debt Trap"

For Pakistan, India and its media hype the "debt trap theory" of BRI, which is consistent with their consistent understanding, because India opposes the "China Pakistan Economic Corridor" (CPEC) which goes through the Pakistan-controlled Kashmir.[27] On October 9, 2018, the *Hindustan Times* published an article stating that China was defending CPEC after Pakistan decided to cut investment in and review billions of dollars of projects. According to the report, the new government under the leadership of Pakistani Prime Minister Imran Khan is worried about the huge loans under the CPEC, fearing that this will push Pakistan into a "debt trap".[28] Sheikh Rashid, Pakistan's railway minister, announced that the cost of a railway project in the CPEC would be cut from 8.2 billion to 6.2 billion USD, saying that Pakistan could not afford huge loans. Meanwhile, Imran Khan has said that the CPEC is under review.[29] The *Hindustan Times* reported that the new government led by populist Prime Minister Imran Khan had strengthened its resistance. He was wary of the rising debt level and said that the country must get rid of foreign loans. He exaggeratedly believed that the new Pakistani government wanted to review all BRI contracts.[30] It is also reported that in 2017, Pakistan rejected the funding provided by China for a giant dam project worth 14 billion USD in the Himalayas, because it was worried that if Pakistan could not repay the loan, Beijing might eventually own Pakistan's important state-owned assets, just like a port in Sri Lanka.[31]

3.3.4 Hype Nepal's "Debt Trap"

India's "debt trap" hype about Nepal is obviously not as intense as that of other South Asian countries, but in view of its importance between China and India, Indian scholars and their media have not forgotten Nepal. For example, Chelani took Nepal as an example of China's "debt trap diplomacy" towards South Asian countries. He believed that China had won a return by supporting Nepal's election. In September 2018, Nepal gave China a project worth 2.5 billion dollars, but the project did not conduct an open bidding. Chelani claimed that Nepal's critics said that China made the cost of the project overinflated, causing difficulty for Nepal to repay Chinese loans.[32] If we look ahead, with the deepening cooperation between China and Nepal, India may strengthen speculation on Nepal's "debt trap theory".

---

[27] Fearing Debt Trap (2018a).

[28] Ibid.

[29] Ibid.

[30] Fearing Debt Trap (2018c).

[31] Ibid.

[32] Chellaney (2018a).

3.4 Features of India's "Debt Trap Theory" of BRI in South Asia

3.4.1 "Internal" and "External" Linkage

The so-called "internal" mainly refers to India (specifically including politicians, scholars and the media), while the "external" mainly refers to the external politics of the hyped country. Although most of the hype and propaganda by Indian scholars and media are nonsense, the chaotic and complex political situation in South Asian countries provides conditions for spreading this "debt trap theory". For example, some officials in Pakistan have complained about the debts of some Chinese projects, which are easily amplified by Indian scholars and media. For example, the aforementioned Pakistan Railway Minister Sheikh Rashid, who claimed that India could not afford huge loans. Some Pakistani officials said that some people worried that some agreements of the CPEC were badly negotiated, too costly, or too biased towards China. Pakistan is still committed to attracting Chinese investment but wants to make greater efforts in terms of price and affordability and re-examine the CPEC. Islamabad tried to readjust the CPEC, but it has become more difficult because it relies on Chinese loans to support its fragile economy.[33] Some officials in Pakistan even said, "We have reservations, but no other countries come to invest in Pakistan. What can we do?".[34]

In the Maldives election in 2018, the opposition made full use of the "debt trap theory". Former President Abdullah Yameen was not only labeled as "pro China", but also recognized as responsible for bringing Maldives into the "debt trap". For example, former President Mohamed Nahid of Maldives publicly claimed that China has "seized" 17 small islands in Maldives.[35] He also accused that "China set up a debt trap for Maldives and used debt as a tool to discipline the Malaysian. The projects undertaken by China in Malaysia were not tendered and transparent".[36] It can be seen that "debt trap theory" hyped by India has become the topic of internal power struggle in the Maldives, and former President Abdulayamin, who works with China, has also drawn sharp criticism from the domestic opposition and India. In particular, it was believed that the former Maldives government had received a lot of loans from China, sending Maldives into a debt trap.[37] Sri Lanka also happened a similar situation. Sirisena also said during his presidential campaign that Chinese investment projects are putting Sri Lanka into the "debt trap".[38]

[33] Fearing Debt Trap (2018c).

[34] Ibid.

[35] Chellaney (2018a).

[36] Libin (2018).

[37] Ibid.

[38] Chellaney (2015).

3.4.2 Interaction Between India and the West

At present, most domestic public opinions believe that the "debt trap theory" was hyped by the West, especially the US. This view is reasonable. From the internal of the country, to the regional, and then to the global, the "debt trap theory" has formed a delicate speculation chain. India is very important in this chain. In other words, in the process of hyping, India handed the hammer to the West, or reminded the West that it presences. As mentioned above, Indian scholars and their media not only took the lead in hyping the "debt trap theory", but also continuously contributed to the flames. Chelani is the most active Indian scholar who hyped the "debt trap theory". From 2015 to 2018, he has published dozens of papers or comments related to the "debt trap theory" of BRI.[39] In 2009, Chellaney raised the issue of China using debt to increase its influence, but then the topic was Sino-US relations.[40] Starting from 2015, Chellaney began to use the term "debt trap" in the cooperation between China and South Asian countries, the earliest being Sri Lanka.[41] At the beginning and end of 2017, Chellaney published "China's Debt Trap Diplomacy" and "China's Debt Imperialism" which are the two most influential papers on "debt trap".[42] The Indian official, Modi also alluded to the debt problem of China's BRI at the 2018 Shangri-la dialogue meeting. He said "All interconnection must be based on trust and respect for sovereignty, rather than placing the country under an unbearable debt burden".[43]

The "debt trap theory" of BRI hyped by Indian scholars and media has been sought after by Western media and politicians since 2018, such as *Washington Post, Washington Times, Pacific Forum.* In May 2018, Harvard University released the *Debt Trap Diplomacy Report*, the core points of which copied the statement of Indian scholar Chellaney. With the increasingly tense Sino-US relations and the start of the trade war, the "debt trap theory" has gradually become global propaganda as a public opinion in the US and other Western countries. U.S. Vice President Burns even publicly attacked China's "debt trap diplomacy". Australian Senator Constable Ferrantiwells declared in the Australian newspaper that Papua New Guinea was "a channel for Beijing to enter the Pacific region" and that China was carrying out "debt trap diplomacy".[44] The BRI's "debt trap theory" is so influential that some scholars regard the so-called "debt trap diplomacy" as one of the three mirror images to understand China's strategy.[45] Objectively, India and Western powers of the "debt

---

[39] Chellaney (2009, 2015); China'Sole Ally (2016); The Bull in the China Shop (2017); China's Creditor Imperialism (2018); How Can America Change Pakistani Behavior (2018); China Ensnares Vulnerable States (2018; Why the South China Sea (2018); Beijing Loses a Battle (2018); The China Backlash (2018); China's Imperial Project Runs (2018); Democracy in Danger (2018); Belt and Roadblocks (2018); Chellaney (2018d); Insecurity in India's Maritime Backyard (2018).

[40] Chellaney (2009).

[41] Chellaney (2015).

[42] Chellaney (2017a, b).

[43] Modi (2018).

[44] Australian Parliamentarians (2018).

[45] Hendler (2018).

trap theory" hype has reached the climax, and both sides can form a close interaction on this issue, mainly because India and the US are anxious about the rise of China, the US is worried about China to challenge its power and status in the global, India not only worried about its power in South Asia is weakened by China, and in the whole Asia to compete with China.

3.5 "Debt Trap Theory": India's New Strategy for Pursuing Regional Power

The so-called "dual strategy" of India towards China refers to: on the one hand, in high-level political exchanges, the Indian government, led by Modi, has lowered its stance and actively developed friendly relations with China; On the other hand, India has attached various labels to China to weakenand eliminate China's influence in South Asia. For example, Modi publicly accused China's debt trap diplomacy towards South Asian countries. He used some euphemistic words, suggesting that South Asian countries have "unbearable debt burden" under China's control. This shows that the "debt trap theory" hyped by Indian scholars and media has affected Indian leaders and internalized India's foreign strategy. The Indian Ministry of Foreign Affairs has repeatedly accused the Yameen government of Maldives of being anti-democratic, which implies that China supports the authoritarian government in South Asia. Modi said to Saleh that he congratulated Maldives on its successful and peaceful transition to democracy.[46] In this context, the struggle between the two lines is clearly divided by India, that is, "Saleh India" versus "Yameen China". Obviously, influenced by the regional power struggle, BRI's "debt trap theory" has become an integral part of India's "dual strategy" towards China, in which the "debt trap theory" is the key element of India's power rivalry with China in South Asia and other regions. This is fully illustrated in the power and political change of Maldives in 2018. The specific process can be seen in the following analysis.

In fact, Indian scholars and media are not as free from the influence and control of the government as they say. The Indian government also intends to use them as a foreign strategic tool. For example, in the border conflict between China and India, Indian media has a subtle relationship with the Indian government. In other words, when India needs to be hard on China or show off its leadership prestige, the negative views of Indian scholars and media towards China will be constantly amplified, just as they were during the "Donglang confrontation" between China and India. When India needs to cooperate with China, Indian scholars and media will restrain their behaviors. Of course, this is just a rough observation, which may be simple. It cannot be ignored that Indian scholars and media are important components of India's national machinery, and they certainly represent India's national interests. For BRI's "debt trap theory", at this stage, with the political exchanges between China and India in a better period, the attitude of Indian political elites towards the

[46] Joint Statement (2018).

"debt trap theory" is "dark", but it is actively used in the regional power struggle. Indian scholars and the media are "bright" to expand China's negative image. With the changes in China India relations, "bright" and "dark" will also change, depending on the specific changes in China India relations. However, it can be concluded that "debt trap theory" has become a new strategy for India to pursue regional power.

In the context of power, India has a common identity with Sri Lanka, Maldives, Pakistan and Nepal, the targets of the "debt trap theory" of BRI: India's backyard. Chelani described India's foreign policy in six words since independence: embrace and then repent. He believed that Indian leaders were too enthusiastic in diplomatic activities, but they often encountered betrayal.[47] This statement is obviously inaccurate. Realistic power politics is the core of India's foreign policy since independence. From Nehru's attempt to establish an Asian federation, he controlled South Asian neighbors through various military and diplomatic, and Indira Gandhi's South Asian version of "Monroe Doctrine" which means, at the beginning of independence, all of these show that it is Indiabelieves in realistic power politics. With this traditional thinking, as Indian scholars pointed out, since the late 1990s, with the rise of China and the increasing interest of the Chinese government in the Indian Ocean, Sri Lanka and Maldives have become part of the traditional power struggle between China and India for decades. For Beijing, as Maldives and Sri Lanka are located along the maritime traffic routes of Africa and the Persian Gulf, they are regarded as resource security centers. While India happens to cross the above sea traffic lines, it is inevitable that the competition between China and India on Maldives and Sri Lanka will intensify.[48]

3.5.1 Maldives' Special Position in the Logic of Indian Power Politics

First, Maldives has a prominent geopolitical position. Reja Mohan pointed out that although only a few islands in Maldives are inhabited, standing here, you can rule the main navigation routes in the Indian Ocean. Therefore, in the colonial era, Maldives attracted the attention of maritime powers.[49] Australian scholars also pointed out that although the population is small, Maldives is very important for India's strategic aspirations. The east–west route of the Indian Ocean passes through the Maldives, while the former British air force and naval base in Kam Island provides a potential basis for controlling the middle of the Indian Ocean.[50] In view of this, India has always insisted that Maldives cannot accept safe exchanges with Pakistan and China, and has said to Male that it will meet all needs of Maldives.[51] Indian officials believe that

---

[47] Chellaney (2018e).

[48] Mohan (2014, p. 122).

[49] Ibid.

[50] Brewster (2016, p. 82).

[51] Lei Jia Mohan: *The Grand Maritime Strategy of China and India*, p. 123.

India and Malaysia have shared ethnic, linguistic, cultural and commercial ties long ago…Maldives is a key member and partner in the Indian Ocean region, ruling the strategic maritime transport lines in this region.[52]

Second, the Maldives is also an important part of India's "backyard". India takes for granted that the Republic of Maldives is in its South Asian sphere of influence.[53] In India's view, India inherited British privileges in South Asia, the whole of which belonged in India. Even for a long time, India thought that Pakistan separated from India which was temporary, and that Pakistan would sooner or later return to India. In this regard, the Maldives is not different from that of other South Asian countries. As some scholars have pointed out, as early as 1947, Nehru gave high praise to the "Monroe Doctrine" that it ensured the Americas from foreign aggression. Clearly, following the legacy of British India, Nehru and subsequent Indian leaders have established a rigid strategic vision of the subcontinent as their sphere of influence and the Indian Ocean as the "ocean of India".[54] In 1983, Indira Gandhi proposed "Indiralism", namely the Indian version of "Monroe Doctrine", the core of which is not to allow foreign powers to interfere in the internal affairs of countries in South Asia.[55] But in reality, India must adjust it. For example, India conducted cooperation with the US in the Indian Ocean in the 1990s, and in recent years, Japan, France and other countries are welcome to cooperate in the Indian Ocean. In this process, China became an "exceptionalism", where India showed an unusual exclusion of its possible role in South Asia and in the Indian Ocean. This is why China's interaction with the Indian Ocean island nation of the Maldives not only makes India anxious, but it is also ready to pull the Maldives into its own track.

Third, Maldives is the core of Indian power. India has got profits of power in Maldives through the "Cactus Action". In November 1988, 80–200 mercenaries from the Sri Lankan Tamil rebel organization, the Tamil Eelam People's Liberation Organization, infiltrated into Male, Maldives and took control of key locations in the city. President Gayoom requested foreign military assistance, including the US, India, Britain, Pakistan, Sri Lanka, Malaysia and other Asian countries. New Delhi responded to the crisis with high speed and decision-making, believing that this is India's privilege and responsibility. Within a few hours, the Indian army took control of Male and rescued the trapped President Gayoom. Then the navy sent out to take the escaped rebels back for trial.[56] This action is called "Cactus Action", which has brought India high international praise. U.S. President Ronald Reagan said that this has made an important contribution to regional stability. The Indian Cabinet Secretary B.G. Deshimuk said "The Cactus Operation has greatly enhanced India's prestige and demonstrated the efficiency and ability of our successful military operations in a

---

[52] Ibid, p. 124.

[53] Brewster (2016, p. 82).

[54] Li Zhonglin, A Review of the Monroe Doctrine in India, *Asian-African Review*, No. 4, 2013, p. 15.

[55] Ibid.

[56] Brewster (2016, p. 84).

short period of time. This region has widely recognized our polices."[57] This success continues to this day. In the change of power in Maldives in 2018, Indian scholars suggested that New Delhi should immediately punish Maldives in the face of a series of practices of President Abdullah Yamin (putting justices and opposition leaders in prison). In the face of political turmoil in Sri Lanka, Indian scholars have given the following advice: Wait and see.[58] Because if Maldives is the core of Indian power, Sri Lanka is the stain on the history of Indian power. During the civil war in Sri Lanka from 1987 to 1990, India carried out large-scale military to achieve peace, but it ended in failure.[59]

3.5.2 Maldives Sends Signals and the Use of Indian Power

Based on the above understanding, India cannot tolerate China's activities in its backyard. Moreover, India believes that such activities have affected India's regional power. As early as September 2012, when China announced to provide the Maldives with a loan of 500 million USD, Indian scholars believed that this huge sum would greatly enhance China's political influence. During the period of President Abdullah Yamin, India deemed that it was challenged by China, such as China's island investment in Maldives (Indian scholars and media believed that these islands were mostly used for military purposes) and the signing of a free trade area agreement between China and Maldives. Obviously, India is not able to clearly distinguish the economic relationship between Maldives and China and the security relationship with India as Maldives thinks.[60]

As mentioned above, the "debt trap theory" is conditional on the non-unity of the target domestic ministry politics, which is well reflected in the Maldives. The political power of the Maldives are well aware that India has long promoting China's BRI's "debt trap theory", and as long as the Maldives caters to India's "debt trap theory", India will inevitably support it. Objectively speaking, the opposition in Maldives can only blame China's "debt trap", because Maldives is very clear that India's propaganda about China's military intentions and purposes in Maldives is groundless, but the debt is real. As for whether it is a "trap", it is not important.

In this backdrop, the Maldivian opposition threw the "debt trap theory" in power change. Mr. Saleh's party has criticized China's activities in the Maldives during the change of power, and the new government is expected to review the cooperation projects.[61] Former Maldives President Mohammad Nasheed has also accused China

[57] Ibid.

[58] Constantino Xavier, "New Delhi Can't Hope to do a Male in Colombo", *Hindustan Times*, October 31, 2018, https://www.hindustantimes.com/analysis/new-delhi-can-t-hope-to-do-a-male-in-colombo/story-EoYKpms3TZIe6VMzvhJKzL.html.

[59] Mohan (2014, p. 122).

[60] Brewster (2016, p. 89).

[61] Chaudhary and Marlow (2018).

of causing the Maldives to fall into a "debt trap".[62] Although whether the Maldives is trapped in the "debt trap" is not really the focus of India, the "debt trap theory" provides an opportunity for India to pull the Maldives into the "double priority" track again.[63] With this opportunity, India maximizes power in the change of power in the Maldives. From February to September 2018, India issued seven statements on the change of power in the Maldives, which demonstrated India's "power over power" interference in the political developments in the Maldives. In a statement dated 2 February 2018, India claimed that, in the spirit of the democratic rule of law, all organs of the Maldives government must respect and obey the orders of the Supreme Court.[64] We also hope that the Maldivian authorities will ensure the safety of the Indian expatriates in the Maldives under any circumstances. As a close and friendly neighbor, India wants a stable, peaceful and prosperous Maldives.[65] On February 6, India again issued a statement on the Maldivian situation, said "the Maldivian government on February 1 refused to comply with the unanimous ruling after declared emergency and suspend the Maldivian constitutional rights, India will also continue to focus on the Supreme Court chief justice and political arrest."[66]

On February 20, India once again pointed out whether Maldives would end the emergency on time and expected that the Maldivian government would not extend the emergency so that the political process in Maldives could resume immediately. At the same time, we urge Maldives to quickly continue to safeguard democracy and law, so as to meet the aspirations of the people of Maldives and alleviate the concerns of the international community.[67] On February 21, when the Maldivian extended the emergency for about 30 days, India was "disappointed".[68] India welcomes the lifting of the emergency in Maldives one month later and calls on Maldives to restore all the provisions of the Constitution, allow the Supreme Court and other judicial departments to operate fully independently, promote and support the free and proper functioning of Parliament, implement the Supreme Court's "All Judges Order" of February 1, 2018, and support genuine political dialogue with all opposition parties. The Government of Maldives must ensure the credible restoration of the political process and the rule of law before the elections this year. As a neighbor whose security is close to Maldives, India hopes to see a stable, peaceful and prosperous Maldives to meet the aspirations of its citizens.[69] On June 14, India again issued the Maldives' political situation, saying that since the beginning of the Maldives political crisis, India

[62] Maldives Election Changing Days (2018).

[63] Double priority refers to India's "neighbour first" and the Maldives' "India first".

[64] On February 1, 2018, the Maldives Supreme Court acquitted former President Nasheed and opposition leaders from President Yameen and government authorities, triggering ongoing political conflict in the Maldives.

[65] Press Release on India's Reaction (2018).

[66] Situation in Maldives (2018).

[67] Press Release on Situation in Maldives (2020), https://www.mea.gov.in/press-releases.htm?dtl/29501/Press_Release_on_situation_in_Maldives.

[68] Press Release on the situation in Maldives (2018).

[69] Revocation of State of Emergency (2018).

has constantly advocated that the Maldives government should allow all institutions, including the high court, and parliament, to work in a way of free, independent, and allow real political dialogue between all parties. This is also a general demand of the international community. In turn, India was frustrated by the former President of the Maldives and the Chief Justice of the Supreme Court to prolonged imprisonment without a fair trial. This doubts whether the Maldivian government can uphold the rule of law and whether the presidential election will be credible in September, 2018. India believes that a democratic, stable and prosperous Maldives is in the interests of all its neighboring countries and friends in the Indian Ocean. India has once again recommended that the Maldives government immediately release political prisoners, including former President Gayoom and Chief Justice Abdulasyoud, and create the conditions for all political forces to participate in the presidential elections.[70] On September 23, the change of power in the Maldives ended, and the opposition leader Ibrahim Mohammed Saleh won. India responded quickly, congratulated on Saleh's election and urged the Maldives Election Commission to formally confirm it as soon as possible. It was also claimed that the election not only marked a victory for the democratic forces of the Maldives, but also reflected a firm commitment to democracy and the rule of law.[71] Under its neighborhood priority policy, India wants to develop close partnerships with the Maldives which can see India's eagerness.

From a series of interference statements in India, many words are closely associated with "power", such as "must", "hope", "advice", "urge", "advocate", etc. And in its tradition of pursuing regional power, if the regime change in the Maldives fails to follow, direct interference is highly likely to appear. This is also why, in the change of power in the Maldives, Indian scholars dare to preach that India should conduct the "big stick policy" in the Maldives. Cherani believes that India's past use of only "carrots" in the Maldives has encouraged Abdulayamin to move closer to China, such as signing a free trade agreement with China. India must use the stick to impose penalties and sanctions, and China's growing presence in the Indian Ocean threatens not only India's security but also the regional excellence of the British-American Navy centered on Diego Garcia.[72] Objectively speaking, India does have a lot of means to punish the Maldives, including military interference, economic sanctions and blockade and embargo. This time, however, India has used its "soft interference" to recover the "lost land" of the Maldives.[73]

---

[70] Press Release on the Political Situation in the Maldives (2018).

[71] Government of India (2018).

[72] Chellaney (2018a).

[73] "The Maldives's New Regime (2018).

3.5.3 India and Maldives's Echo and Results in the "Debt Trap"

Although China wasn't surprised at the regime change in Maldives, it mainly responded to the West when refuting the "debt trap theory", and did not publicly mention India. However, from the official to the media, India is excited about the change of regime in Maldives. Modi immediately telephoned Saleh'selection as President and wished for strengthening democracy, peace and prosperity in Maldives under the leadership of Mr. Saleh. Saleh invited Modi to his inauguration ceremony, and Modi readily agreed.

On November 17, 2018, Modi attended the swearing in ceremony of the new President of Maldives, which is symbolic and sends a signal to Indian media and scholars that India has once again defeated China's penetration into its maritime neighbors. There are also views that Modi's participation in the inauguration ceremony of the new President of Maldives aims to ensure that Yameen can peacefully transfer power to the winner Saleh, and at the same time send a signal to Yameen that there can be no other choice but to accept this result.[74] During the interaction of the two leaders, the two sides discussed how to get rid of the so-called "debt trap" of China. In the joint statement between India and Malaysia, Saleh briefed Modi on the severe economic situation faced by the country during his inauguration. The two leaders discussed how to continue to develop its partnership for India, especially to help the new government fulfill its commitments to the people of Maldives. In particular, President Saleh stressed the urgent need to develop housing and infrastructure, as well as the water and sewage systems in remote islands. Modi assured Saleh that India firmly helps Maldives achieve sustainable social and economic development. He also said that India was willing to help in all possible ways and suggested that the two sides meet as soon as possible to formulate details according to Maldives.[75] It appearsthat the leaders used "recovery" when describing India Malaysia relations in the statement. Modi believed that with Mr. Saleh's election as President of Maldives, the cooperation and friendship will continue.[76] It can be seen that India is very bitter about China Malaysia relations during the Abdullah Yameen period. The joint statement also fully reflects India's desire to completely replace China in Maldives, and the best way is to help Maldives solve the "debt trap" made by China.

Subsequently, Abdulla Shahid, the Foreign Minister of Maldives, continued this idea during his visit to India. Shaheed made it clear that India is the best friend of Maldives, and promised that Indian military equipment and personnel can remain in Maldives.[77] Ibrahim Mmeer, the finance minister of Maldives who accompanied his visit, announced that the new government had confirmed that the prices of many projects under construction were artificially high, and was reviewing the transactions

---

[74] Chellaney (2018c).

[75] Joint Press Statement (2018).

[76] Ibid.

[77] India Our Best Friend (2018).

with China to assess the debt, because China's investment projects were concluded in secret.[78] Indian Foreign Minister Sushma Swaraj promised that India is ready to fully support the social and economy of Maldives according to India's "neighbor priority" policy.[79] India assured Maldives of its support in implementing its development priorities and ensuring financial and budgetary stability.[80] Of course, in this interaction, India also got what it wanted: the Maldives' renewed commitment to "India first" and the Maldives government will remain sensitive to India's security and strategic concerns.[81] On November 28, 2018, the Japanese media revealed that India would give Maldives a loan of 1 billion USD, three times the amount required by Maldives, to repay its Chinese debt. It is pointed out that India is aimed at "buying Maldives to leave China", while the more incisive view is that it is to let Maldives change from a "debt trap" to another "debt trap".[82] From December 16 to 18, 2018, Maldives' new President Saleh visited India. Modi personally announced that he would grant Maldives a loan of 1.4 billion USD, more than the previously reported 1 billion USD. The main purpose is to help Maldives repay its 1.5 billion USD debt to China.[83]

Here, we can briefly sort out the "debt trap theory" adopted by India: first, India hyped the "debt trap theory" of China's BRI, then the opposition in Maldives accepted the signal and sent a feedback of "debt trap theory" to India in the political struggle. India intervened in the domestic politics of Maldives to support the opposition, and finally the opposition won, and the Indian government fulfilled its commitments, to helping Maldives "get rid of" the so-called "debt trap". In this process, the "debt trap theory" is not a goal, but a strategy for both sides to pursue power. The opposition in Maldives seeks domestic political power, while India seeks regional domination power, or security power in the Northern Indian Ocean. In the joint statement of India and Malaysia, the two sides expressed their agreement on maintaining peace and security in the Indian Ocean region, and reiterated their commitment to pay attention to each other's concerns and aspirations for stability in the region and not allow their respective territories to be used for any activities that harm the other side.[84] Among the strategies of "debt trap theory", China's investment in Maldives Island is one of the focuses that India pays the most attention to. This time, it is deliberately emphasized in the joint statement, which is self-evident that it is meaningful and targeted.

[78] "Tried to Play (2018).

[79] Visit of Foreign Minister of Maldives to India (2018).

[80] Ibid.

[81] Ibid.

[82] India (2018).

[83] Ranjan (2018).

[84] Joint Statement (2018).

3.6 Conclusion

The "security dilemma" of China-India relations is largely reflected in the "mutual trust dilemma". In the context of both sides, China tends to promote cooperation with India and believes that India should and may participate in active bilateral and regional cooperation; India tends to think that China's cooperation is not intentional. In particular, the regional cooperation plan aims to seek regional and even global power. In the process of promoting the cooperation agenda, India believes that China has harmed India's interests, such as violating South Asia and engaging in a pearl chain strategy to encircle India in the Indian Ocean. In other words, the two sides may have a consensus on regional cooperation, but it is difficult to really conduct cooperation, because China hopes to solve the problem with international cooperation and interdependence, while India is used to using realistic power politics to maintain its regional hegemony. This is the real reason why India used the realistic power politics strategy "debt trap theory" to cheat and alienate China from other South Asian countries. Objectively speaking, it is difficult for China to change India's strategic thinking. As pointed out in the paper, the current "debt trap theory" is mainly hyped and influenced by Sri Lanka, Pakistan, Maldives and Nepal. However, with the promotion of cooperation, Bangladesh, Afghanistan, etc. may also become a means for India to use the "debt trap theory" to weaken or eliminate the so-called Chinese influence in South Asia. From the perspective of the consequences of the "debt trap theory", China is the first victim and has been crowned with various indecent reputations; the impact on China-India relations will also exist for a long time, which may not be obvious, but will subtly influence the "non-mutual trust" that affects China India strategy. At the regional level, it is pointed out that India will respond to the increasing interaction between China and the Indian Ocean and South Asian countries in a three-pronged approach: first, pay close attention to Beijing's activities; Second, promote their own projects and commitments; The third is to educate and inform neighboring countries of the consequences of interaction with China. The first two are understandable, but the latter reveals India's obsession with power. In the short term, India may benefit more from such a strategy, but in the long run, it may also be backfired. For other South Asian countries, it is in their best interests to implement a balanced strategy between China and India, and this role of balance and counterbalance will change with the needs of these countries, leading to uncertainty or challenges to regional stability. India should understand that the paranoid concept of power is a serious threat to regional cooperation, peace and prosperity. In the future, China and India can truly create the "China India Century" in the twenty-first century only by "breathing together and sharing a common destiny". For China, to avoid unnecessary losses of China's BRI projects in relevant South Asian countries, we need to start with the preconditions for the "debt trap theory" of BRI to take effect, that is, how to evaluate and stabilize the internal politics of cooperation partners and maintain their loyalty to cooperation, how to counteract the close interaction between India and other South Asian countries against China and how to calm the tension between China and its partners must be seriously considered.

References

Amit Ranjan, "A New Chapter in India-Maldives Relationship," ISAS Brief, No. 632-19, (2018, December). https://www.isas.nus.edu.sg/wp-content/uploads/2018/12/ISAS-Briefs-No.-632-A-New-Chapter-in-India-Maldives-Relationship-1.pdf.

Archana Chaudhary and Iain Marlow, PM Narendra Modi Heads to Maldives as Island Shifts toward India from China, *Hindustan Times*, (2018, Nov. 17). https://www.hindustantimes.com/search?q=PM%E2%80%89Narendra-Modi-heads-to-Maldives-as-island-shifts-toward-India-from-China.

Australian Parliamentarians Say China Engages in 'Debt Trap Diplomacy' in South Pacific, *People's Daily News*, (2018, October 5). http://m.people.cn/n4/2018/1005/c203-11696216.html.

"Beijing Loses a Battle in the Maldives-but the Fight for Influence Goes on", September 26, 2018. https://chellaney.net/?s=Beijing+Loses+a+Battle+in+the+Maldives+—+but+the+Fight+for+Influence+Goes+on&submit=Search.

"Belt and Road blocks", November 1, 2018. https://chellaney.net/?s=The+China+Backlash&submit=Search.

Brahma Chellaney, "Power Shifts in Asia", January 13, 2009, https://chellaney.net/?s=Power+shifts+in+Asia&submit=Search

Brahma Chellaney, What are Chinese submarines doing in the Indian Ocean? (2015, May 24). https://chellaney.net/2015/05/24/what-are-chinese-submarines-doing-in-the-indian-ocean-far-from-chinas-maritime-backyard/.

Brahma Chellaney, China's Debt-Trap Diplomacy, (2017a, January 25). https://chellaney.net/2017/01/25/chinas-debt-trap-diplomacy/.

Brahma Chellaney, *China's Debt-Trap Diplomacy, World Press Syndicate*, (2017b, 23 January). https://www.project-syndicate.org/commentary/china-one-belt-one-road-loans-debt-by-brahma-chellaney-2017-01/chinese?barrier=accesspaylog.

Brahma Chellaney, India must Impose Punishing Sanctions on the Maldives, (2018, Feb. 20). https://www.hindustantimes.com/opinion/india-must-impose-punishing-sanctions-on-the-maldives/story-wN5ZLTBZCzkV1EFoE7MPTL.html.

Brahma Chellaney, *China's Imperial Project Runs into Resistance*, (2018a, Oct. 3). https://www.chinausfocus.com/finance-economy/chinas-imperial-project-runs-into-resistance.

Brahma Chellaney, *China's Creditor Imperialism*, (2018b, Jan. 1). https://chellaney.net/2018/01/01/chinas-creditor-imperialism/.

Brahma Chellaney, China's Muscle has Forced India to Rethink its Maritime Strategy, (2018c, Nov. 15). https://www.hindustantimes.com/search?q=China's-muscle-has-forced-India-to-rethink-its-maritime-strategy.

Brahma Chellaney, "Maldives: India should not Rest on its Oars", *Hindustan Times*, October 9, 2018d, https://www.hindustantimes.com/search?q=Maldives:-India-should-not-rest-on-its-oars.

Brahma Chellaney, Has India Played into China's Hands in Wuhan. *Hindustan Times*, (2018e, May 7). https://www.hindustantimes.com/opinion/has-india-played-into-china-s-hands-in-wuhan/story-Yzu9I7JFqKK3YZQEfLWuKI.html

"China Ensnares Vulnerable States in a Debt Trap", February 24, 2018. https://chellaney.net/?s=China+Ensnares+Vulnerable+States+in+a+Debt+Trap&submit=Search.

"China's Creditor Imperialism", January 1, 2018. https://chellaney.net/?s=China's+Creditor+Imperialism&submit=Search.

"China's Imperial Project Runs into Resistance", October 4, 2018. https://chellaney.net/2018/10/04/chinas-imperial-project-runs-into-resistance/.

"China'Sole Ally in Asia Might Get More than it Wished for", November 7, 2016. https://chellaney.net/2016/11/07/chinas-sole-ally-in-asia-might-get-more-than-it-wished-for/ "China's Debt-Trap Diplomacy", January 25, 2017. https://chellaney.net/?s=China's+Debt-Trap+Diplomacy&submit=Search.

Constantino Xavier, "New Delhi Can't Hope to do a Male in Colombo", *Hindustan Times*, October 31, 2018, https://www.hindustantimes.com/analysis/new-delhi-can-t-hope-to-do-a-male-in-colombo/story-EoYKpms3TZIe6VMzvhJKzL.html.

David Brewster: *The Indian Ocean* (translated by Du Youkang and Mao Yue), Social Science Academic Press, 2016.

"Democracy in Danger in yet another Asian Nation", November 16, 2018. https://chellaney.net/2018/11/16/democracy-in-danger-in-yet-another-asian-nation/.

Debt-trap Diplomacy. https://en.wikipedia.org/wiki/Debt-trap_diplomacy.

"Fearing Debt Trap, Pakistan Rethinks Chinese 'Silk Road' Projects", *Hindustan Times*, September 30, 2018c, https://www.hindustantimes.com/world-news/fearing-debt-trap-pakistan-rethinks-chinese-silk-road-projects/story-vXKGyGkmuFWrvmf0d0oaPP.html.

Fearing Debt Trap, Pak Cuts Spending on CPEC Project; China Downplays Matter, Indo Asian News Service, Beijing, (2018a, Oct. 9). https://www.hindustantimes.com/world-news/fearing-debt-trap-pak-cuts-spending-on-cpec-project-china-downplays/story-.

Fearing Debt Trap, Pakistan Rethinks Chinese 'Silk Road' Projects, *Reuters*, (2018b, Sep 30). https://www.hindustantimes.com/world-news/fearing-debt-trap-pakistan-rethinks-chines-silk-road-projects/story-vXKGyGkmuFWrvmf0d0oaPP.html

Government of India, Press Release on Presidential Elections in Maldives, Ministry of External Affairs, (2018, September 24). https://www.mea.gov.in/press-releases.htm?dtl/30424/press+release+on+presidential+elections+in+maldives.

Karl Hendler, "Reading the Belt and Road Tea Leaves: Aggression, Explitation, or Prosperity?" (2018, August 8). https://www.pacforum.org/analysis/pacnet-56-reading-belt-and-road-tea-leaves-aggression-exploitation-or-prosperity.

"How Can America Change Pakistani Behavior?" January 30, 2018. https://chellaney.net/?s=How+Can+America+Change+Pakistani+Behavior&submit=Search.

India Our Best Friend: Maldives Foreign Minister's Message to China, *Hindustan Times*, (2018, Nov. 26). https://www.hindustantimes.com/india-news/india-our-best-friend-maldives-foreign-minister-s-message-to-china/story-XwEDXVAxBNzdXoWiCR5eiN.html. Under President Abdullah Yameen, India was asked to withdraw military installations and personnel.

India wants to give 1 billion to help 'little brothers' repay China's loans, but there is a condition, *China.com*, (2018, November 30). https://news.china.com/international/1000/20181130/34551082_all.html.

"Insecurity in India's Maritime Backyard", November 15, 2018. https://chellaney.net/2018/11/15/insecurity-in-indias-maritime-backyard/.

Joint Press Statement after talks between Prime Minister Narendra Modi and President of Maldives Ibrahim Mohamed Solih, Ministry of External Affairs, Government of India, (2018, November 17). https://www.mea.gov.in/bilateral-documents.htm?dtl/30605/joint+press+statement+after+talks+between+prime+minister+narendra+modi+and+president+of+maldives+ibrahim+mohamed+solih.

Joint Statement on the Occasion of State Visit of the President of the Republic of Maldives to India, Ministry of External Affairs, Government of India, (2018, December 17).

Lei Jia Mohan: *The Grand Maritime Strategy of China and India* (translated by Zhu Xianchao and Zhang Yumei), Beijing, China Publishing Group Corporation, China Democratic Legal Publishing House, 2014.

Li Zhonglin, *A Review of the Monroe Doctrine in India*, Asian-African Review, No.4, 2013.

Tang Libin: *China set "traps"? The West smears and hypes China, which is overthrown by facts*, *News Network*, (June 15), 2018. http://column.cankaoxiaoxi.com/2018/0615/2280860_4.shtml.

Maldives Election Changing Days' Foreign Media Involved in China-India Competition, *Global Network*, (2018, September 25).

"Modi Sends out a Clear Message at the Shangri-La Dialogue," *The Hindustan Times*, (2018, Jun. 4). https://www.hindustantimes.com/editorials/modi-sends-out-a-clear-message-at-the-shangri-la-dialogue/story-VZx9KOod8dPxSkFKcDtd8I.html.

Hans Morgenthau: *Interstate politics: power struggles and peace (*Translated by Xu Xin, Hao Wang and Li Baoping), Peking University Press, 2006.
Press Release on India's Reaction over Evolving Situation in Maldives after Order of the Supreme Court of Maldives, Ministry of External Affairs, Government of India, (2018, February 2). https://www.mea.gov.in/press-releases.htm?dtl/29409/Press_Release_on_Indias__over_evolving_situation_in_Maldives_after_order_of_the_Supreme_Court_of_Maldives.
Press Release on Situation in Maldives, Ministry of External Affairs, Government of India, (2018, February 20). https://www.mea.gov.in/press-releases.htm?dtl/29501/Press_Release_on_situation_in_Maldives.
Press Release on the Political Situation in the Maldives, Ministry of External Affairs, Government of India, (2018, June 14). https://www.mea.gov.in/pressreleases.htm?dtl/29977/Press_Release_on_the_Political_Situation_in_the_Maldives.
Press Release on the situation in Maldives, Ministry of External Affairs, Government of India, (2018, February 21). https://www.mea.gov.in/press-releases.htm?dtl/29505/Press_Release_on_the_situation_in_Maldives.
Press Release on the situation in Maldives, Ministry of External Affairs, Government of India, February 18, 2020. https://www.mea.gov.in/press-releases.htm?dtl/29505/Press_Release_on_the_situation_in_Maldives.
Kartikeya Ramanathan, *Maldives Close to Free Trade Agreement with China*, India Caught Unaware, (2017, Dec. 1). https://www.hindustantimes.com/world-news/maldives-close-to-free-trade-agreement-with-china-india-caught-unawares/story-u0qLPWNMv7SZT6QMxmCqvN.html.
Revocation of State of Emergency in Maldives, Ministry of External Affairs, Government of India, (2018, March 22). https://www.mea.gov.in/press-releases.htm?dtl/29705/Revocation_of_State_of_Emergency_in_Maldives.
Ni Shixiong: *Contemporary Western International Relations Theory, Fudan University Press*, 2016.
Situation in Maldives, Ministry of External Affairs, Government of India, (2018, February 6). https://www.mea.gov.in/press-releases.htm?dtl/29415/Situation_in_Maldives.
"The Bull in the China Shop", June 29, 2017. https://chellaney.net/?s=The+Bull+in+the+China+Shop&submit=Search.
"The China Backlash", September 28, 2018. https://chellaney.net/2018/09/28/the-china-backlash/.
The Maldives's New Regime is an Opportunity for India to Regain its Lost Ground, (2018, Nov. 21). https://www.hindustantimes.com/editorials/the-maldives-new-regime-is-an-opportunity-for-india-to-regain-its-lost-ground/story-A3pSSkeVFr6Doru3MOtL5N.html.
Tried to Play India against China as a 'Puppet Master': Maldives Foreign Minister on Ex-president Yameen, *Press Trust of India*, (2018, Nov. 27). https://www.hindustantimes.com/india-news/tried-to-play-india-against-china-as-a-puppet-master-maldives-foreign-minister-on-ex-president-yameen/story-QCjc7VhCsg94eK6Lw8AnDI.html.
Visit of Foreign Minister of Maldives to India, Ministry of External Affairs, Government of India, (2018, November 26). https://www.mea.gov.in/press-releases.htm?dtl/30640/Visit_of_Foreign_Minister_of_Maldives_to_India.
"Why the South China Sea is Critical to Security," March 30, 2018. https://chellaney.net/?s=Why+the+South+China+Sea+is+Critical+to+Security&submit=Search.

Chapter 4
Debt Issue and BRI-CMEC in Myanmar

Myint San

Abstract The main objective of this chapter is to highlight the importance of the China-Myanmar Economic Corridor (CMEC) project and its opportunities and challenges, especially in the debt issue of Myanmar. As a gateway of the Belt and Road Initiative (BRI), the CMEC is one of the most important parts of BRI, which aims to improve connectivity between China and Myanmar through infrastructure investment, economic development, and regional cooperation. In particular, the CMEC transport corridor provides China with overland access to the Indian Ocean, and it is also expected to boost landlocked Yunnan's economy. In addition, the *Kyaukphyu* Deep Sea port is also critical for China's energy security. However, the CMEC is surrounded by some serious challenges ranging from regional geo-politics, social and environmental impacts, and internal instability to political discontent. Moreover, BRI spending in developing countries has raised serious concerns about debt sustainability. As a result, policy-makers in Myanmar have cautioned about BRI-CMEC project activities and learned lessons from the experience of the debt issues in other developing countries. As the "debt trap" is complex and controversial, the responsibilities will have on both sides, creditor and debtor. Greater debt transparency and international standards of lending are critical in addressing the risks posed by rising debt in many developing countries. Presently, because of the COVID-19 pandemic and changing global geo-politics, Myanmar is facing difficulties in servicing its debt obligations to China. China is also trying to help Myanmar restructure its debt, including through partial debt forgiveness, with a case-by-case method.

Keywords BRI · CMEC · Debt · Trap · China · Myanmar

M. San (✉)
Dawei SEZ Management Committee, Yangon, Myanmar
e-mail: dr.myintsan85@gmail.com

N. Peng and M. Y. Cheng (eds.), *The Reality and Myth of BRI's Debt Trap*, Indo-Pacific Focus, https://doi.org/10.1007/978-981-97-1056-0_4

4.1 Introduction

China's Belt and Road Initiative (BRI) aims to improve connectivity between China and other countries, the developing/underdeveloped countries in particular, through infrastructure investment and regional integration. It could promote trade, more efficient resource reallocation and strengthen economic growth across the region. It could also encourage countries to coordinate economic policy and improve regional collaboration.

Myanmar is one of the neighboring countries of China, and the CMEC is also one of the most important parts of BRI. However, BRI spending in developing countries has raised serious concerns about the debt sustainability, and there is no exception in Myanmar. As a result, policy-makers in Myanmar have cautioned about BRI-CMEC project activities and debt issues based on the experience of other countries, such as Sri Lanka, Pakistan and Laos. It is necessary to consider both the creditor and the debtor sides. The higher interest rate, lack of credit governance such as transparency, accountability, and noncompetitive nature of the projects as well as the international standard of lending practices such as Paris Club are major issues of China's lending. On the other hand, white elephant megaprojects by governments in developing countries, the savings-gap and foreign exchange gap problems, the balance of payment problems, poor and mismanagement in the local economy, corruption and the neglect of debt sustainability are major issues on the debtor side. To solve the debt issues in developing countries, it deserves attention and should be addressed in a coordinated manner by all parties worldwide.

4.2 BRI and "Debt Trap"

The BRI is a massive program launched in 2013 and tries to build a network of infrastructure, such as ports, railways, and roads, linking China more closely with the rest of Asia, Africa, and Europe. The objective of BRI is creating networks that will allow for a more efficient and productive free flow of trade as well as further integration of international markets both physically and digitally. Thanks to the BRI, Chinese construction, transportation, and communication companies are engaging tremendously in construction work across the globe. If infrastructure is a critical engine of growth in developing countries, then debt financing is the fuel for that engine. Public borrowing to support productive investment is central to the development narratives of today's wealthy countries, and it continues to drive growth in emerging economies.

However, there is also considerable evidence indicating significant negative impacts on countries and their people when governments incur too much debt. Low-income countries (LICs) face significant challenges in meeting their development objectives, including the Sustainable Development Goals (SDGs), while at the same time ensuring that their external debt remains sustainable. Carrying out normal credit activity is essential to economic growth, but its availability is uneven across countries, especially for developing countries. Therefore, access to concessional financing is critical for achieving the two goals of debt sustainability and progress toward reaching development goals.[1] In particular, financing infrastructure projects is important for addressing a country's development bottleneck, upgrading industries, and promoting sustainable development. However, such projects are generally characterized by a long payback period. As Uhuru Kenyutta, President of Kenya, said, the debt problem in essence concerns not the occurrence of debt but the use of debt.[2]

International lending has always been a risky business. Information asymmetry between lenders and borrowers incentivizes the latter to misuse loans and mismanagement, while lenders lack credible enforcement power over international loan contracts. The history has shown that over-exuberant lending on the part of transnational banks and investors regularly contributes to the boom-and-bust cycles of what many have termed "casino capitalism."[3] Similar to these historical episodes, China's excessive capital supply and saturated domestic markets led many Chinese lenders to look outward for new borrowers in the Global South, despite the high risks. What is distinct about BRI is that it is a state-led lending initiative aimed at exporting not only China's excess capacity and capital but also the Chinese economic growth model centered on infrastructure investment. However, expanding this model internationally entails a high degree of financial risk, particularly in the Global South, where many countries have a record of debt defaults and debt distress.[4]

Since 2017, China has faced criticism from foreign officials and academics for using its financing and infrastructure projects to ensnare poor countries with heavy debt loads and thereby win strategic leverage. A "debt-trap" situation is one where: "the creditor country is said to extend excessive credit to a debtor country with the intention of extracting economic or political concessions when the debtor country becomes unable to meet its repayment obligations. "Debt-trap diplomacy" is a term in international finance that describes a creditor country or institution extending debt to a borrowing nation partially, or solely, to increase the lender's political leverage.[5] They document the large scale of China's lending boom from 2000 to 2017 and find that approximately 50% of China's lending was not captured by the most widely used international debt statistics. "Hidden debts" are a significant challenge to international surveillance and the pricing of risk.

According to the International Monetary Fund (IMF), from 2013 to 2016, China's contribution to the public debt of heavily indebted poor countries nearly doubled from 6.2 to 11.6%. China's lending is expanding even more through the BRI. These types of loans are described as a vicious cycle, and taking out external loans to promote development and well-being with the purpose of self-perpetuating growth not only

[1] John Hurley, (2018).

[2] The so-called China's debt trap is a narrative trap (2022).

[3] Liao, (2021).

[4] Ibid.

[5] Horn Sebastian & Carmen M. Reinhart & Christoph Trebesch, China's Overseas Lending, *Journal of International Economics*, Vol.133, https://www.nber.org/papers/w26050.

Table 4.1 Selected debt figures for developing countries significantly or highly vulnerable to debt distress (millions USD)

Country	GDP	PPG Debt	PPG ED	Debt to China	BRI lending pipeline	PPG ED/ GDP	Debt to China/ PPG ED
	(1)	(2)	(3)	(4)	(5)	(6) = (3)/ (1)	(7) = (4)/ (3)
Djibouti	1,727	1,496	1,464	1,200	1,464	84.77	81.96
Kyrgyzstan	6,551	4,068	3,976	1,483	4,564	60.69	37.30
Laos	15,903	10,782	8,604	4,186	5,471	54.10	48.65
Maldives	4,224	2,775	879	240	1,107	20.81	27.30
Mongolia	10,951	9,583	7,392	3,046	2,469	67.50	41.21
Montenegro	4,374	3,412	2,406	200	1,535	55.01	8.31
Tajikistan	6,952	2,906	2,252	1,197	2,807	32.39	53.15
Pakistan	278,913	195,239	58,014	6,329	40,021	20.80	10.91
Sri Lanka	81,322	6,9,286	32,565	3,800	2,136	40.04	11.67

Note PPG Debt = Public and publicly guaranteed debt; ED = External debt; PPG ED = Public and publicly guaranteed external debt. All GDP and debt statistics reflect 2016 or end-2016 values, with the exception of the lending pipeline, which reflects estimated value post-2016
Source John Hurley, Scott Morris, and Gilyn Porte lance, 2018

does not work but also turns into perpetual debt with an enormous capital flow to creditors. These debts should be enabled by the governments, as is most of the time the case; the reality of it on the local economy is crushing. Debt must be dealt with. But to achieve this, a new political and social consensus must emerge.

A recent Center for Global Development report found that eight BRI recipient countries, namely, Djibouti, Kyrgyzstan, Laos, the Maldives, Mongolia, Montenegro, Pakistan, and Tajikistan, are at a high risk of debt distress due to BRI loans,[6] as shown in Table 4.1. These countries will face rising debt-to-GDP ratios beyond 50%, with at least 40% of external debt owed to China once BRI lending is completed. The IMF has also scrutinized multiple aspects of the BRI, repeatedly warning of unsustainable debt levels, predatory lending, and the lack of project transparency.[7] An IMF program should include BRI debt restructuring or reevaluating proposed infrastructure investments to determine if they are financially sound. At a minimum, the IMF will need to see the terms of BRI loans to complete the necessary debt sustainability analysis.[8]

[6] John Hurley (2018).

[7] Christine Lagarde (2018).

[8] Constanța Botnar (2020).

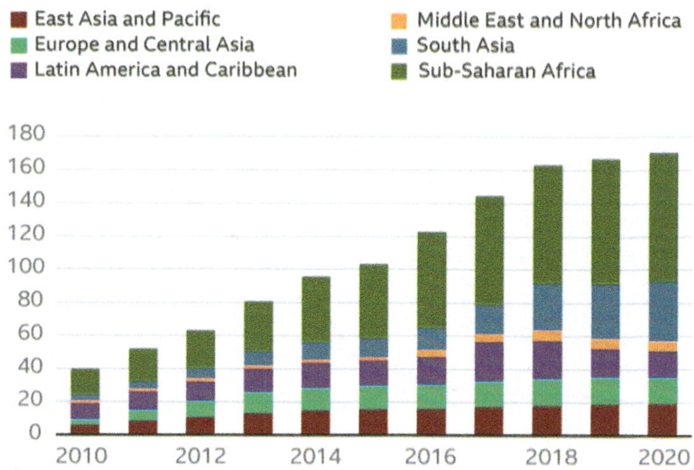

Fig. 4.1 China's lending to developing countries (2010–2020). *Source* World bank international debt statistics

In addition, according to the World Bank (WB),[9] of the 35 billion USD that the world's 74 low-income nations will owe in debt service payment in 2022, approximately 37% or 13.1 billion USD is owned by Chinese entities. At the end of 2020, of the 97 countries for which data were available, those with the highest external debt to China were all involved in the project.[10] China has been seeing the Association of Southeast Asian Nations (ASEAN) as an important region for its massive infrastructure-building BRI.[11] According to Refinitiv, BRI-related funding for the 10 ASEAN countries since 2013 has amounted to 304.1 billion USD, equivalent to half their annual fiscal spending. Of them, Myanmar, Laos, and Cambodia are the three countries that rely heavily on China. Although the funding for Myanmar at 21.7 billion USD is less than one-third the size for Indonesia, all three of the mainland Southeast Asian countries have accepted Chinese investment and loans that are 1.6 to 2 times larger than their annual fiscal expenditures. China is one of the world's largest single creditor nations. Its loans to lower- and middle-income countries have tripled over the past decade, reaching 170 billion USD by the end of 2020. There are now more than 40 low- and middle-income countries, according to Aid Data, whose debt exposure to Chinese lenders is more than 10% of the size of their annual economic output (GDP) as a result of this "hidden debt (Fig. 4.1)".[12]

Governments around the world responded to the COVID-19 pandemic with massive fiscal, monetary, and financial stimulus pacxfvfgbkages. While these measures were aimed at addressing the health emergency, cushioning the impact of the pandemic on the poor and vulnerable and putting countries on a path to recovery,

---

[9] Shabtai Gold (2022).

[10] The Country Most in Debt to China (2022).

[11] Iori Kawate & Yuichi Nitta (2021).

[12] China: Is it burdening poor countries with unsustainable debt (2022).

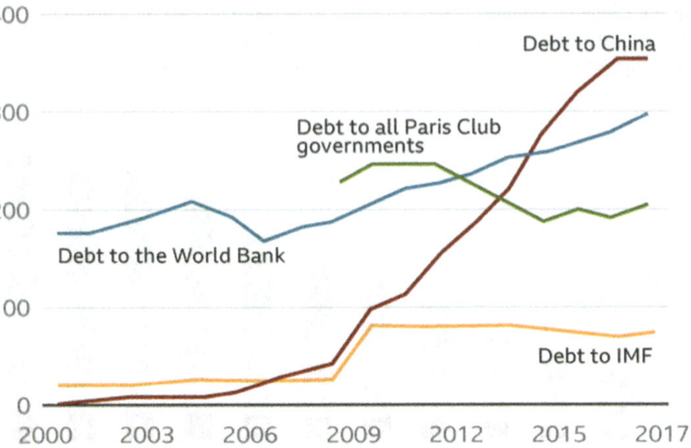

Fig. 4.2 Aggregate external public debt (Billions, USD). *Source* world bank international debt statistics; Paris club

the resulting debt burden of the world's low-income countries rose 12% to a record 860 billion USD in 2020, according to a World Bank report (Fig. 4.2).[13]

However, China's overall lending commitments are likely to be significantly greater than these figures suggest. Research by AidData, an international development body at William & Mary University in the US, finds that half of China's lending to developing countries is not reported in official debt statistics. Much of the debt owed to China relates to large infrastructure projects such as roads, railways, and ports and to the mining and energy industry under BRI. China does not publish records of its foreign loans, and the majority of its contracts contain nondisclosure clauses that prevent borrowers from revealing their contents. It argues that such confidentiality is common practice for international loan contracts. Moreover, much of China's development financing is fundamentally a commercial operation. In addition, China tends to lend at higher rates of interest than Western governments. At approximately 4%, these loans are close to commercial market rates and approximately four times that of a typical loan from the WB or an individual country such as France or Germany. The needed repayment period for a Chinese loan is also generally shorter than 10 years, compared to approximately 28 years for other lenders' concessional loans to developing countries.[14]

However, labeling BRI a "debt trap" not only insults the borrowing countries but also neglects the domestic root of the debt problem. "Debt trap diplomacy" is a severe concern for developing countries. Beyond this, a 'strategic trap' is another dimension to consider in many other BRI nations that could fall into the same political-economic

[13] Low-Income Country Debt Rises to Record $860 Billion in 2020, (2021).

[14] Ibid.

crisis as Sri Lanka.[15] Development holds the key to addressing the debt problem of developing countries. A concerted global effort is needed to balance the supply and demand for development financing. To this end, the Chinese President Xi Jinping proposed the 'Global Development Initiative' with a gathering greater global support for development. In addition, China is committed to helping developing countries ease their burden. For example, in the wake of the COVID-19 pandemic, China implemented the debt relief initiatives of the G-20 and signed a debt relief agreement or reached a consensus with 19 African countries. China is now the country with the most debt relief among G-20 members.[16]

Many more countries are in a situation where their debt is unsustainable. Often, these nations took on debt before COVID-19 hit, and now there is 'just not going to be enough money for them to pay the debt. Moreover, Beijing-controlled creditors have continued to take 'full payments' during the pandemic, despite an effort to freeze, such as transfer with the world economy in turmoil.[17] "The pandemic has accelerated China's pivot toward 'soft' infrastructure such as health services and the digital economy as new priorities in its economic engagement with the region," Wang said in the report, pointing to the increased prominence of the "health silk road" and "digital silk road" on Beijing's BRI agenda.[18]

According to *Cui Can*,[19] BRI has showcased resilience and vitality in boosting economic development amid the COVID-19 pandemic and assisted participating countries in stabilizing their economies. Over the years, several low-income and emerging economies have been experiencing daunting debt risks owing to the COVID-19 pandemic and global political uncertainties. As a result, it is necessary to adopt appropriate measures to sort out the debt repayment issues of such countries with concerted efforts from all parties, said *Zhou Xiaochuan*, former governor of China's central bank, at the Boao Forum for Asia Annual Conference 2022.[20] "The BRI is by no means a 'debt trap' that participating countries could fall into," *Zhou* stressed, "In fact, China has been an active participant in the G-20 initiative on postponing debt repayments for the world's least-developed countries."[21] The country ranked first among the G-20 members in debt deferral amounts, making significant contributions to addressing the short-term liquidity needs of most impoverished countries, according to a recent press briefing by China's foreign ministry. Moreover, *Hu Xiaolian*, a Chinese expert on economic issues, pointed out that the critical path for low-income countries to solve debt issues is development. "Debt

[15] Asanga Abeyagoonnasekera, "Sri Lankan Crisis between Debt-trap and Strategic-trap: The Chinese Stake", ISDP, https://isdp.eu/sri-lankan-crisis-between-debt-trap-and-strategic-trap-thechinese-stake/.

[16] The so-called China's debt trap is a narrative trap (2022).

[17] Ibid.

[18] China's Belt and Road plans for Southeast Asia face uncertain 'long-term prospects' as social, environment concerns persist: study (2022).

[19] Cui Can (2022).

[20] Ibid.

[21] Ibid.

problems, including those related to countries along BRI, are complicated, and debt restructuring may not be the priority choice for these countries".[22] Jones and Hameiri find that controversial BRI projects were often initiated by recipient governments, and the perceived debt problems arose mainly because of the misconduct of the local elites.[23] Cui Can explained that to develop themselves and eliminate poverty in the future, such countries still need financial support from the international community. However, debt restructuring may lower the sovereign rating and increase financing costs when these countries borrow debt or attract foreign investment in infrastructure construction projects.

Pradumna Bickram Rana and Ji Xianbai conducted an online perception survey of opinion leaders (defined as policymakers, academics, and representatives of businesses and media) from a wide range of stakeholder countries, 26 Asian countries that have signed the BRI MoU with China. Over 1200 opinion leaders responded to the survey questionnaire. The key findings of their survey are as follows: After having considered both the benefits and costs of BRI, 41.6% of the respondents to survey stakeholders believed that BRI represented a net benefit for their countries, while only 14.8% said that it was a net cost. A total of 40.6% noted that it was too early to tell. The strongest endorsements for BRI came from Bangladesh (64.5%), Pakistan (59.7%), and Nepal (58.8%), while the opinion leaders from the Philippines were the least receptive to BRI. The Korean, Myanmar, and Vietnamese opinion leaders took a more neutral stance, saying that it was too early to ascertain whether BRI was a net opportunity or cost to their respective countries.[24] According to their findings, some respondents noted that domestic factors that were in the purview of host governments (such as corruption and a reckless propensity to borrow) were responsible for rising debt levels rather than Chinese BRI financing. They also found that three out of the five South Asian countries for which data are available are presently facing debt distress. These are Sri Lanka, Pakistan, and Maldives. Presently, because of the ongoing pandemic, many BRI projects are on hold, and a number of BRI countries are facing difficulties in servicing their debt obligations to China.

China is helping these countries restructure their debt, including through partial debt forgiveness. In countries suffering from debt distress, the Chinese have provided debt relief in an ad hoc case-by-case manner. China has also demonstrated a willingness to provide additional credit so that a borrower can avoid default.[25] Moreover, the G-20 Agenda toward a More Stable and Resilient International Financial Architecture was carried forward in 2017 to include "G-20 Operational Guidelines for Sustainable Financing", which provide a detailed, multifaceted approach to improve debt sustainability and the debt restructuring process.[26]

[22] Ibid.

[23] Ibid.

[24] Pradumna Bickram Rana & Jason Ji Xianbai (2020).

[25] John Hurley (2018).

[26] Ibid.

Table 4.2 Major BRI-CMEC projects in Myanmar

No	Name of project	Status of project
1	*Kyaukphyu* deep seaport and special economic zone (SEZ)	Framework agreement signed in 2018
2	The muse-mandalay railway project	MoU signed in 2020
3	Three border economic zones in Shan and Kachin States	MoU for the Muse-Ruili zone signed in 2020
4	The New Yangon City development project	Letter of Intent signed in 2020

Note BRI: belt & road initiative and MoU: memorandum of understanding
Source SiuSue Mark, Indra Overland, and Roman Vakulchuk (2020)

4.3 BRI-CMEC in Myanmar

Myanmar occupied a unique geographical position in China's BRI, laying at the junction of South Asia and Southeast Asia and between the Indian Ocean and south-western China's landlock Yunnan Province. Moreover, China is one of the major investors, lenders and trading partners of Myanmar.[27] Yunnan Province holds a critical position in border trade and investment, accounting for 70% of Myanmar's border trade. The CMEC starts from Yunnan Province, which shares a border with Myanmar. From Ruili city on the China-Myanmar border, the corridor would head toward Mandalay, the second largest city of Myanmar. From there, it will extend toward the east and west to Yangon city and the *Kyaukphyu* SEZ in Rakhine State. The CMEC is part of China's broader strategy of investing widely to diversify its sources of importing energy to enhance its economic integration with Myanmar.

It is estimated that under the elaborate plan, China is targeting a massive investment of approximately 100 billion USD in Myanmar, which exceeds the cost of China-Pakistan Economic Corridor (CPEC) funding (62 billion USD)[28] Of the 38 projects that China has proposed under CMEC, Myanmar has approved only nine thus far. The agreement involved the development of the Kyaukphyu deep seaport and special economic zone (SEZ), development of the New Yangon city project, development of three economic border zones in the Shan and Kachin States of Myanmar and a feasibility study of the Muse-Mandalay Railway project. The major CMEC projects are given in Table 4.2. Chinese leaders and officials wanted to get Myanmar to reaffirm commitment to the CMEC. An important item on Wang's agenda during his recent visit was to get Myanmar to expedite project implementation. Myanmar is also interested in benefiting from BRI-CMEC.

Kyaukphyu is key to the BRI and CMEC, as it sits on the Bay of Bangal and will provide strategic geo-economic access to the Indian Ocean, where China wants to develop marine infrastructure. Kyaukphyu Deep Sea Port could be taken to circumvent the Malacca Straits, while the Kyaukphyu SEZ could be a key to Myanmar,

[27] Myint San (2019).
[28] Yan Naing (2020).

Bangladesh and the Northeast India Economic Corridor. The 10 billion USD Kyaukphyu project includes a port that costs 7.3 billion USD and a special economic zone pegged at 2.7 billion USD. There are doubts over the economic viability of the SEZ at Kyaukphyu, as it is poorly connected to other commercial centers in Myanmar. In 2015, the deep-water port in the Kyaukphyu project was delayed after critics raised concern that the deal could land Myanmar into excessive debt to China, as it would cost 7.5 billion USD and give Chinese developers an 85% share. In the wake of criticism, Myanmar negotiated with a consortium led by the China Communications Construction Company (CCCC) to reduce the initial project cost from 7.5 billion USD to 1.3 billion USD and raise its own share from the previous 15 to 30%.

Similarly, the 431 km of the Muse-Mandalay railway project connects China's Yunnan Province and the trading post-Muse on the China-Myanmar border. It has no forward movement. The estimated cost for this project will be 9 billion USD. In particular, local communities are opposing the project and have complained that they were not consulted for the project's Environment Impact Assessment (EIA) study. Will the railway project provide fuel to an already raging armed conflict in the Shan state and provide Shan rebels with new targets to hit?[29] Myanmar's government also split up the tender processes for the New Yangon City Project (a megacity project in Yangon), the largest urban center and commercial city of the country. The 1.5 billion USD project to cover 20,000 acres has been a source of controversy and criticism due to the selection of the CCCC, a Chinese state-owned firm blacklisted by the World Bank (WB) from 2015 to 2017 as the frontrunner in the tender. The single tender for the entire project would require the bidding firms to have a large initial investment and may deter other investors.

Importantly, the Myanmar government was having dealt with strong opposition to projects from its people. Local lives and livelihoods are likely to be adversely affected by infrastructure projects, and people are angry that they have not been consulted. There is the question of environmental degradation too that is of concern to local communities and activists. Much opacity shrouds project terms adding to unease over Chinese intentions. There have been several mass protests against CMEC projects, and this could prove particularly troublesome in ethnic states that are roiled in conflicts. People in the Kachin and Shan states, for instance, have long protested against not only their oppression and exclusion by the Myanmar state but also the exploitation of their natural resources by the Chinese. CMEC projects, several of which are located in these states, are seen as yet more collusion between the two.

Regarding BRI and CMEC projects, a famous Myanmar Economist, U Myint (2019), also pointed out the following points: the CMEC, like any other project, will have its costs and benefits. The standard economic cost/benefit principle is to proceed with a project if its benefits are larger than its costs. It is important to measure costs and benefits, as well as clearly identify who benefits and who bears the costs. In May 2019, the government of Myanmar set out the terms upon which it would negotiate BRI project agreements with China. These include stipulations that Myanmar should be allowed to do the following: (a) seek financing from international

[29] Sudha Ramachandran (2021).

financial institutions to implement the projects. (b) invite international tenders to ensure international investment in the projects. (c) choose projects that create mutual benefits for both sides.[30]

Recently, a Myanmar-based think-tank Institute for Strategy and Policy (ISP-Myanmar)[31] released a survey report examining elite attitudes toward China and the current state of China-Myanmar relations. Stakeholders' opinions are also critical for the implementation of BRI and CMEC projects. The report by the ISP-Myanmar surveyed 215 representatives from civil society organizations, political parties, business associations, and ethnic armed organizations in February and March 2022, a year after the military's coup. According to their survey findings, the most common public concern regarding the CMEC among the participants was China's growing geopolitical influence over the region (34%). The second most common concern was a debt trap (18%), followed by concerns over socioenvironmental impacts (17%) and then China's economic domination (16%). Only 6% answered political influence, while 3% indicated they had no concerns over the CMEC. According to Khine Win, the executive director of Sandhi Governance Institute, a local organization that monitors joint ventures between the government and private groups, said compartmentalization of the project reduced the risk for Myanmar.[32]

4.4 Debt Issues in Myanmar

4.4.1 Debt Sustainability

In 2021, Myanmar's total public debt was estimated to be 27.6 million USD. It covered public domestic debt (60.5% of total), and public and publicly guaranteed (PPG) debt was 39.5%. Most PPG external debt is held by bilateral creditors, and China (11.3% of total) and Japan (12.7% of total) are the largest creditors. Among the multilateral creditors, the International Development Association (IDA) and the Asian Development Bank (ADB) were the largest, as given in Tables 4.5 and 4.6. All external PPG debt indicators remain below the policy-relevant thresholds in the baseline scenario.

These thresholds include the present value (PV) of the external-debt-to-GDP ratio, the PV of the external-debt-to-exports ratio, the external-debt-service-exports ratio, and the external-debt-service-to-revenue ratio. According to the IMF's estimation, the PV of the PPG external debt-to GDP ratio is gradually declining from 11.3% of GDP in 2019/20 to approximately 9.2% of GDP in 2029/30. As shown in Table 4.3,

[30] U Myint (2019).

[31] Myanmar's Key Stakeholders and Their Perceptions of Sino-Myanmar Relations-A Survey 2022, (2022)

[32] Khine Win (2019).

Table 4.3 Total public and publicly guaranteed debt in Myanmar

Particular	2019		2021	
	US$ Million	Percent of total	US$ Million	Percent of total
Total external debt	10.1	38.2	10.9	39.5
1.1. Bilateral creditors	8.1	30.6	8.4	30.3
Paris club	4.2	16.0	5.0	18.0
Of which: Japan	2.9	10.9	3.5	12.7
Non-Paris club	3.9	14.6	3.4	12.2
Of which: China	3.4	13.0	3.1	11.3
1.2. Multilateral creditors	2.0	7.5	2.5	9.2
Of which: ADB	0.6	2.2	0.6	2.2
Of which: IDA	1.4	5.2	1.5	5.6
Of which: IMF	0.0	0.0	0.4	1.3
Commercial creditors	0.0	0.1	0.0	0.1
2. Domestic debt	16.3	61.8	16.7	60.5
3. Total debt	26.4	100.0	27.6	100.0

Source IMF and Myanmar authority

both debt service-to-exports and the debt service-to-revenue ratio decline starting in 2026, reflecting the end of the repayment period under the DSSI.[33]

Thus, despite the expected increase in the current account and budget deficits and additional borrowing, external and public debt should remain robust to shocks, and the overall risk of debt distress should be low. Standardized stress tests show that an export slowdown shock has the greatest impact. It increases the PV of the external debt-to-GDP ratio, the external debt-to-exports ratio and the debt service-to-exports ratio the most, highlighting the need to expand the export base. The standardized stress test also shows that the debt service-to-revenue ratio is most affected by depreciation. According to the study of the World Bank and IMF, Myanmar has a low-income status because its CPIA is less than 3.25 (Table 4.4).

Table 4.6 also provides the debt burden of some Asian countries, including Myanmar. According to this table, Myanmar is the lowest position in debt burden, with 17% of GDP and 120 USD per capita debt, compared to other Asian countries. As an LDC country, Myanmar needs to borrow external loans because of budget and trade deficits, declines in domestic production, requirements for infrastructure and development projects and other factors. Myanmar needs to consider the following factors when she borrows the loan from external sources: (1) external loan should be commercially viable, with a good rate of return from the projects, and concessional loan; (2) careful attention to losses of debt; (3) evaluation and monitoring of loan

[33] IMF Country Report, (2020).

Table 4.4 External debt in Myanmar (2000–2019)

No	External indebtedness (Millions USD)	2000	2005	2010	2015	2019
1	Total debt outstanding and disbursed	6,482.2	7,177.9	10,164.2	10,292.8	11,114.4
2	Long-term debt	5,899.3	6,327.6	8,607.1	9,853.2	10,708.5
3	Public and publicly guaranteed					
4	Short-term debt	526.3	788.2	1,178.6	99.0	66.1
5	Use of IMF credit	56.6	62.1	378.5	340.6	339.8
6	External debt (% of GNI)	72.8	59.9	20.5	15.6	15.2
7	Total long-term debt (% of total debt)	91.0	88.2	84.7	95.7	96.3
8	Short-term debt (% of total debt)	8.1	11.0	11.6	1.0	0.6
9	Debt service (% of exports of goods and services)	1.0	0.6	3.1	3.6	3.8

Source ADB (2021): Key Indicators for Asia and the Pacific

Table 4.5 Debt sustainability indicators in Myanmar

Indicator	Actual		Projection								
	2017	2018	2019	2020	2021	2022	2023	2024	2025	2030	2040
PV of PPG external-debt-to-GDP ratio	–	–	11.8	12.8	12.8	12.1	11.5	10.9	10.4	9.4	9.4
PV of PPG external debt to export ratio	–	–	53.7	72.4	72.3	66.2	61.6	58.1	55.6	47.1	41.7
PPG debt-service-to-export ratio	4.5	5.2	4.2	6.0	6.2	6.8	6.3	6.5	5.5	4.3	3.4
PPG debt-service-to-revenue ratio	5.5	7.0	5.9	7.4	7.7	8.4	7.6	7.7	6.4	4.9	3.9

Note PV means present value. PPG means public and publicly guaranteed
Source IMF (2020)

and performance; (4) regular payment of interest and principal; (5) review of existing external loans; (6) renovation of existing external loans; (7) establishing a good debt management system; and (8) check and balance between the government and the parliament regarding external loans.[34]

[34] Win Shen (2020).

Table 4.6 Debt burden in some Asian countries

No	Country	Year	External debt US$ (Billion)	Percent of GDP	Per capita debt (US$)
1	Myanmar	2015	6.40	17	120
2	Cambodia	2016	9.82	57	600
3	Laos	2016	12.00	53	1,700
4	Vietnam	2015	50.90	26	500
5	Bangladesh	2021	78.40	22	460
6	Sri Lanka	2016	46.60	68	2,200
7	Pakistan	2021	122.00	43	554

Source Wikipedia: list of countries by external debt

4.4.2 Chinese Debt in Myanmar

According to WB, Myanmar's outstanding debt to China was 3.34 billion USD at the end of 2019, down 26% from the end of 2015, immediately before the NLD government came to power. This is in contrast to the 72% and 34% increases in neighboring Laos and Cambodia, respectively, over the same period. Additionally, China's share of external debt fell from approximately 45% in 2015 to approximately 30% in 2019.[35] If the country falls into default, there is a risk of falling into a "debt trap" in which it is forced to hand over critical infrastructure to China. In addition, Myanmar has been keenly aware of this.

Already, Myanmar is heavily indebted to China; approximately 40% of its total foreign debt of 10 billion USD is owed to China. Myanmar is keen to avoid going Sri Lanka's way, i.e., it would like to avoid falling into a Chinese "debt trap". It is therefore being more careful in signing on to the Chinese-proposed projects, preferring to accept only those projects or project components that will benefit Myanmar.

According to former Auditor General,[36] Myanmar's current national debt stands at approximately 10 billion USD, of which 4 billion USD is owed to China. The truth is that loans from China come at higher interest rates than loans from financial institutions such as WB or IMF. The country has to repay as much as 500 million USD annually to China in both principal and interest. As a result, he cautioned the government about continued reliance on Chinese loans, both pre-BRI and BRI loans.

The former Deputy Minister of Planning and Finance and Chairperson of the *Kyaukphyu* SEZ Management Committee has warned against falling into the "debt trap". He has stressed that Chinese projects must have commercial viability and benefit Myanmar. Myanmar officials said that Myanmar will only implement projects that can guarantee mutual benefits for both sides. The previous government set up a 20-member commission including the chief minister of Kachin State to review the project, including its environmental and social impacts. The official explained that

[35] Iori Kawate & Yuichi Nitta (2021).

[36] Myanmar's auditor general cautions own govt against Chinese loans (2020).

the government developed the Myanmar Sustainable Development Plan (MSDP) to ensure better projects and is scrutinizing projects to determine their financial feasibility and relevance for the MSDP. Once a project is included in the project bank, it is considered for funding either via public or private–public channels or in the form of official development assistance (ODA).[37]

One example of the change in policy was the revised plan to build a deep port in Kyaukphyu, Rakhine State. The scale of this project was initially planned at 7.2 billion USD but was reduced to 1.3 billion USD when the basic agreement was reached in November 2018. The project's details were changed at Myanmar's request, and additional investment will be decided on once demand for the port is known. Analysts have pointed out that Myanmar's involvement in China's BRI-CMEC meant that it continued to take new debts to finance its enormous infrastructure projects.[38]

4.4.3 Causes of External Debt

The original reasons for taking external loans are undoubtedly deficiencies in one's own capital and aspirations related to development, consumption and expansion. The experience of debtor countries indicates that budget-deficit policy, when applied, has a direct and indirect bearing on deepening the external imbalance. We can discuss the direct influence when a country takes an external loan to cover some part of the deficit caused by current expenses.

The fiscal deficit in Myanmar widened to 6% of GDP in 2021 from 5% in 2020. Declining revenue widened the deficit despite lower public expenditure. Tax revenue slumped 36.7%. External trade was also hit hard by mobility restrictions to contain the spread of COVID-19 and quell domestic political tensions. The US dollar value of merchandise exports declined by 13% in 2021 on weaker earnings from most major export categories. Import growth fell by 23%, mostly on lower demand for capital and investment goods. Because of these factors, the current account deficit, as a percentage of GDP, narrowed from 2.5% in 2020 to 1.1% in 2021. Foreign direct investment commitments fell by 31.4% in 2021 due to ongoing political uncertainty. The deteriorating business environment affected new company registrations, which dropped by 42.8% in 2021 according to the ADB.

Another reason is that developing countries such as Myanmar are undeniably in need of infrastructure upgrades to promote economic development and improve the living standard of the people, but there are key questions surrounding the ownership, operation and terms of these projects. In addition, the reasons for running into debt depend mainly on the level of development of a country; thus, they differ for economically well-developed countries and for developing countries. In addition, the ongoing COVID-19 pandemic, global recession due to the Russia-Ukraine war

[37] SiuSue Mark & Indra Overland & Roman Vakulchuk (2020).

[38] Dipanjan Roy Chaudhury (2020).

Table 4.7 Selected economic indicators for Myanmar

Indicators	2020	2021	2022	2023
GDP growth	3.2	−18.4	−0.3	2.6
Inflation	5.7	3.6	8.0	8.5
CAB/GDP	−2.5	−1.1	−0.8	−1.3

Note CAB = current account balance, GDP = gross domestic product. The fiscal year data for 2022 and 2023 are estimated

Source Central bank of Myanmar; Central statistical organization; Asian development bank estimates

and internal political instability have also greatly affected economic development, budget deficits, balances of payment and debt payments.

According to the Asian Development Outlook (ADO), Myanmar's GDP is estimated to have contracted by 18.4% in fiscal year 2021 after shrinking to 3.2% in 2020 (Table 4.7). All major sectors led to the decline in GDP except agriculture. Political instability weighed heavily on business sentiment, and the COVID-19 pandemic created both demand and supply shocks in the economy. The kyat, the local currency, depreciated by 32.6% against the US dollar over 2021 on declining export earnings and lower capital inflows. Consumer prices, including food and beverages, started to increase sharply in the third quarter of 2021, mainly due to the highly volatile kyat and logistics disruptions. Inflationary pressure from higher prices of fuel and other commodities, combined with weaker kyat, was countered by lower consumer confidence and enormous income losses. An estimated 1.6 million jobs were lost in 2021 due to the dual shocks of the COVID-19 pandemic and political tensions.

According to WB's Myanmar Economic Monitor in January 2022,[39] Myanmar's economy and people continue to be severely tested by the ongoing impacts of the military coup and the surge in COVID-19 cases in 2021. The WB projects grow by 1% in the year to September 2022. While reflecting recent signs of stabilization in some areas, the projection remains consistent with a critically weak economy, approximately 30% smaller than it might have been in the absence of COVID-19 and the February 2021 coup. The near-term outlook will depend on the evolution of the pandemic and the effects of conflict, together with the degree to which foreign exchange and financial sector constraints persist, as well as disruptions to other key services, including electricity, logistics and digital connectivity. Ongoing economic pressures have a substantial effect on vulnerability and food security, particularly for the poor. The share of Myanmar's population living in poverty is expected to have more than doubled compared to pre-COVID-19 levels.

[39] Myanmar Economic Monitor: Contending with Constraints (2022).

4.4.4 *Solution for External Debt*

When faced with the occurrence of grave difficulties pertaining to the repayment of debt, a country can act in a threefold manner: (1) Not discharging the defaults being valid within, (a) Repudiation- terminating (invalidating) the obligations conferred upon the debtor Party at some time and the total cessation of paying debts, which entails the repressions on the part of creditors, (b) Moratorium-demanding the renegotiation of the original contract of credit; (2) Continue the payment at any cost; (3) Restructuring the debt.

Paris Club creditors provide debt treatments to debtor countries in the form of rescheduling, which is "debt relief" by postponement or, in the case of concessional rescheduling, reduction in debt service obligations during a defined period (flow treatment) or as of a set date (stock treatment). For example, in January 2013, the Paris Club treated 10 billion USD of debt owed by Myanmar to the Paris Club, canceling 50% of arrears and rescheduling the rest over 15 years, including 7 years of grace.

One devastating impact of the global COVID-19 pandemic is the inability of an increasing number of countries, especially low-income countries, to make principal and interest payments on their external debts. To avoid defaulting, which would produce economic turmoil and suffering, these countries are turning to the Paris Club for debt relief. China is also cooperating with debt relief and other measures to ease the debt burden of developing countries, especially BRI countries. In sum, from the sustainable development point of view, implementing any project including BRI projects in developing countries should be economically viable, socially equitable and environmentally sustainable.

4.5 Conclusion

CMEC would be a game changer for Myanmar and for the region as well by playing a pivotal role through economic incentives and regional integration in the form of networks, connectivity and partnerships. With the development of the *Kyaukphyu* deep seaport, Myanmar will become the hub of regional economic activity, and more so, it also has the potential to be an economic and energy corridor. There will be a net of railway lines, gas pipelines and economic zones. The CMEC should be equally beneficial to China and Myanmar. It is expected that both China and Myanmar will be able to play more active roles in the regional and international spheres. However, the progress of CMEC project activities is slow because of the Myanmar government's caution about the "debt trap" issue. Moreover, global geo-political change and global recession due to the Russia-Ukraine war as well as political tension, instability and conflicts are critical challenges for the implementation of BRI and CMEC projects.

References

Asanga Abeyagoonnasekera, "Sri Lankan Crisis between Debt-trap and Strategic-trap: The Chinese Stake", ISDP, https://isdp.eu/sri-lankan-crisis-between-debt-trap-and-strategic-trap-thechinese-stake/

Constanța Botnar, Debt Trap Diplomacy: Measuring China's Reach and Projection of Influence, Master Thesis and HD Thesis, 2020, https://projekter.aau.dk/projekter/en/studentthesis/debt-trap-diplomacy-measuring-chinas-reach-and-projection-of-influence(abb03ee0-bb29-4180-ac8c-b769ff91398d).html

China: Is it burdening poor countries with unsustainable debt, *BBC*, January 6, 2022, https://www.bbc.com/news/59585507

China's Belt and Road plans for Southeast Asia face uncertain 'long-term prospects' as social, environment concerns persist: study, *South China Morning Post*, 2 June 2022, https://www.scmp.com/week-asia/economics/article/3180162/chinas-belt-and-road-plans-southeast-asia-face-uncertainlong?module=perpetual_scroll_1&pgtype=article&campaign=3180

Christine Lagarde, "Belt and Road Initiative: Strategies to Deliver in the Next Phase", International Monetary Fund (IMF), April 12, 2018, https://www.imf.org/en/News/Articles/2018/04/11/sp041218-belt-and-road-initiative-strategies-to-deliver-in-the-next-phase

Cui Can, "BRI is a boost for economic development, not a debt trap", *China.org.cn*, April 24, 2022, http://www.china.org.cn/business/2022-04/24/content_78184261.htm

Dipanjan Roy Chaudhury, "Myanmar pushed back against China funded economic corridor inspired by debt trap", *Economic Times*, 2020, https://economictimes.indiatimes.com/news/international/world-news/myanmars-pushback-against-china-funded-economic-corridor-inspired-by-debt-trap-in-s-asian-states/articleshow/7

Horn Sebastian & Carmen M. Reinhart & Christoph Trebesch, China's Overseas Lending, *Journal of International Economics*, Vol.133, https://www.nber.org/papers/w26050.

IMF Country Report, No 20/215 Myanmar, International Monetary Fund (IMF), December 21, 2020.

Iori Kawate & Yuichi Nitta, "Myanmar's Debt to China Decrease 26% Under Ousted Suu Kyi", *Nikkei Asia*, February 7, 2021, https://asia.nikkei.com/Spotlight/Datawatch/Myanmar-s-debt-to-China-decreases-26-under-ousted-Suu-Kyi)

Jessica C. Liao, "How BRI Debt Puts China at Risk", *The Diplomat*, October, 27, 2021, https://thediplomat.com/2021/10/how-bri-debt-puts-china-at-risk/

John Hurley etc., "Examining the Debt Implications of the Belt and Road Initiative from a Policy Perspective", Center for Global Development Policy Paper, No.121, 2018, https://www.cgdev.org/sites/default/files/examining-debt-implications-belt-and-road-initiative-policy-perspective.pdf.

Khine Win, China-Myanmar Sustainable Development and Cooperation Under CMEC Forum, Yangon, July 8, 2019.

Low-Income Country Debt Rises to Record $860 Billion in 2020, Press Release, World Bank, 2021, https://www.worldbank.org/en/news/press-release/2021/10/11/low-income-country-debt-rises-to-record-860-billion-in-2020#:~:text=Overall%2C%20in%202020%2C%20net%20inflows,highes.

Myanmar Economic Monitor: Contending with Constraints, World Bank, January 2022, https://www.worldbank.org/en/country/myanmar/publication/myanmar-economic-monitor-january-2022-economic-activity-in-myanmar-to-remain-at-low-levels-with-the-overall-outlook-blea.

Myanmar's auditor general cautions own govt against Chinese loans, *Economic Times*, June 12, 2020, https://economictimes.indiatimes.com/news/international/business/myanmars-auditor-general-cautions-own-govt-against-chinesloans/articleshow/76346777.cms?utm_source=contentofinterest&utm_medium=text&utm_campaign=cppst.

Myanmar's Key Stakeholders and Their Perceptions of Sino-Myanmar Relations-A Survey 2022, ISP-Myanmar, August 2022, https://www.ispmyanmar.com/burmese/wp-content/uploads/2022/08/China-Survey-English.pdf

Myint San, "The Role of Cross-Border Economic Zones and Special Economic Zone: The Case of CMEC", September 26, 2019, Yunnan.

Pradumna Bickram Rana & Jason Ji Xianbai, "BRI's 'Debt Trap Diplomacy': Reality or Myth?", RSIS, November 4, 2020, https://www.rsis.edu.sg/rsis-publication/cms/bris-debt-trap-diplomacy-reality-or-myth/#.Yqgrv3ZBy3A

Shabtai Gold, China is owned 37% of poor countries' debt payment in 2022, World Bank, 2022, www.devex.com.

SiuSue Mark & Indra Overland&Roman Vakulchuk, Sharing the Spoils: Winners and Losers in the Belt and Road Initiative in Myanmar, *Journal of Current Southeast Asian Affairs*, Vol. 39, No.3, 2020, pp.381-404.

Sudha Ramachandran, "Myanmar wary of Chinese debt trap, goes slow on CMEC", *India Narrative*, 2021, https://www.indianarrative.com/world-news/myanmar-wary-of-chinese-debt-trap-goes-slow-on-cmec-63467.html.

The Country Most in Debt to China, *Forbes*, August 19, 2022, http://www.forbes.com.

The so-called China's debt trap is a narrative trap, *Brussels Times*, August 25, 2022, https://www.brusselstimes.com/278603/the-so-called-chinas-debt-trap-is-a-narrative-trap.

U Myint, "Thinking, Fast and Slow" on the Belt and Road: Myanmar's Experience with China, *Perspective*, No.90, October 29, 2019, Institute of Southeast Asian Studies, Singapore.

Win Shen, Situation of State's External Debt and Experience Debt Clearance with Paris Club, Yangon, 2020.

Yan Naing, "Rescuing Myanmar From the Chinese Debt Trap", *Irrawaddy*, August 21, 2020, https://www.irrawaddy.com/opinion/guest-column/rescuing-myanmar-chinese-debt-trap.html

Chapter 5
Debt Management and the BRI in Cambodia

Neak Chandarith and Sok Sothearak

Abstract Cambodia's economy has grown impressively in recent years. This growth has been partly supported by external debt due to an infant debt market and lack of domestic capital. However, external public debt stocks, reaching 9.97 billion USD or 33% of GDP in 2022, to some critiques, have raised concerns over debt sustainability and China's growing influence on the country. This chapter argues that the risk of Cambodia's external public debt is low. First, most of the debt has been used for prioritized infrastructure projects implemented under public–private partnership schemes, meaning that the risk of debt overspiling to state coffers is slim. Second, Cambodia has a well-regarded debt management framework with specific conditions, indicators, and ceilings. Third, the country's external public debt has been very conservative and highly concessional. Fourth, Cambodia has a large foreign exchange reserve compared to its public debt and debt obligation. Finally, the kingdom has been using a diversification strategy as its agency for bargaining. However, there are some potential risks. The first is private debt, which is unpredictable and for which there is no management framework in place yet. The second is the exposure of Cambodia's GDP to export shock, as the country relies heavily on exports of goods. The third is suboptimal government revenue mobilization.

Keywords Cambodia · Chinese debt · Debt trap · Debt management · BRI

N. Chandarith (✉) · S. Sothearak
Institute for International Studies and Public Policy, Royal University of Phnom Penh, Phnom Penh, Cambodia
e-mail: neak.chandarith@rupp.edu.kh

S. Sothearak
e-mail: sok.sothearak@rupp.edu.kh

N. Peng and M. Y. Cheng (eds.), *The Reality and Myth of BRI's Debt Trap*, Indo-Pacific Focus, https://doi.org/10.1007/978-981-97-1056-0_5

5.1 Introduction

Cambodia's GDP had been growing at an average rate of 7% annually between 2010 and 2019 but dropped to -3% in 2020 due to the COVID-19 pandemic.[1] The post pandemic recovery seemed relatively robust as GDP growth rebounded to 3% and 5.2% in 2021 and 2022, respectively. Cambodia's GDP growth is expected to reach 5.5% in 2023, 6.1% in 2024, and 6.3% in 2025, a gradual increase but below the prepandemic level.[2] Exports of garments, travel goods, and footwear helped push for the recovery of the economy, while the reviving traveling and tourism sectors (as a result of "living with COVID-19 strategy") improved the current account balance.[3] These sectors, along with construction and real estate, have been the main engine of Cambodia's economic growth in the last decade. In addition, external debt has played a crucial role in paying for rehabilitation and development projects in the country due to the lack of domestic capital stocks and the small and inexperienced internal debt capital market. Cambodia's external debt stocks have gradually grown in size from 2 billion USD in 2000 to 22.4 billion USD in 2022.[4] Among this, 9.97 billion USD is public debt (public and publicly guaranteed, PPG).[5] This accounts for 33% of the country's GDP during that period (Table 5.1).

This chapter is written as an evidence-based argument against Cambodia's "debt trap" narrative. Many opinions and concerns have emerged regarding the current state of Cambodia's external public debt. It is believed that Cambodia's reliance on external debt, especially Chinese debt, to finance development projects would lead the country to the brink of default and eventually to the relinquishment of some state assets, such as ports, to pay for borrowed funds. However, as you will see in the following sections, there are many reasons to believe that at best, it shows that those who uphold this idea do not have a comprehensive understanding of how public loans are being managed, assessed, and used. In addition, it also shows that they do not fully grasp how some countries who had borrowed money from China had defaulted on their debt purely due to their own mismanagement. At worst, the fear of Cambodia being pulled into a debt trap, probably based on data jugglery, has been politicized and used as propaganda to attack the government and to discriminate against China. As such, this chapter will provide an overall picture of the debt policy and practice in Cambodia, elaborate on debt management strategy and regulations, and examine the risk of debt default, specifically the extent to which Cambodia is likely to fall into a Chinese debt trap. This would contribute to a wide literature on small states' dilemmas in having to choose between debt-financing development and

[1] GDP growth (annual %)-Cambodia. The World Bank. (n.d.). https://data.worldbank.org/indicator/NY.GDP.MKTP.KD.ZG?locations=KH.

[2] Cambodia Economic Update (2023).

[3] Cambodia Economic Update (2022).

[4] See Cambodia external debt. CEIC. (n.d.). https://www.ceicdata.com/en/indicator/cambodia/external-debt.

[5] See External debt stocks, public and publicly guaranteed (PPG) (DOD, current US$)-Cambodia, The World Bank, https://data.worldbank.org/indicator/DT.DOD.DPPG.CD?locations=KH.

Table 5.1 Cambodia's external debt stock, PPG

Year	External debt stocks, public and publicly guaranteed (PPG) (DOD, current US$ billion)	External debt stocks, PPG (% of GDP)
2000	2.01	55.14
2001	2.08	52.20
2002	2.27	53.08
2003	2.56	54.85
2004	2.77	51.88
2005	2.83	44.99
2006	3.01	41.38
2007	2.22	25.74
2008	2.54	24.57
2009	2.75	26.41
2010	3.06	27.22
2011	3.46	26.99
2012	4.29	30.51
2013	4.81	31.62
2014	5.25	31.45
2015	5.64	31.24
2016	5.83	29.13
2017	6.58	29.66
2018	6.99	28.47
2019	7.56	27.91
2020	8.76	33.87
2021	9.45	35.06
2022	9.97	33.28

Source The World Bank, https://data.worldbank.org/. and Cambodia Public Debt Statistical Bulletin, Ministry of Economy and Finance, https://gdicdm.mef.gov.kh/en/cat/documents-and-publications/bulletins

being left behind in this technologically competitive and climate-vulnerable world. The content in this chapter is structured as follows. The second section will introduce the size of Cambodia's public loans from China along with the introduction to some projects under the Belt and Road Initiative in Cambodia. The third section describes Cambodian people's views on Chinese debt to Cambodia. The debt management framework in Cambodia will be discussed in the fourth section, with a specific emphasis on legal mechanisms, public debt thresholds, and risk indicators. On the same note, an analysis of how unlikely Cambodia is to fall into a debt trap is provided by looking at the increasing size of the country's foreign exchange reserve and the

Table 5.2 Cambodia's Public External Debt by Top Three Creditors

Year	China		Asian Development Bank (ADB)		Japan	
	US$ million	% of External Debt, PPG	US$ million	% of External Debt, PPG	US$ million	% of External Debt, PPG
2015	3,406.50	44.50	1,878.27	24.54	724.63	9.47
2016	3,599.89	43.32	2,001.11	24.08	899.07	10.82
2017	4,052.90	41.84	2,119.27	21.88	1,235.01	12.75
2018	4,620.17	40.56	1,399.70	23.23	1,347.92	11.83
2019	4,865.99	38.50	2,914.39	23.06	1,399.70	11.08
2020	5,255.26	34.94	3,475.83	23.11	2,000.48	13.30
2021	5,415.71	34.84	3,743.26	24.08	1,855.23	11.93
2022	4,001.72	40.14	2,051.15	20.57	1,077.66	10.80

Source Cambodia Public Debt Statistical Bulletin, Ministry of Economy and Finance, https://gdicdm.mef.gov.kh/en/cat/documents-and-publications/bulletins

use of agency in debt management. Last but not least, this chapter will try to speculate which aspect of external debt might become a potential hazard for Cambodia.

5.2 Chinese Debt in Cambodia

In recent years, there has been a trend that a sizeable proportion of public external debt Cambodia accrued came from China. This led to discussion and concern, especially from the Western counterparts and media, that Cambodia is pivoting too close to China and sinking into a "debt trap".[6] By 2022, for instance, China provided 4 billion USD in public loans to Cambodia, amounting to approximately 40% of total external public debt and overshadowing other bilateral development partners by a large margin. Table 5.2 summarizes the size and percentage of Cambodia's external public debt by three main creditors. Since 2015 (the earliest publicly available data), Chinese loans have made up 35% to 45% of Cambodia's external public debt. The second next main creditor, the Asian Development Bank (ADB) (multilateral partner), accounted for only 20% to 25%, while the third main creditor, Japan, accounted for less than 15% during the same period.

[6] See Mengheng Seng, "Concern Over Cambodia's Climbing Debt", *Kiripost*, February 10, 2023, https://kiripost.com/stories/concern-over-cambodias-climbing-debt; Shaun Turton, "Cambodia's Hun Sen defends succession plan, denies China 'debt trap'", *Nikkei Asia*, May 27, 2022, https://asia.nikkei.com/Spotlight/The-Future-of-Asia/The-Future-of-Asia-2022/Cambodia-s-Hun-Sen-defends-succession-plan-denies-China-debt-trap; Narin Sun, "Cambodia Seeks New Financing from Beijing Amid Fears of 'Debt Trap'", *Voice of America (VOA)*, February 7, 2023, https://www.voanews.com/a/cambodia-seeks-more-loans-from-beijing-amid-fears-of-debt-trap-/6943062.html.

Chinese lending to Cambodia has been viewed as a part of the Belt and Road Initiative (BRI), proposed by Chinese President Xi Jingping in 2013 as an ambitious transcontinental connectivity plan. In general, BRI is a broad framework encompassing infrastructure projects that aim at connecting China with the participating countries. To achieve this connectivity, enormous investment capital is needed for the development of physical transport infrastructure (ports, roads, tunnels, and bridges) and energy infrastructure (power plants, energy storage, and distribution networks). Chinese sources have provided funding for these projects.

On the one hand, there is no clear rule or definition for defining which project can be regarded as a part of BRI. On the other hand, there is no limitation on the scope and scale of the BRI project specification officially provided either. Any Chinese-funded projects on foreign soil are usually perplexingly regarded as BRI projects. Therefore, a clear framework for project identification is needed. To avoid labeling all Chinese-funded projects as BRI projects, Wang adopted a set of criteria for defining a project as a part of BRI: (1). it must be reported on the official BRI's website (the Belt and Road Portal); and (2). It must receive investment from Chinese sources.[7] Wang further distinguished BRI projects into four types: projects financed by loans of Chinese financial institutions, projects invested in by Chinese firms (partially or wholly), projects invested in by Chinese-local joint ventures, and projects of China's foreign assistance program.[8]

BRI projects in Cambodia mainly involve physical infrastructure development. The Reconnecting Asia Project of the Center for Strategic and International Studies (CSIS) tracked the development of BRI projects in Cambodia until 2020. However, only transportation and energy infrastructure projects were recorded in its database.[9] Table 5.3 below lists the BRI projects announced, under construction, or completed. As of mid-2021, 3,287 km of road and eight main bridges were built in the country.[10] Major and recent projects include a 190-km first-ever expressway connecting the capital city with the major port city of Sihanoukville in the southwest, Sihanoukville Special Economic Zones, a 700-megawatt power plant, a building at the Cambodia-China Friendship Preah Kossamak Hospital, and two new international airports.[11] Most of the transport infrastructures in Cambodia under the BRI are public–private

[7] Wang Zheng (2022).

[8] Ibid.

[9] Reconnecting Asia Project Database (2021).

[10] Vannarith Chheang (2021).

[11] See Vannarith Chheang, "BRI Projects in Cambodia and Laos Roll on Despite Covid-19", ISEAS Perspective, No.99, July 27, 2021, https://www.iseas.edu.sg/articles-commentaries/iseas-perspective/2021-99-bri-projects-in-cambodia-and-laos-roll-on-despite-covid-19-by-vannarith-chheang/; Jayant Menon, "The Belt and Road Initiative in Cambodia: Costs and Benefits, Real and Perceived", ISEAS Perspective, No.1, March 2023, https://www.iseas.edu.sg/wp-content/uploads/2023/03/ISEAS_EWP_2023-1_Menon.pdf; Wang Zheng, "Assessing the Belt and Road Initiative in Southeast Asia amid the COVID-19 Pandemic (2021-2022)", ISEAS Perspective, No.57, May 26, 2022, https://www.iseas.edu.sg/articles-commentaries/iseas-perspective/2022-57-assessing-the-belt-and-road-initiative-in-southeast-asia-amid-the-covid-19-pandemic-2021-2022-by-wang-zheng/.

Table 5.3 BRI projects in cambodia as of 2022

Name	Infrastructure type	Funding sources	Contractors
Siem reap new international airport, siem reap	Intermodal	The Export–Import bank of China	
Stung tatay river hydropower dam, Koh Kong	Powerplant	The Export–Import bank of China	China Gezhouba group corporation
Kamchay hydroelectric power plant	Powerplant	The Export–Import bank of China	Sinohydro
National road 51 rehabilitation, Kampong Speu	Road		
National highway No. 5 improvement project[12]	Road	China	Shanghai Construction Group
National road project no. 11	Road	China	
National road 58	Road	The Export–Import Bank of China	Shanghai Construction Group Co. Ltd.
National road 6A, siem Reap—Kampong cham expressway	Road		Shanghai Construction Group
Mekong bridge project, stung treng	Road	China	Shanghai Construction Group
4th Cambodia-China friendship bridge	Road	China	Shanghai Construction Group Co. Ltd.
Phnom Penh—Sihanoukville expressway	Road		China Communications Construction Company
National road (NR) 57B project, battambang	Road	The Export–Import Bank of China	China Road and Bridge Corporation
7th Cambodia-China friendship bridge (Koh Thom Bridge), Kandal	Road	The Export–Import Bank of China	China Road and Bridge Corporation

(continued)

[12] The road construction had been funded by Japan, whereas road improvement was funded by China. See Michelle Vachon, "National Road Number 5″-the Side Story of a Years-Long Road Improvement Project", *Cambodianess*, February 12, 2022, https://cambodianess.com/article/national-road-number-5-the-side-story-of-a-years-long-road-improvement-project.

Table 5.3 (continued)

Name	Infrastructure type	Funding sources	Contractors
National road No. 55 expansion project	Road	China	China Road and Bridge Corporation
Expansion of national road No. 51	Road	The Export–Import Bank of China	China Road and Bridge Corporation
Hun Ty agricultural industrial park phase I	Agriculture		China Civil Engineering Construction Corporation Ltd.
Hun Ty agricultural industrial park phase II	Agriculture		China Civil Engineering Construction Corporation Ltd.
Celimo tires	Chemicals		Hodo Group
Royal skyland project	Construction		China Metallurgical Group
Techo international airport	Construction		China State Construction Engineering
500 kV power transmission and transformation project (Phnom Penh Section	Energy		China National Machinery Industry Corporation
Rural water supply project phase II	Energy		China Jiangxi International Economic
Sihanouk 2 × 350 MW Coal-fired power plant unit 2	Energy		Power Construction Corporation of
Upper stung tatay hydropower BOT investment project	Energy		China National Machinery Industry
Cambodian national stadium	Entertainment		China State Construction Engineering
Cambodia-China friendship preah kossamak hospita	Health services		China State Construction Engineering
Cambodia highway 41 upgrade project 1B	Transportation		China Communications Construction
Cambodian national highway No. 11 reconstruction and expansion project	Transportation		China Communications Construction

(continued)

Table 5.3 (continued)

Name	Infrastructure type	Funding sources	Contractors
Eighth Cambodia-China friendship bridge	Transportation		Shanghai Construction Group
National road 7 upgrade project	Transportation		Shanghai Construction Group
Phnom Penh-Sihanoukville expressway	Transportation		China Communications Construction Company, Ltd.
Techo airport B500 lake development project phase I	Transportation		China National Machinery Industry Corporation

Source Reconnecting Asia Project, https://reconasia.csis.org/reconnecting-asia-map/; Chanrith Ngin (23 August 2022). The Undetermined Costs and Benefits of Cambodia's Engagement with China's Belt and Road Initiative. *ISEAS Perspective, 84*(2022), 1–15
https://www.iseas.edu.sg/wp-content/uploads/2022/07/ISEAS_Perspective_2022_84.pdf

partnership (PPP) projects. PPP means that these projects were initiated by the Royal Government of Cambodia (RGC) and were then contracted to companies who had won the construction bidding before seeking financial support from Chinese sources. These major projects are usually developed under the build-operate-transfer (BOT) scheme, in which the contracting company is responsible for the construction of the project, for the operation of the infrastructure over the agreed-upon period, and for transferring its ownership to the RGC at no cost.[13] The fact that external public debt in general makes up a 'sizeable' portion of Cambodia's GDP and the fact that Chinese loan specifically makes up a relatively large proportion of the public debt stir up concerns, however unfounded they might be, domestically and internationally.

5.3 Cambodian Perceptions of Chinese Debt

Many Cambodians have grown increasingly concerned in recent years about Cambodia's debt to China. Doubts concerning Cambodia's sovereignty and economic viability have been expressed as a result of China's status as the nation's biggest creditor. This section will investigate how Cambodians regard Chinese debt by looking at a number of sources, including academic research, news articles, and interviews with locals. It contends that opinions among Cambodians are divided about China's debt, with some seeing it as a chance for economic growth while others worry about the dangers of becoming overly reliant on Beijing.

In recent years, China has grown to be a significant economic partner for Cambodia. It is the main source of foreign aid and investment in the country. The

[13] Subdecree (1998).

construction of Cambodia's much-needed infrastructure has been aided by Chinese funding. It has also accelerated economic growth and the creation of jobs. Those who see Chinese debt favorably contend that it is essential for Cambodia's economic growth.[14] They highlight China's significant infrastructure investment in Cambodia, which has encouraged economic growth and created jobs. They also contend that China is Cambodia's trustworthy partner. China has offered financial support and development aid to Cambodia without putting as many restrictions on it as other development partners did. Chinese debt critics contend that Cambodia is becoming overly dependent on China as a result.[15] They are concerned that China would use its economic clout to wrest control of Cambodia's vital infrastructure, entrap the country in a "debt trap", or otherwise exert political influence in the Southeast Asian nation.

According to a 2022 survey by the ISEAS-Yusof Ishak Institute,[16] 38% of Cambodians and 64% of Chinese respondents say China has a high or very high political influence in their nation. According to the survey, 52% of Cambodians are worried about their country's debt to China, and 32% think that the nation is in danger of getting caught in a financial trap. The author conducted interviews with a range of Cambodian citizens to better understand how they felt about Chinese loans. A 35-year-old Phnom Penh man who was interviewed expressed anxiety over Cambodia's debt to China. He was concerned that China may try to sway Cambodian politics through its economic clout. Additionally, he expressed alarm over the environmental effects of some Chinese-funded projects in Cambodia. For instance, he said that certain dams financed by China have uprooted local populations and harmed the ecosystem. A 27-year-old Siem Reap resident who was also interviewed claimed that she saw the possibility presented by Chinese loans for economic growth. She claimed that Chinese investment has aided in constructing Cambodia's desperately needed infrastructure. She said that she was certain that the Cambodian government would be able to responsibly manage its debt to China. Divergent opinions exist on Cambodia's reliance on Chinese loans. To promote openness regarding its debt to China and diversify its sources of foreign investment and development assistance, the Cambodian government should take the necessary action. Additionally, it is crucial to guarantee that projects funded by China are completed in a sustainable and responsible manner.

There are geopolitical concerns in addition to the economic, political, social, and environmental concerns that are related to Chinese debt. Given that Cambodia is indebted to China and that the country is situated in a strategically significant area, there are worries about China's expanding regional influence. According to some analysts,[17] China may use its economic clout to exert pressure on Cambodia to support its geopolitical objectives, such as its claims in the South China Sea (SCS).

---

[14] See Pheakdey Heng and Vannarith Chheang (2019).

[15] See Yalirozy Teng (2023).

[16] Vannarith Chheang (2022).

[17] See Anaig Williamson, The economic and political implications of China's foreign aid in Cambodia, *Moussons*, No.41, 2023, pp.133–150.

Particularly since The Wall Street Journal reported that China had inked a covert arrangement to permit its military to use the station in 2019,[18] the US has charged Cambodia with allowing China to utilize its Ream Naval base. Again, in 2022, a Western official acknowledged that China and Cambodia were moving through with plans to establish a base for their navy at Ream Naval Base and were trying to conceal their activities.[19] The US has continued to express alarm about the expanding Chinese military presence in the area despite Cambodia's repeated denials of these allegations. To prove that the report was false and groundless, the government even extended an invitation to journalists to inspect its Ream Naval site in July 2019.[20] The complicated connection between the US and Cambodia must be noted. The US's claims against Cambodia in relation to the Ream Naval Base are a part of a larger US strategy to oppose China's expanding influence in the Indo-Pacific region. Ironically, the US has been bolstering its regional ties and partnerships while also stepping up its military involvement elsewhere in the region.

5.4 Debt Management Framework in Cambodia

5.4.1 Cambodia's Debt Management Framework

Before illustrating how Cambodia's public debt level, specifically that provided by China, should not be alarming, it is worthwhile to examine Cambodia's debt management framework. The RGC, with the Ministry of Economy and Finance as its sole implementing body of public debt management, laid out its detailed public debt management framework in the Strategic Document on Public Debt Management 2011–2018. The document, first, listed key policies and principles for public debt management: (1). loans must be proportionate to and in accordance with the strength of economic and budgetary situations; (2). RGC must accept only highly concessional loans and maintain transparent and effective use of debt; (3). RGC must continue the centralization of public debt management and improve risk evaluation and monitoring mechanisms; and (4). Loans must be used only for prioritized sectors that support growth sustainability and economic productivity, such as transport infrastructure, energy infrastructure, irrigation systems, and clean water supplies. Second, it set forth disciplining policies such as (1). The borrowing ceiling for 2011–2018 was set at 400 million SDR (Special Drawing Right) per year and increased to 700 million SDR in accordance with budgetary needs and the macroeconomic situation. (2). no government bonds would be issued during this period; and (3). The Minister of

[18] See Jeremy Page & Goldon Lubold & Rob Taylor," Deal for naval outpost in Cambodia furthers China's quest for military network", *The Wall Street Journal,* July 21, 2019, https://www.wsj.com/articles/secret-deal-for-chinese-naval-outpost-in-cambodia-raises-u-s-fears-of-beijings-ambitions-11563732482.

[19] See Ellen Nakashima & Cate Cadell (2022).

[20] See Dara Mech (2019).

Economy and Finance is the sole individual capable of making public borrowing and debt guarantees. All of these aimed to achieve three main development targets: maintaining economic growth of 6% to 7% annually, maintaining government revenue of 13.5% to 15% of GDP per year, and poverty reduction of at least 1% a year. Third, the document also registered useful information about the characteristics of Cambodia's public debt (by 2010). Accordingly, the majority of public debts were concessional loans with an annual interest rate of 0% to 2%, 20-to-40-year amortization periods, and a 7-to-15-year grace period.[21]

In 2015, the RGC came up with a new strategic document for debt management: Strategic Document on Public Debt Management 2015–2018. The majority of principles and mechanisms laid down in this strategic document mirror those of the previous document except for the debt ceiling and, to some extent, the inclusion of new sectors (sewage treatment plants and vocational training for the industrial sector) into the list of prioritized infrastructures. The RGC continued to accept only highly concessional loans, but the debt ceiling was raised to 700 to 800 million SDR per year for the 2016–2018 period (600 million SDR for 2015). The document also directed the government to focus more on the public–private partnership (PPP) framework and preparation for the creation of a contingency fund for the development of infrastructure, taking note of the significant reduction of grants to the country.[22]

The latest debt management policy document, Public Debt Management Strategy 2019–2023, further increases the debt ceiling and puts forth more specific public debt indicators. The debt ceiling was set at 1.5 to 2 billion SDR, increased to 3 billion SDR per year for the 2019–2023 period, but the aggregate external debt during this period must not exceed 11 billion SDR (equivalent to USD 15 billion). Ceilings for other public debt indicators include the following:

(1) The present value of the total public and publicly guaranteed debt (PPG)-to-GDP ratio must remain below 55%.
  a. The present value of the external PPG to GDP ratio must remain below 40%.
  b. The present value of the domestic PPG to GDP ratio must remain below 15%.
(2) The present value of the external PPG to exports ratio must remain below 180%.
(3) The ratio of external PPG debt servicing to export must remain below 15%.
(4) The ratio of external PPG debt servicing to the government's revenue must remain below 18%.
(5) The debt guarantee ceiling must remain at or below 10% of the government's revenue.[23]

Figure 5.1 illustrates the ratio of external PPG debt to GDP from 2013 to 2023, which has remained below the 40% threshold. Furthermore, the RGC created the Public Debt Management Commission led by the Minister of Economy and Finance

[21] Strategic Document on Public Debt Management (2012).
[22] Strategic Document on Public Debt Management (2018).
[23] Public Debt Management Strategy (2019).

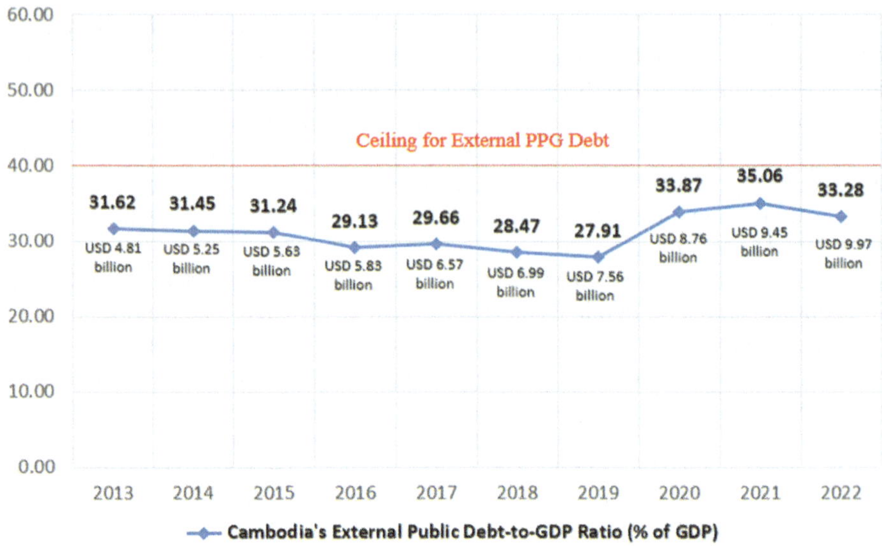

Fig. 5.1 Cambodia's External Public Debt to GDP. *Source* Compiled by the authors using Cambodia Public Debt Statistical Bulletin, Ministry of Economy and Finance, https://gdicdm.mef.gov.kh/en/cat/documents-and-publications/bulletins

in 2019 to supervise PPG debt in the country. RGC also issued the first batch of government bonds denominated in national currency in September 2022 to reduce its reliance on external debt, but this domestic public debt is meager compared to the external one-27 million USD in the first issue and 200 million USD target.[24] The debt management policy of Cambodia since 2018 has been highly rated by the World Bank's Country Policy and Institutional Assessments (CPIA) index. According to the CPIA debt policy rating (Table 5.4), Cambodia's debt management framework received a 5 rating on a 1-to-6 scale (1 being the lowest and 6 being the highest).[25]

5.4.2 Situation of External Public Debt in Cambodia

The table below summarizes the main indicators for the PPG debt of Cambodia. The debt ceilings from 2015 to 2022 conformed with those predetermined in the Public Debt Management Strategies. Noticeably, the ceiling for 2020 was raised to 1.9 billion SDR before coming down a year afterwards.[26] The present value of the external PPG debt to GDP ratio has stayed below the determined threshold by 15 to

[24] Cambodia issues Government Bond (2023).

[25] See CPIA debt policy rating (1 = low to 6 = high) – Cambodia, World Bank, https://data.worldbank.org/indicator/IQ.CPA.DEBT.XQ?locations=KH.

[26] Cambodia Public Debt Statistical Bulletin (2023).

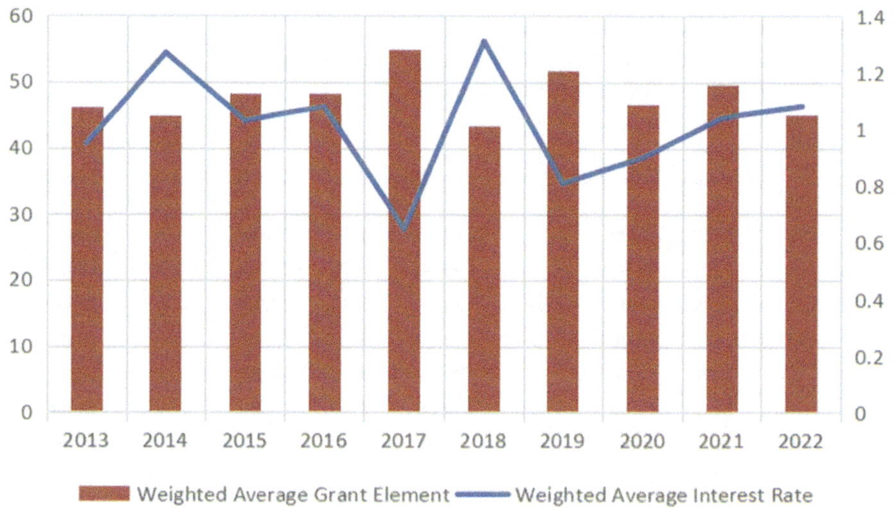

Fig. 5.2 Cambodia's PPG Debt, WA grant element & WA interest rate *Source*: Compiled by the authors using Cambodia Public Debt Statistical Bulletin, Ministry of Economy and Finance, https://gdicdm.mef.gov.kh/en/cat/documents-and-publications/bulletins

Table 5.4 The World Bank's CPIA Rating of Cambodia's Debt Policy, 2010–2022

Year	Cambodia's CPIA rating
2010	3.5
2011	3.5
2012	4
2013	4
2014	4
2015	4.5
2016	4.5
2017	4.5
2018	5
2019	5
2020	5
2021	5
2022	5

Source The World Bank, https://data.worldbank.org/indicator/IQ.CPA.DEBT.XQ?locations=KH

20 percentage points since 2015, while the present value of external PPG compared to exports has remained 4 to 6 times the fraction of the threshold. The main concern in regard to PPG debt is not the size of the outstanding debt itself but the size of the debt servicing that a country has to pay annually. For Cambodia, as shown in the table

Table 5.5 Cambodia's external PPG debt

Year	Debt Ceiling (million SDR per year)	PV of External PPG to GDP ratio (%)		PV of External PPG to Exports ratio (%)		External PPG Servicing to Exports ratio (%)		External PPG Servicing to Government's Revenue ratio (%)	
		Actual	Threshold	Actual	Threshold	Actual	Threshold	Actual	Threshold
2015	600	23.20	**40.00**	33.50	**150.00**	1.30	**20.00**	5.70	**20.00**
2016	700	22.50	**40.00**	31.60	**150.00**	1.30	**20.00**	4.90	**20.00**
2017	700	22.80	**40.00**	30.80	**150.00**	1.30	**20.00**	4.70	**20.00**
2018	1,514	21.40	**40.00**	30.40	**180.00**	1.50	**15.00**	5.30	**18.00**
2019	1,400	20.80	**40.00**	26.70	**180.00**	1.50	**15.00**	4.50	**18.00**
2020	1,900	24.00	**40.00**	32.80	**180.00**	1.80	**15.00**	6.30	**18.00**
2021	1,500	24.40	**40.00**	35.60	**180.00**	2.00	**15.00**	7.00	**18.00**
2022	1,600	24.90	**40.00**	33.90	**180.00**	2.10	**15.00**	7.80	**18.00**

Source Compiled by the authors using Cambodia Public Debt Statistical Bulletin, Ministry of Economy and Finance, https://gdicdm.mef.gov.kh/en/cat/documents-and-publications/bulletins

below, the ratio of external PPG debt servicing compared to the government's revenue has remained in single digit since 2015. This indicates that it has not imposed much stress on the state's coffer. In addition, compared to exports, Cambodia's external PPG servicing accounts for less than 3% of export value annually, indicating further absorption and repayment capacity the country's economy has to offer. In addition, the fact that the RGC set up specific effective thresholds against excessive debt servicing risk provides protection against the country falling into public debt stress, debt trap, or sovereign default (Table 5.5).

The conditionality for Cambodia's PPG debt is summarized in the following table, and the changes are represented in the following graph. The summary table shows that most of Cambodia's external loans have been long-term and highly concessional loans, having an annual interest rate of less than 2% and a grace period from 7 to 9 years on average. These rates and grace periods are concessional loan conditionalities according to the Asia Development Bank's classification.[27] In addition, this grace period allows for the development projects, mostly infrastructure, to materialize and start earning revenue for amortization after the grace period. Furthermore, what is even more interesting is that the grant element accounts for approximately 50% of the debt. Overall, Cambodia's debt was categorized as low by the latest Joint World Bank-IMF Debt Sustainability Analysis (Table 5.6).[28]

[27] See Lending Policies and Rates, International Monetary Fund (IMF), https://www.adb.org/what-we-do/public-sector-financing/lending-policies-rates.

[28] Cambodia Joint World Bank-IMF (2022).

Table 5.6 Conditionality for cambodia PPG debt

Year	Weighted average interest rate (%)	Weighted average maturity (Year)	Weighted average grace period (Year)	Weighted average grant element (%)
2013	0.95	27.63	8.65	46.18
2014	1.27	28.23	8.52	44.77
2015	1.03	29.31	8.62	48.32
2016	1.08	28.81	8.5	48.32
2017	0.65	32.94	9.3	54.97
2018	1.31	27.38	7.55	43.27
2019	0.81	28.51	7.87	51.62
2020	0.9	26.31	7.64	46.5
2021	1.04	31.01	8.78	49.54
2022	1.08	26.77	8.35	45.01

Source Compiled by the authors using Cambodia Public Debt Statistical Bulletin, Ministry of Economy and Finance, https://gdicdm.mef.gov.kh/en/cat/documents-and-publications/bulletins

5.4.3 Cambodia's Foreign Exchange Reserves

The foreign exchange reserve of a country refers to the amount of foreign currency reserves (including SDR) and gold reserves that the central bank of the country accumulates. Foreign exchange reserves play a crucial role in the economy and the financial system of a country by providing foreign currency liquidity for government transactions, meeting the demands of the global financial market, maintaining the exchange rate, intervening in the foreign exchange market, financing the balance of payment, and providing space for monetary intervention. In terms of debt, foreign exchange reserves are also used as a buffer against debt repayment shock or default. The Guidotti-Greenspan rule of foreign exchange reserves, which provides a general economic guideline, dictates that the amount of foreign exchange reserves a country should hold must equal 100% of short-term external debt (debt with maturity of one year or less).[29] If we apply this rule to Cambodia, we see that foreign exchange reserves exceed this threshold.

Table 5.7 shows the number of total reserves (including gold) of Cambodia in current US dollars and in the percentage of external PPG debt from 2010 to 2021. This debt is total external PPG debt and not just short-term debt as dictated by the Guidotti-Greenspan rule. In recent years, the country has accumulated reserves of more than 200% of PPG external debt. Thus, it is reasonable to say that Cambodia has more than enough reserves as a buffer against external public debt and that the fear of moving toward debt traps might have been exaggerated.

[29] Olivier Jeanne & Romain Rancière (2006).

Table 5.7 Cambodia's total reserves

Year	Total reserves (includes gold, current US$)	Total reserves (% of total external debt stocks, PPG)
2010	3,817,077,827.48	124.74
2011	4,061,810,700.02	117.30
2012	4,759,658,458.02	111.01
2013	4,997,891,277.03	103.81
2014	6,108,231,224.39	116.28
2015	7,375,682,885.25	130.82
2016	9,113,957,299.04	156.29
2017	12,201,741,896.49	185.53
2018	14,630,894,026.00	209.18
2019	18,771,430,900.21	248.24
2020	21,328,475,092.66	243.36
2021	20,269,721,097.82	214.46

Source The World Bank, https://data.worldbank.org/indicator/FI.RES.TOTL.CD?locations=KH

5.4.4 Cambodia's Agency in Debt Management

Agency in our context refers to the action or intervention of the government of a BRI-participating country in influencing the outcome of a project. Ngin documented how some governments in Southeast Asia influenced or changed the outcome of BRI projects, especially the negotiation on project financing, in their countries.[30] Four case studies were mentioned: Myanmar, Laos, Indonesia, and Malaysia. 'Strategic selection' was used in the case of Myanmar when the National League for Democracy (NLD) government successfully renegotiated to reduce the cost of a deep-sea port to USD 1.3 billion. The project had been negotiated and approved by the previous military regime at the cost of 7.5 billion USD.[31] Likewise, Malaysia's East Coast Rail Link was also renegotiated due to the change of the government. The new government led by Mahathir Mohamad suspended the project, and the renegotiation reduced the cost of the project and changed the route of the rail link. When Mahathir was replaced by Muhyiddin, the project reverted back to its original route. In Laos, the government also renegotiated the funding conditions for Laos-China High-Speed Rail with a loan from China. The project, planned for construction in 2010, was postponed until late 2016 due to the terms of the contract (hiring too many Chinese workers for the project). In Indonesia, on the other hand, the tension between the central government, the subnational government, and the military provided 'leverage' for the renegotiation of the Jakarta-Bandung High Speed Rail project.[32] These four case

[30] Chanrith Ngin (2023).

[31] Ibid.

[32] Ibid.

studies show the circumstances or agencies used to renegotiate the conditionality of some BRI projects in Southeast Asia. Such renegotiations, however, were not observed in Cambodia. The country has been using a different strategy or agency: diversification. Although Chinese loans make up a large proportion of Cambodia's PPG external debt, China is not the only development partner that Cambodia has relied on. France, Germany (through KfW), India, Japan, the Republic of Korea, and Thailand are other main state creditors, while the Asian Development Bank, World Bank, and European Investment Bank are the main institutional creditors.[33]

In fact, Chinese loans as the proportion of Cambodia's total external PPG debt have been declining since 2015. Table 5.2 above shows that Chinese loans made up approximately 45% of total PPG loans in 2015, and it continues to decline to approximately 35% in 2021, a 10-percentage-point drop in 6 years. In contrast, ADB loans have remained at 23%-24%, and Japanese loans have remained at 11%-13% during the same period (Table 5.2). Cambodia also 'allocates' major infrastructure projects to and sources of funding from development partners other than China.

Japan, for example, provided the loan for the construction of a 90-km stretch of National Road 5 in northwestern Cambodia. The road, also called Asian Highway 1, is a primary regional road linking Thailand's capital Bangkok with Vietnam's Ho Chi Minh City while passing through Cambodia's capital city.[34] Japan also provides 383 million USD loans for the development of Cambodia's major port, Sihanoukville Autonomous Port, into a deep-sea port.[35] Another major project, the Neak Loeung Bridge or Tsubasa Bridge, the longest bridge in Cambodia, crossing the Mekong River, was also funded by Japan.[36] This is not to mention the assistance the Japan International Cooperation Agency (JICA) has been providing in flood protection and drainage improvement in the capital city.[37]

Likewise, the Republic of Korea is also a main development partner in infrastructure development in Cambodia. National Roads 2 and 22, connecting Cambodia's capital to the border with Vietnam, were funded by a loan from the Republic of Korea and built by a Korean construction company.[38] Fund diversification is a basic strategy to avoid overreliance on a single source of external funding and an agency for bargaining in loan negotiations.

5.4.5 Cambodia's Potential External Debt Risks

The analysis of Chinese public loans to Cambodia is the analysis of Cambodia's overall debt. No distinction should be made between Chinese loans and loans from

[33] Cambodia Public Debt Statistical Bulletin (2023).
[34] Samean Lay (2022).
[35] Raksmey Chhorn (2022).
[36] Sokheng Vong and Rebecca Moss (2015).
[37] Opening Ceremony (2020).
[38] Socheata Van (2023).

other development partners since the conditionality for providing and accepting loans is based on financial and economic rationales. Trying to spotlight Chinese financial assistance from other countries' financial assistance is politically motivated and absurd. Although we were not able to find a detailed conditionality of Chinese loans to Cambodia, we can assume that it is at least as favorable as other countries' loans. The fact that the size of Chinese loans is larger than other countries' loans might imply a more favorable conditionality. As such, would it not be good for Cambodia's economy to accept more favorable financing, given the absorption and repayment capacities?

However, there are still potential risks (for its external debt from all sources) that Cambodia should be cautious about. First, Cambodia's external public debt (PPG) should not be a cause of concern for the country given the reasons provided in the above sections. External private debt (private nonguaranteed or PNG), on the other hand, needs to be monitored closely. The table and figure below show the amount of PNG debt the country has accumulated since 2010. Although it only accounts for less than 30% of total external debt, its wild fluctuation throughout the years (Fig. 5.3) is very worrying. The growth rates of the external PPG debt have been steadily below 20% (except for 2012), whereas the growth rates of PNG debt have been relatively unpredictable. This can be problematic for debt forecasts and policy planning. Moreover, the fact that Cambodia has not had a clear policy for external private debt management makes it even more vulnerable (Table 5.8).

In addition, the Joint World Bank-IMF Debt Sustainability Analysis shows that Cambodia's external debt-carrying capacity (private and public) is vulnerable to

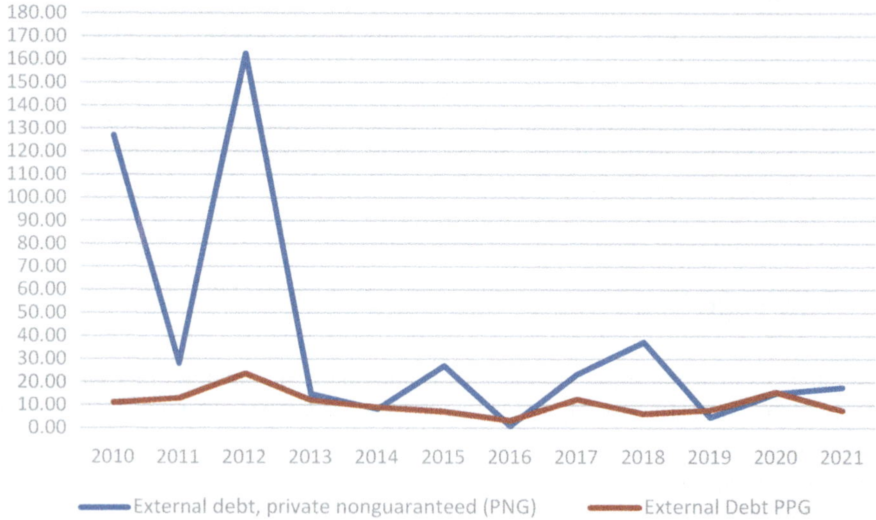

Fig. 5.3 Growth rate of cambodia's external private development and external public debt. *Source* The World Bank, https://data.worldbank.org/indicator/DT.DOD.DPNG.CD?locations=KH

Table 5.8 Cambodia's external private debt

Year	External debt, private nonguaranteed (PNG)			External debt, PPG
	DOD, current US$	% of total external debt	Growth Rate	Growth Rate
2010	442,209,000.00	11.03	127.46	11.37
2011	567,107,000.00	12.18	28.24	13.16
2012	1,489,881,000.00	22.07	162.72	23.82
2013	1,712,935,000.00	22.48	14.97	12.29
2014	1,856,620,000.00	22.32	8.39	9.11
2015	2,362,000,000.00	25.03	27.22	7.33
2016	2,388,290,000.00	23.74	1.11	3.43
2017	2,950,639,000.00	25.83	23.55	12.78
2018	4,055,507,000.00	29.97	37.45	6.35
2019	4,251,778,000.00	27.71	4.84	8.11
2020	4,901,666,000.00	27.90	15.29	15.90
2021	5,779,214,000.00	28.87	17.90	7.84

Source The World Bank,https://data.worldbank.org/indicator/DT.DOD.DPNG.CD?locations=KH

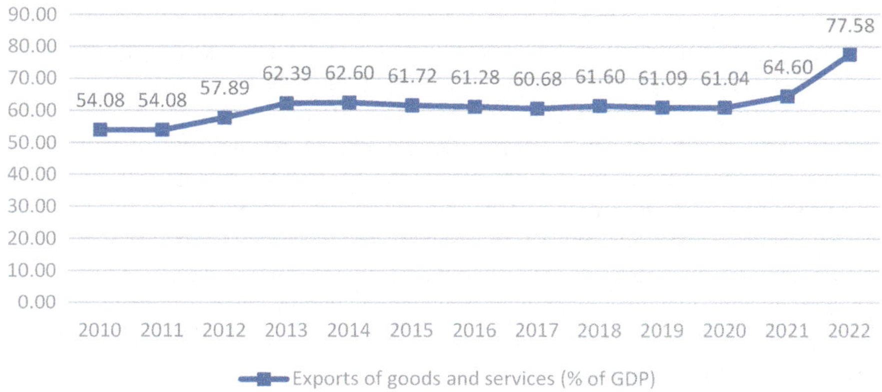

Fig. 5.4 Cambodia's exports of goods and services as percentage of GDP. *Source* The World Bank, https://data.worldbank.org/indicator/NE.EXP.GNFS.ZS?locations=KH

export shock.[39] The stress test run by this analysis indicates that the ratio of the present value of external debt to GDP breached its simulation threshold in terms of the export stress test, implying that the debt servicing capacity of Cambodia is vulnerable to a decrease in the country's exports. This is particularly important, as exports make up between 60 and 70% of the country's GDP (Fig. 5.4). However, the test also shows that the breach is brief and small.[40]

[39] Cambodia Joint World Bank-IMF (2022).

[40] Ibid.

Table 5.9 CPIA Rating for Cambodia's Revenue Mobilization

Year	Cambodia's CPIA rating for revenue mobilization
2010	3
2011	3.5
2012	3.5
2013	3.5
2014	3.5
2015	3.5
2016	3.5
2017	3.5
2018	3.5
2019	3.5
2020	3.5
2021	3.5
2022	3.5

Source The World Bank, https://data.worldbank.org/indicator/IQ.CPA.REVN.XQ?locations=KH

Last but not least, another potential risk that can make external debt and debt servicing problematic for Cambodia is the revenue collection capacity of the RGC. Although the data discussed in the above section (Table 5.5) show that the annual debt servicing obligation of the RGC has remained small compared to the government's revenue and well below the threshold, the government's revenue collection efficiency has remained below the optimum. The World Bank's CPIA rating for revenue mobilization for Cambodia has remained at a medium rating of 3.5 (1 being the lowest, 6 being the highest) throughout the last decade.[41] This CPIA rating for revenue mobilization assesses the pattern of revenue collection of the government in terms of tax and nontax sources. Being at a medium level means that the revenue collection of the RGC has not been efficient enough, and debt servicing can be vulnerable to shocks in revenue collection (Table 5.9).

5.5 Conclusion

Cambodia's economy has been growing at an impressive rate during the last decade. Sectors such as garments, footwear, travel goods, construction, and tourism have been the main catalysts for growth and development. The dependence on external debt has been prominent in this growth journey, owing to the lack of domestic capital stocks and the infant debt market in the country. The steady growth of external public debt (PPG) stocks, reaching 9.97 billion USD or 33% of GDP in 2022, becomes a cause

[41] Cambodia Economic Update (2023).

of concern for many, national and foreign alike. Even more irritating, especially for the West, is the fact that a sizeable proportion of Cambodia's external public debt has been from China. There is a common belief that because of this, Cambodia is being pushed further into the Chinese orbit and is being swallowed by the so-called "debt trap" of China's BRI.

This concern might have been exaggerated as the risk of Cambodia's external public debt is low. First, most of Cambodia's external public debt has been used for prioritized infrastructure projects that usually pay for themselves in the medium to long run. These projects have been implemented under the PPP scheme, meaning the risk of debt overspill from any project to the state's coffer is very slim. In other words, the PPP scheme makes them self-contained development projects. Second, Cambodia has a well-regarded debt management framework (5 CPIA ratings by the World Bank) with specific conditions, indicators, and ceilings for disciplining its borrowing behavior. Third, the external public debt of the country has been very conservative (remaining within every indicator's threshold) and highly concessional (long-term loan with low-interest rate, long grace period, and high level of grant element). Fourth, Cambodia has a large foreign exchange reserve compared to its public debt and debt obligation. This acts as a buffer and credibility against any economic downturn and debt default risk. Finally, the kingdom has been using a diversification strategy as its agency for bargaining.

Although all data and indicators indicate good performance for public debt management, there is a possibility that the country still faces problems with its external debt. The first potential risk concerns private debt because of the unpredictable characteristics of this kind of debt and the absence of a private debt management framework. The second potential risk arises from the exposure of Cambodia's GDP and debt obligation to export shock, as the country depends heavily on the export of goods and services. The last potential risk is caused by suboptimal government revenue mobilization.

As policy recommendations, the RGC needs to establish and follow the suggestions below. It must increase revenue mobilization and strengthen fiscal restraint. Financial goals should be established and closely adhered to. This entails controlling budget deficits, bringing down the national debt, and increasing the effectiveness of government spending. It should increase the tax base, streamline the filing process, and minimize tax exemptions to increase revenue. This will support boosting tax collection for the government and lowering its dependency on debt. Second, it must comply rigidly with macroprudential controls. It must employ macroprudential policies to reduce volatility in the housing market and lower the possibility of a bubble. This may entail actions such as increasing the capital requirements for banks, limiting lending to the real estate industry, and setting a restriction on the debt-to-income ratio for mortgages. These will eventually put a stop to the nation's uncontrollably rising private debt. In the same line, it ought to enhance banks' and other financial institutions' capacity for risk management. Finally, accountability and openness need to be improved. This involves actions such as enhancing the control of public expenditure and providing timely and accurate budget data as well as disclosing the terms and conditions of the public debt. The sustainability of Cambodia's debt, however, is also significantly influenced by Chinese creditors and investors. The sustainability of the nation's debt as well as the dangers connected to certain projects must be taken into consideration initially. They should also collaborate with the Cambodian government to restructure the country's existing debt in a way that lessens its debt load and fosters sustainable growth. Last but not least, the Chinese government and investors might transfer technical know-how to Cambodia in sectors such as public finance, debt management, and financial sector regulation and supervision. By doing so, Cambodia will be better able to manage its economy and lower the risk of going into debt.

References

Cambodia Economic Update: Navigating Global Economic Headwind. World Bank Group. (1 November 2022). https://documents.worldbank.org/en/publication/documents-reports/documentdetail/099240011302241362/p17734004eeaaf0ee08c1e01df07b5a22df

Cambodia Economic Update: Post-COVID-19 Economic Recovery. World Bank Group. (16 May 2023). https://documents.worldbank.org/en/publication/documents-reports/documentdetail/099051523221517821/p17734003f2bcf02b0a89500f61b1f3ff7b

Cambodia external debt. CEIC. (n.d.). https://www.ceicdata.com/en/indicator/cambodia/external-debt

Cambodia issues Government Bond of $27 million in H1. *Khmer Times*. (1 August 2023). https://www.khmertimeskh.com/501334815/cambodia-issues-government-bond-of-27-million-in-h1/

Cambodia Joint World Bank-IMF Debt Sustainability Analysis. World Bank-IMF. (November 2022). https://documents1.worldbank.org/curated/en/099220002082341012/pdf/BOSIB053b9ddd307508e0e0ea3991f19d4d.pdf

Cambodia Public Debt Statistical Bulletin. Ministry of Economy and Finance. (2023). https://gdicdm.mef.gov.kh/en/cat/documents-and-publications/bulletins

Chheang, V. (25 April 2022). Cambodian perception of the new Chinese. *ISEAS Perspective*, *42*(2022), 1–11. https://www.iseas.edu.sg/articles-commentaries/iseas-perspective/2022-42-cambodian-perception-of-the-new-chinese-by-vannarith-chheang/.

Chheang, V. (27 July 2021). BRI Projects in Cambodia and Laos Roll on Despite Covid-19. *ISEAS Perspective*, *99*(2021), 1–9. https://www.iseas.edu.sg/articles-commentaries/iseas-perspective/2021-99-bri-projects-in-cambodia-and-laos-roll-on-despite-covid-19-by-vannarith-chheang/

Chhorn, R. (8 August 2022). Japan to Loan $383 m to Develop Sihanoukville Port. *Kiripost*. https://kiripost.com/stories/japan-to-loan-383m-to-develop-sihanoukville-port

Chanrith Ngin, "How Recipient Countries in Southeast Asia Manage 'Belt and Road Initiative' Projects", *ISEAS Perspective*, No.99, October 10, 2022, https://www.iseas.edu.sg/articles-commentaries/iseas-perspective/2022-99-how-recipient-countries-in-southeast-asia-manage-belt-and-road-initiative-projects-by-chanrith-ngin/

CPIA debt policy rating (1=low to 6=high) – Cambodia. The World Bank. (n.d.). https://data.worldbank.org/indicator/IQ.CPA.DEBT.XQ?locations=KH

External debt stocks, public and publicly guaranteed (PPG) (DOD, current US$) - Cambodia. The World Bank. (n.d.). https://data.worldbank.org/indicator/DT.DOD.DPPG.CD?locations=KH

GDP growth (annual %) - Cambodia. The World Bank. (n.d.). https://data.worldbank.org/indicator/NY.GDP.MKTP.KD.ZG?locations=KH

Heng, P., & Chheang, V. (2019). The Political Economy of China's Maritime Silk Road Initiative in Cambodia. In: Jean-Marc Blanchard (eds) China's Maritime Silk Road Initiative and Southeast Asia. Palgrave Studies in Asia-Pacific Political Economy. Palgrave Macmillan, Singapore. https://doi.org/10.1007/978-981-32-9275-8_6

Jeanne, O., & Rancière, R. (2006). The Optimal Level of International Reserves for Emerging Market Countries: Formulas and Applications. International Monetary Fund. https://www.imf.org/external/pubs/ft/wp/2006/wp06229.pdf

Lay, S. (10 January 2022). PM opens stretch of Japan-funded National Road 5. *The Phnom Penh Post*. https://www.phnompenhpost.com/national/pm-opens-stretch-japan-funded-national-road-5.

Lending Policies and Rates. International Monetary Fund. (n.d.). https://www.adb.org/what-we-do/public-sector-financing/lending-policies-rates.

Mech, D. (29 July 2019). Journalists invited to tour ream naval base. *The Phnom Penh Post*. https://www.phnompenhpost.com/national-politics/journalists-invited-tour-ream-naval-base.

Menon, J. (March 2023). The Belt and Road Initiative in Cambodia: Costs and Benefits, Real and Perceived. *ISEAS Perspective, 01*(2023). https://www.iseas.edu.sg/wp-content/uploads/2023/03/ISEAS_EWP_2023-1_Menon.pdf

Nakashima, E. & Cadell, C. (6 June 2022). China secretly building naval facility in Cambodia, Western officials say. *The Washington Post*. https://www.washingtonpost.com/national-security/2022/06/06/cambodia-china-navy-base-ream/

Ngin, C. (10 October 2022). How Recipient Countries in Southeast Asia Manage 'Belt and Road Initiative' Projects. *ISEAS Perspective, 99*(2022), 1–14. https://www.iseas.edu.sg/articles-commentaries/iseas-perspective/2022-99-how-recipient-countries-in-southeast-asia-manage-belt-and-road-initiative-projects-by-chanrith-ngin/

Opening Ceremony of Full-scale Mechanical Screen of the Project for Flood Protection and Drainage Improvement in Phnom Penh Capital City Phase 4. Japan International Cooperation Agency. (2 June 2020). https://www.jica.go.jp/Resource/cambodia/english/office/topics/200602.html

Olivier Jeanne & Romain Rancière, The Optimal Level of International Reserves for Emerging Market Countries: Formulas and Applications. International Monetary Fund (IMF), 2006, https://www.imf.org/external/pubs/ft/wp/2006/wp06229.pdf

Page, J., Lubold, G., & Taylor, R. (21 July 2019). Deal for naval outpost in Cambodia furthers China's quest for military network. *The Wall Street Journal*. https://www.wsj.com/articles/secret-deal-for-chinese-naval-outpost-in-cambodia-raises-u-s-fears-of-beijings-ambitions-11563732482

Public Debt Management Strategy 2019–2023. Ministry of Economy and Finance. (2019). https://gdicdm.mef.gov.kh/en/2020/01/17/10115.html

Reconnecting Asia Project Database. Center for Strategic and International Studies. (14 May 2021). https://reconasia.csis.org/reconnecting-asia-map/

Raksmey Chhorn, "Japan to Loan $383 m to Develop Sihanoukville Port", *Kiripost,* August 8, 2022, https://kiripost.com/stories/japan-to-loan-383m-to-develop-sihanoukville-port

Samean Lay, "PM opens stretch of Japan-funded National Road 5", *The Phnom Penh Post,* January 10, 2022, https://www.phnompenhpost.com/national/pm-opens-stretch-japan-funded-national-road-5.

Seng, M. (10 February 2023). Concern Over Cambodia's Climbing Debt. *Kiripost*. https://kiripost.com/stories/concern-over-cambodias-climbing-debt

See Ellen Nakashima & Cate Cadell, "China secretly building naval facility in Cambodia, Western officials say", *The Washington Post,* June 6, 2022, https://www.washingtonpost.com/national-security/2022/06/06/cambodia-china-navy-base-ream/

See Dara Mech, "Journalists invited to tour ream naval base", *The Phnom Penh Post,* July 29, 2019, https://www.phnompenhpost.com/national-politics/journalists-invited-tour-ream-naval-base.

See Pheakdey Heng and Vannarith Chheang, The Political Economy of China's Maritime Silk Road Initiative in Cambodia. In: Jean-Marc Blanchard (eds) *China's Maritime Silk Road Initiative and Southeast Asia*, Singapore: Palgrave Macmillan, 2019

Sokheng Vong and Rebecca Moss, "Bridge spanning Mekong River opened", *The Phnom Penh Post,* April 7, 2015, https://www.phnompenhpost.com/national/bridge-spanning-mekong-river-opened

Socheata Van, "National roads 2, 22 construction to be completed 'end of March'", *The Phnom Penh Post,* February 15, 2023, https://www.phnompenhpost.com/national/national-roads-2-22-construction-be-completed-end-march

Strategic Document on Public Debt Management 2011–2018. Ministry of Economy and Finance. (2012). https://gdicdm.mef.gov.kh/en/2018/10/05/2268.html

Strategic Document on Public Debt Management 2015–2018. Ministry of Economy and Finance. (2015). https://gdicdm.mef.gov.kh/en/2018/10/05/2272.html

Subdecree NO. 11 on Build-Operate-Transfer (BOT). Royal Government of Cambodia. (1998). https://data.opendevelopmentcambodia.net/laws_record/sub-decree-on-construction-contract-corperation-and-transferability#:~:text=This%20sub-decree%20applies%20on%20Build-Operate-Transfer%20contracts%20between%20the,not%20applicable%20on%20such%20contracts%20between%20private%20entities

Sun, N. (07 February 2023). Cambodia Seeks New Financing from Beijing Amid Fears of 'Debt Trap.' *Voice of America (VOA).* https://www.voanews.com/a/cambodia-seeks-more-loans-from-beijing-amid-fears-of-debt-trap-/6943062.html

Teng, Y. (9 February 2023). Debt fear as Hun Sen cements China ties. *Cambodianess.* https://cambodianess.com/article/debt-fear-as-hun-sen-cements-china-ties

Turton, S. (27 May 2022). Cambodia's Hun Sen defends succession plan, denies China "debt trap." *Nikkei Asia.* https://asia.nikkei.com/Spotlight/The-Future-of-Asia/The-Future-of-Asia-2022/Cambodia-s-Hun-Sen-defends-succession-plan-denies-China-debt-trap

Vannarith Chheang, "BRI Projects in Cambodia and Laos Roll on Despite Covid-19", *ISEAS Perspective*, No.99, July 27, 2021, https://www.iseas.edu.sg/articles-commentaries/iseas-perspective/2021-99-bri-projects-in-cambodia-and-laos-roll-on-despite-covid-19-by-vannarith-chheang/.

Vachon, M. (12 February 2022). "National Road Number 5" – the Side Story of a Years-Long Road Improvement Project. *Cambodianess.* https://cambodianess.com/article/national-road-number-5-the-side-story-of-a-years-long-road-improvement-project

Van, S. (15 February 2023). National roads 2, 22 construction to be completed 'end of March.' *The Phnom Penh Post.* https://www.phnompenhpost.com/national/national-roads-2-22-construction-be-completed-end-march

Vannarith Chheang, 2022/42 "Cambodian perception of the new Chinese", ISEAS-Yusof Ishak Institute, April 25, 2022, https://www.iseas.edu.sg/articles-commentaries/iseas-perspective/2022-42-cambodian-perception-of-the-new-chinese-by-vannarith-chheang/

Vong, S., & Moss, R. (7 April 2015). Bridge spanning Mekong River opened. *The Phnom Penh Post.* https://www.phnompenhpost.com/national/bridge-spanning-mekong-river-opened

Williamson, A. (2023). The economic and political implications of China's foreign aid in Cambodia. Moussons, (41), 133-150. https://doi.org/https://doi.org/10.4000/moussons.10476

Wang Zheng, "Assessing the Belt and Road Initiative in Southeast Asia amid the COVID-19 Pandemic (2021–2022)", *ISEAS Perspective*, No.57, May 26, 2022, https://www.iseas.edu.sg/articles-commentaries/iseas-perspective/2022-57-assessing-the-belt-and-road-initiative-in-southeast-asia-amid-the-covid-19-pandemic-2021-2022-by-wang-zheng/

Yalirozy Teng, Debt fear as Hun Sen cements China ties, *Cambodianess,* February 9, 2023, https://cambodianess.com/article/debt-fear-as-hun-sen-cements-china-ties

Zheng, W. (26 May 2022). Assessing the Belt and Road Initiative in Southeast Asia amid the COVID-19 Pandemic (2021–2022). *ISEAS Perspective*, 57(2022), Art. 57. https://www.iseas.edu.sg/articles-commentaries/iseas-perspective/2022-57-assessing-the-belt-and-road-initiative-in-southeast-asia-amid-the-covid-19-pandemic-2021-2022-by-wang-zheng/

Chapter 6
Laos-China Railway: Legal, Social, Economic and Environmental Perspectives

Sypha Chanthavong

Abstract The Laos-China railway is one of the results of the Laos-China cooperation policy. This railway links China to the capital of Lao PDR, Vientiane, and passes five provinces, namely, Luangnamtha, Oudomxay, Luang Prabang, Vientiane, and Vientiane Capital. This railway plays a significant role in the economic integration of Laos with neighboring countries and serves the passing service policy of the government. Millions of passengers use this train to travel to world cultural heritage sites such as Luang Prabang and end up on the Laos-China borders or crossing the border to China or Laos. Aside from passengers, a large number of goods were transported by trains, for example, from China to Laos and Thailand, from Laos to China, or from Thailand to China. Both state and local people generate income from the train.

Keywords Laos · China · Railway · BRI · Economic · Integration

6.1 Introduction

Lao People's Democratic Republic (hereinafter called Lao PDR or Laos) is a landlocked country in mainland Southeast Asia that shares a border with five neighboring countries, namely, China to the north, Vietnam to the east, Thailand to the west, Myanmar to the northwest, and Cambodia to the south. Since 1986, the Government of Lao (GoL) has had to change the status of landlocked to land link country, which introduced the concept of "passageway service" in the second National Socio-Economic Development Plan of Lao PDR.[1] After that, the "passageway service country" concept was widely discussed in each five-year national social and economic development plan. For example, the 6th National Socio-Economic Development Plan (2006–2010) acknowledges the link between the railway between Lao PDR

[1] *The Second National Socio-Economic Development* Plan, (1986).

S. Chanthavong (✉)
Faculty of Law and Political Science, National University of Laos, Vientiane Capital, Lao PDR
e-mail: chantavongsy@yahoo.com

N. Peng and M. Y. Cheng (eds.), *The Reality and Myth of BRI's Debt Trap*, Indo-Pacific Focus, https://doi.org/10.1007/978-981-97-1056-0_6

and Thailand.[2] While the high-speed railway between Lao PDR and China was officially introduced in the 7th National Socio-Economic Development Plan in 2011, the GoL would like to promote logistics based on the north–south and east–west corridor policies for linking with the region in terms of transportation, including the China-Laos border at Boten International Checking Point or the Boten-Vientiane Capital high-speed railway project.[3]

The Laos-China railway was again promoted in the 8th National Socio-Economic Development Plan in 2016 under the main concept of regional and international integration. Within this plan, the GoL promotes the railway, which links to Boten. Vientiane Capital, Vientiane Capital-Thakek-Mouya (Laos-Viet Nam border), from Thakek-Savannakhet-Champasack-Nongnokkhien international checkpoint (border between Laos and Cambodia) and Champasack-Vangtao international checkpoint (border with Thailand).[4]

Aside from the internal policies, it is important to note that Lao PDR has a railway with a link between the Nong Khai northeast province of Thailand and the Vientiane capital, which is 3.5 km long. One of the most significant for Lao PDR to decide linking transportation is the ASEAN[5] Framework on Multimodal Transport, which was signed in Vientiane, Lao PDR on 17 November 2005.[6] This framework requires the ASEAN Member States to realize multimodal transportation to enable door-to-door delivery of goods and passenger travel among the ASEAN and the partner countries.[7] The Laos-China railway project was constructed on 25 December 2016.[8] This project costs 5.9 billion USD and is 414 km long. The railway has a size of 1,435 m according to the railway standard, with a total of 33 stations, 75 tunnels (total length of 183.9 km, accounting for 43% of the total route), and 170 bridges (length of 69.2 km, accounting for 15.8% of the total route).[9] The GoL and the project building company approximate that the income of the project will be 3.98 million USD per year for domestic rail passengers, while 8.62 million passengers are expected.[10] The Laos-China Railway is concessed for 50 years after the commencement date.[11] However, it is argued that the Laos-China Railway project has two sides. First, the project will link Laos to China and other countries as the priority of the GoL. Second, the project will generate income in terms of trading, transportation, investment, and tourism

[2] Report of the Six National Socio-Economic Development Plan, (2011).

[3] The Seven National Socio-Economic Development Plan, (2011).

[4] The Seven National Socio-Economic Development Plan, (2016).

[5] ASEAN is abbreviation of the Association of Southeast Asian Nations; more detail please refer to https://asean.org.

[6] Ministry of Public Works and Transport, report on the draft of the railway law (2018).

[7] See more detail in implementation framework of the ASEAN framework agreement on multimodal transport, https://asean.org/wp-content/uploads/2019/11/Implementation-Framework-AFAMT_FINAL.pdf.

[8] Deputy Minister (2018).

[9] Somsack Pongkhao (2021).

[10] Jasmina Yap (2017).

[11] Lao Government and the Laos-China Railway Company Limited, (2016).

in the tourism destinations in the northern part of Lao PDR, namely, Vang Vieng and Luangprabang. On the other hand, the Laos-China Railway project generates negative impacts on society and the environment, mainly in areas nearby or adjacent to the railway.

This chapter examines the legal and both positive and negative impacts of the Laos-China Railway Project by dividing it into three main sections. The first is to examine the Laos-China Cooperation Policy to frame how the railway was built. The second is to identify the legal to deal with the railway project. This is because the railway is very new for the GoL, so how the GoL drafts the law to manage the railway is very important for understanding. Third, the social and environmental concerns of the Laos-China Railway Project, mainly the resettlement program and social and environmental impacts during construction and operation, will be carefully examined. To understand the legal, social, and environmental perspectives regarding the Laos-China railway project, the paper will carefully examine the relevant documents and use empirical surveys and observations. Empirical data are scrutinized by the relevant people who are working directly with the management of the railway project and people who identified themselves as directly and indirectly impacted by the construction and operation of the railway. The observations were carried out through the railway service and the livelihood of people near both the railway station and along the railway. This chapter collects the relevant information from many sources as a desk review, and interviews were conducted from May to September 2023.

6.2 Chinese Investment in Infrastructure Sectors in Laos

Historically speaking, Laos and China have a long time of cooperation. However, in the case of investment, for example, the GoL and Chinese government signed an agreement for the promotion and protection of bilateral investment on 31 January 1993.[12] This Agreement is the starting point for Chinese investors to invest in Laos. According to official statistics, Chinese investors rank first, second or third in foreign direct investment in Laos. For example, in 2019, China was ranked second, with 16 projects and an investment value of 1,072,237,229 USD.[13] In 2021, China remained the largest investor in Laos, with 813 projects worth 16 billion USD.[14] The investment of Chinese investors began to play an important role in the regional countries and Lao PDR after the Chinese government announced the policy to promote foreign investment or the "Go Out Policy" in 1999 and the Belt and Road Initiative (BRI) in 2013. China's investment in Lao PDR as of October 2020 has a total of 793 projects

[12] This agreement signed in Vientiane with has 12 articles.

[13] "All approved investment project by country in the year 2019, (2022).

[14] Phayboune Thanabouasy, (2021).

with a total approved value of more than 12 billion USD, ranking first among 32 countries and regions that have invested in Lao PDR.[15]

Many infrastructure projects were developed and funded by the Chinese government and Chinese investors in Lao PDR, including hydropower dam projects, special economic zones, expressways, and railways. In terms of hydropower development projects, according to available data, 17 dams have been allocated to Chinese companies, and 10 out of 17 were developed by the Sinohydro Company, including 7 cascade dams in the Nam Ou River in northern Laos. Datang Overseas provides 81% of the budget for the construction of the Pakbeng Dam in the Mekong River in Pakbeng district, Oudomxay province.[16] For the special economic zone, China has also invested in special economic zones that have been approved for a total of 463 projects with a total approved value of more than 3.1 billion USD.[17]

The expressway from Vientiane to Boten is one of a good examples of the infrastructure with investment by Chinese companies. The expressway project is divided into three phases, namely, Vientiane to Vangvieng, Vang Vieng to Luangprabang and Luangprabang to Boten. Until now, the first phase of the expressway from Vientiane to Vangvieng has been operating. The Vientiane-Vang Vieng expressway project brings benefits in terms of infrastructure, such as transportation routes to facilitate transportation, tourism, trade and investment for business operators, people and the nation. The project is part of the main road network system of the Asian Highway 12 (Natouia-Udomxay-Pak Mong-Luang Prabang-Vientiane-Vientiane-Nong Khai-Udonthany-Khon Kaen). This road is part of the development plan of the Kumming-Bangkok highway, which is the second alternative corridor and is the main line of the road network system in the northern part of Lao PDR according to the development plan of transit services and regional and international integration policy. The Vientiane-Vang Vieng highway has a total length of 109 km and a total budget of 1,297,064,448 USD.[18]

It is observable that the Silk Road policy of China and the regional liking of the Laos policies are merged. Tom Wilms has observed that the rail from Vientiane to Boten is much safer than the existing roads. Traveling by road is time-consuming, for example, 14 h. However, the railway uses only 4 h.[19]

---

[15] Laos-China jointly review economic-commercial and technical work, (2020).

[16] Compilation on Hydropower Project in Lao PDR, (2015).

[17] Laos-China jointly review economic-commercial and technical work, (2020).

[18] Yunnan Construction and Investment Holding Group., Co., LTD, (2017).

[19] Tom Wilms, (2021).

6.3 Laos' Legal Framework and Institutional Arrangement for Railway Management

In Lao PDR, twelve levels of regulation were identified.[20] The highest level of regulation is the Constitution of Lao PDR, and the lowest is village regulations. Regarding railway management, the GoL has prepared both legal and institutional arrangements. In terms of law, the GoL promulgated the Law on Railways in 2019, with 167 articles.[21] At the same time, in terms of institutional arrangement, the GoL has established the railway department under the Ministry of Public Works and Transportation, while the railway police department was established in the Ministry of Public Security. This part of the paper will scrutinize how to manage the railway from legal and institutional points of view.

The railway law provides the objective that "this law determines the principles, regulations and measures on the management, inspection of railway activities for ensure of the railway implementation to be efficient, modern, sustain and environmental friendly to make sure the running of railway activities and transportation by using of railway to be convenient, quick, safe, integrate with the regional and international, contribution to the national defense and social security and national socioeconomic development."[22] From the provisions of this article, one of the main purposes of the law is to link Laos with the regional by using the railway while another one is the national social economic development. Currently, the Laos-China Railway Company has created an application for online ticket booking, which makes people who would like to travel by train more convenient. From the opening date of the Lao-China train until September 17, 2023 can transport a total of 3,197,600 passengers, an average of 4,889 passengers/day and a record of 10,197 passengers/day. Only for more than 8 months in 2023 can 1,759,900 passengers be transported. For the transportation of goods from the day of operation until September 17, 2023, 5,381,900 tons of goods can be exported, an average of 8,229 tons/day and a maximum of 15,250 tons/day. The main types of goods include fruits, potato flour, barley, rubber, beer, iron ore, concentrated iron ore and chemical fertilizers. The goods sent from China to Laos total 770,900 tons, and the goods sent from Laos to China total 4,560,800 tons. Only in 2023, until September 17, export goods reached 3,101,400 tons, an increase of 138% compared to the same period of last year, with an average of 11,928 tons/day, with a maximum shipment of 15,250 tons/day. Among them, 344,700 tons of goods were sent from China to Laos, and 2,752,200 million tons of goods were sent

[20] The Constitution; Laws; Resolutions of the National Assembly; Resolutions of the Standing Committee of the National Assembly; Ordinances of the President of the Republic; Decrees of the Government; Resolutions of the Government; Orders and Decisions of the Prime Minister; Orders, Decisions and Instructions of the Minister and Head of a Government Authority; Orders, Decisions and Instructions of the Provincial Governors and City Governors; Orders, Decisions and Instructions of the District and Municipality Chiefs; Village Regulations.

[21] The law has promulgated by the President of Lao PDR based on Presidential Decree No 151, dated 29 January 2019.

[22] Law on Railway, article 1, (2019).

from Laos to China. Therefore, the Lao-China Railway Company has procured one more EMU train, totaling 6 trains to support the current increase in passengers, especially in preparation for Lao PDR's ASEAN chairmanship and the opening of the Lao Tourism Year in 2024.[23]

Regarding the management of the railway, the GoL is the manager of the railway centralized and unity nationwide, and the GoL assigned power to the Ministry of Public Works and Transportation (MPWT) to be the main responsible and coordinate with the ministries, organization, and local authority. The railway management sector includes MPWT, Provincial Public Works and Transportation (PPWT) and District Office of Public Works and Transportation (OPWT).[24]

Under the law, there is one Prime Minister Decree regarding railway management called "railway staff". The railway staff includes train police and railway officers inspecting the running of trains that are appointed and signed to perform the duties of control, safeguarding, safety and ordering inside the train, station, and railway.[25] The train police have the rights provided in the regulations on train police that are signed by the minister of public security, while the officer inspecting the running of trains is an officer from the public works and transportation sector, which is appointed and assigned by the minister of public works and transportation to perform the duties related to facilitating, managing, inspecting security and order inside of trains, stations and railways.[26] It seems to be that this decree assigned the power to the minister of public security to issue an agreement on the establishment and activity of the train police and its branch at local levels as well as assigning power to the minister of public works and transportation to appoint the staff to work with the railway.

Under the MPWT, the Department of Railways (DRW) was established. The DRW has the duty to research and integrate the policies of the party and the government, the strategic plans of the Ministry of Public Works and Transport regarding the railway works to be deepened. At the same time, the DRW has the duty to create strategic plans and policies, plans, programs, and detailed project periods and guide the implementation of railway works to present the considered and approved minister of public works and transport. The DRW has a duty to develop the policies of the party and the government, as well as the Ministry of Public Works and Transport, regarding railway work to be efficient and highly effective. One of the main tasks of the DRW is to research draft regulations, rules, laws and technical standards regarding the construction, management, use, maintenance, and repair of mechanical vehicles, equipment, and railways and to research and create short-term and long-term strategic plans regarding the expansion of the railway system in the country and explore the design of railway construction according to the technical standards set by the Ministry. The DWR requires finding sources of funding both domestically and internationally to develop railway work and developing a management plan and using

[23] Thanouthong, (2023).

[24] Ibid, article 149.

[25] Governmental "Decree on Railway Officer," No 474/PM, article 2, Prime Minister Office, (2021).

[26] Ibid, article 11.

the budget approved by the government to be highly effective as well as managing the state investment budget, grants, joint ventures, and loans of railway development projects.[27]

The DRW has the main rights to carry out inspections and audits of activities of technical departments, projects and business units depending on their sector. The second is negotiate, negotiate, sign agreements, protocols, or other commitments with related parties both domestically, abroad and with international organizations as approved by the Minister. Third, we propose the use of the budget and mechanical vehicles, materials and equipment as assigned by the Ministry.[28]

There are five divisions under the DRW, but two divisions, namely, the division of engineering and the division of transportation, are directly working with the railways. The engineering division has the rights to collect the economic-technical, technical identification, standard and impacts of railway activities on the social and environment. Inspection, monitoring of the survey, design, construction, maintenance and repair of the railway, equipment and safety instruction and facilitation of the railway. Creating a plan for surveying, designing and constructing railways as well as managing and using railways for efficiency and effectiveness. Management of the enterprise with an offering of the construction and repair of the railways.[29] The division of the transportation in the train has the right to first create the plan for transportation, management, and data collection of the train transportation. The second is creating regulations for the management of train transportation, assessing the environmental impacts of train transportation and safety management and creating plans for domestic and international train transportation. Third is to manage the train transportation of the enterprises.[30] It seems that the two divisions work closely and directly with the railway in Lao PDR as the secretariat to the DRW and MPWT.

Aside from the role of DRW in railway management, the Minister of PWT also has created an agreement on the Establishment and Activities of the Laos-China Railway Project Management Committee (LCRM). The LCRM is secretariate to the Deputy Prime Minister or chairperson of the LCRM and Minister of the PWT in terms of management, inspection and coordination with the Laos-China Railway Company and other organizations to implement the procedure of railway construction to be aligned with the plan.[31] The LCRM has the rights to, first, management, inspection and coordination with the Laos-China Railway Company to ensure project implementation from the starting date to the handover date. The second is to coordinate with the relevant organization at the central and local levels to ensure that project activity implementation is facilitated to reach the goals and objectives of the project. Third is to manage and inspect labor, equipment, machines, and vehicle imports for use in the project. Fourth is to mediate an issue regarding social and environmental

[27] Agreement on Establishment and Activity of Department of Railways, (2017).

[28] Ibid, article 3.

[29] Law on Railway, article 9, (2019).

[30] Ibid, article 10.

[31] Agreement on Establishment and Activities of the Laos-China Railway Project Management Committee, (2020).

impacts, safety management, obstacle resolution, land compensation and concession agreement implementation. The fifth is to coordinate with the relevant sectors in both Laos and China in creating training and human resource upgrading plans regarding railway management.[32] This is comparable to the fact that the LCRM has more power compared with the DWR because the LCRM is chaired by the Deputy Prime Minister, and the Minister of PWT is a deputy and serves as the standing person.

The local PWT, namely, the provincial and district PWT, does not have more power than the DRW and LCRM PWT. For example, the provincial division of the PWT has the right to assist in the management of the railway, including the railway land and railway observation area within the province. At the same time, the provincial division of the PWT also has the right to propose to the MPWT for training and upgrading the staff regarding railway management and regularly report issues regarding the railway to the MPWT.[33] The district office of the PWT has four rights regarding railway management. The first is to disseminate and implement policies, strategies, laws, regulations, plans, programs, projects, orders, and guidelines for railways. The second is railway observation area protection. Third, the relevant organization should coordinate the supply and management of land for railway construction. The fourth is to assist the railway, including the railway land and railway observation area within the district.[34]

It is observable that almost all of the economic activities regarding the construction, management and maintenance of the railway are under the hands of LCRM and DRW, while the local levels of the PWT sectors are only assistance to the central level. Moreover, hard and complicated activities, such as the allocation of land for railway construction, belong to the district office of the PWT. This activity is not easy to find the empty land or avoid from the constructed building is the most activity of the railway construction as well as how to avoid the conflict between landowner and concession company is the most controversial issues.

Separately from the PWT sectors at both the central and local levels in terms of railway management, the role of the train police serves as an important point to mention here. The train police are officers from the Ministry of Public Security, which appoints and assigns to perform the duty in the train and railway station for control of security, order, supervise of forbidding things or illegal and solving any issue regarding to insecurity of the train. The PWT and public security ministry regulate the appointment, rights, and duties of the train police.[35] Train police includes the Department of Train Police under the Ministry of Public Security, the Division of Train Police under the Provincial Police Bureau, and the Unit of Train Police under the District Police Bureau.

The Department of Train Police is an academic police professional. This department has the rights and duties to prevent the railway from trespassing animals or railway stations, to collect negative situations and crime on the railway or station,

[32] Law on Railway, article 3, (2019).

[33] Ibid, article 151.

[34] Ibid, article 152.

[35] Law on Railway, article 2, (2019).

and to advise the train police at the provincial and district levels nationwide.[36] At the same time, the department of train police has the right to use criminal coercive measures in the case of severe crime, immediately and testimony of the suspect person in regard to railway activities. The department of train police also has the rights to cooperate with the department of railway under the ministry of public works and transports, other sectors, railway staff, and solving the accident in railway or station.[37]

The department of train police is the main actor who cooperates with the Laos-China Railway Company in terms of coping with the security of the railway. For example, on 8 February 2022, the department issued a notice on the prohibition of using the railway. This notice prohibits passengers from carrying out guns, bullets, explosives, chemicals, drugs, sharpened materials, animal and smelling foods and drinks. In the case of finding the prohibited belongings, the railway stall can be seized and handed over to the train police for initial investigation based on the relevant laws.

At the provincial level, there is the Division of Train Police (DTP) under the Provincial Police Bureau. This division has the role of being the secretariate to the head of the provincial police bureau in terms of creating the plan and its implementation regarding train safety, such as safeguarding the train station within the province and collecting all relevant negative issues and crimes in the train station and along the railway to prevent, protect, and solve the issues immediately.[38] The DTP has rights and roles. First, it collects and inspects any situation within the train station and along the railway within the province to respond to the negative situation, crime and safeguard the train station. The second is to use coercive measures[39] as provided in the Criminal Procedure Law, such as detention, arresting and initial investigation of suspect persons before being sent to investigation police officers. Third, in the case of accidents or other incidents on the railway, the DTP should cooperate with the railway staff and other sections to solve the case. Fourth, it is necessary to facilitate inspection, advise passengers to violate the law and regulations inside the station and along the railway and to inspect and seize the prohibited belongings of passengers.[40] The district unit train police have the role to be the secretariate of the district police bureau for safeguarding the train way within the boundary of the district. The district unit trained police have the same rights and duties as the DTP. However, such rights and duties are limited within the district boundary.[41] It is important to note that

[36] Agreement on Establishment and Activity of the Department of Train Police, (2021).

[37] Law on Railway, article 3, (2019).

[38] Agreement on Establishment and Activity of the Provincial Division of Train Police and District Unit of Train Police (2021).

[39] There are 7 coercive measures as provided in the Law on Criminal Procedure, 2017, namely, Issuance of warrants; Detention; Arrest; Remand; Presentencing release; Presentencing house arrest; Suspension of position or duties. More detail see Article 136–145 of the Law on Criminal Procedure, (2017).

[40] Agreement on Establishment and Activity of the Department of Train Police, (2021).

[41] Agreement on Establishment and Activity of the Provincial Division of Train Police and District Unit of Train Police, (2021).

DTP and districts that have railways can establish train police, for example, Vientian Capital, Vientiane province, Luangprabang province, Oudomxay province and Luangnamtha province. Other provinces with railways that do not pass the provincial boundary cannot establish train police.

The role of training police in cooperation with training management organizations, mainly public works and transportation, is crucial, as mentioned above. The trespass to the reservation area of land along the railway requires the police professional to cope with this issue.[42] At the same time, stealing the electricity wire and other components of the railway are one of the greatest concerns for the company and government of Lao itself. For example, on 31 December 2021, the Minister to the Prime Minister's Office issued a notice to the Ministry of Public Works and Transport as well as the relevant sector in terms of increasing the inspection of railways by inviting local people at the village level to be joined as well as the professional performance of the train police to ensure the operation of the railway.[43]

6.4 Laos-China Railway, Economic and Local People's Income Generation

The Laos-China railway project is one of the most important economic drivers of both countries, mainly exportation, job creation for the Lao people, and education support of the Lao PDR sectors, for example. In terms of exportation, the exportation statistics increase from the quarter to the quarter of the year. However, this section aims to focus on the real economic return of the railway project rather than on the feasibility study of the project. According to statistics, in mid-December 2021, after opening the Laos-China railway, the trading values between Laos and China were more than 100 million yuan or more than 15 million USD.[44] According to the news from the Laophatthana Newspaper quoted to the vice president of the Laos-China Railway Company, from December 2021 to 2 August 2022, the Laos-China Railway can transport approximately 701,600 passengers and 1.027.000 tons of goods. In terms of passengers, there are three main groups: first, 50% are domestic and neighboring country tourists, 40% are general passengers, and the remaining 10% are state employers. The goods from Laos to China cover 773,400 tonnes and include mainly iron, potassium, black charcoal, rubber, and cassava power. The goods from China to Laos cover 253.600 tonnes, which includes fertilizer, electricity equipment, cloth and so on.[45]

A good example is from Xiengkhouang province, because in 2021, the export values of Xiengkhouang province are approximately 675 billion Kip and in the year 2022 will be 1000 billion Kip, more than fifty percent of the exportation is China

[42] Report on the draft of the railway law, (2018).

[43] Notice on focusing to solve issues regarding to railway, (2021).

[44] Not yet a month, (2021).

[45] Laos-China Railway Company prepare to solve the easy access to ticket, (2022).

mainly after the operation of the Laos-China railway. This is because the railway can save time, consume more resources than the truck, and consume less money.[46] The export of 100 tons of sticky rice to China is one of the good examples for shipping via the Laos-China railway, which can reduce the number of days compared with shipping via Thailand or Vietnam before reaching China, which will take a longer time.[47] Thailand, a neighboring country of Laos, is also using the Laos-China railway for the export of products and goods to China. For example, the *Bangkok Post* was published on 20 January 2022, which provides that the first thousand tonnes of Thai rice were shipped to Chongqing of China via the Laos-China railway, and the Thailand exportation sector will look for exports to China via this channel because the goods will reach China within 1–2 days.[48] The Laos-China railway will be an alternative for goods exportation from Laos, Thailand, Cambodia and Myanmar to China.[49] Of course, for the government of Lao, the Laos-China railway will bring many opportunities for trading and exporting goods to China. However, the opportunities may come with some challenges of the project construction and operation, mainly the issues relevant to compensation and the social and environmental impacts of the railway project, which cannot be avoided.

The Laos-China Railway creates income not only for the company itself but also for local people and business operations. In terms of local people, income comes from several sources. First, during the construction of the railway, thousands of people were hired to work with the project; for example, on 26 February 2020, the Laos-China Railway Company advertised 700 jobs to the Lao people, which was divided into 3 phases. The first phase will offer 300 persons for drivers, controllers, motor mechanics and infrastructure mechanics, and the selected persons will be trained in China for 13–18 months. The remaining jobs will be announced in the second and third phases.[50] At the same time, during the beginning of the grand opening ceremony of the Laos-China Railway, along the road to the Vientiane Railway Station, many local people produced the T-shirt with the Lao language "Laos-China Railway" to sell for passengers and people who drive to see the station. This is because the railway station is a new landscape for people to go there and take a photo as the term in the used "check in". The price of a shirt is ranked from 30.000 LAK to 60.000 LAK or approximately 2–4 USD.

Another job creation is for restaurants along the way to the station, which means that the restaurants have more customers because waiting inside of the station is not allowed before one hour for departure. The best way for passengers to wait nearby the station by using a restaurant, one owner of the restaurant in Vientiane just 2 km from the station observed that almost all of the customers in her restaurant during the morning and evening time or before the departure time of the rail are passengers who will shortly go head to station. However, the station is not allowed to enter inside, and

[46] Laos-China Railway create more exportation opportunity to China, (2022).

[47] Manyphone Vongphachanh, (2022).

[48] First Thai rice shipment delivered using Laos-China railway, (2022).

[49] Somsack Pongkhao, (2022).

[50] Laos-China Railway Company 'open 600–700 jobs, (2020).

there is no rest room service there, so passengers wait in the restaurant, which serves their food, drinks, free rest room, free parking lot and easily reaches the station in a suitable time.

One of the most interesting jobs related to Laos-China Railway operation is snack preparation. This job requires the professional and skill of Lao cookies, bakery and snack making. This is because the snack that sells inside the cargo of trains is made in the Lao style. One of the middle-aged females who was served for snack preparation explained that she had come to work in this job since the beginning of railway operation or after the snack preparation company advertised the job or at the end of 2021. She further explained that she normally comes to work daily with other staff, but most of the staff are female and working hours starting from 10 am-6 pm. The wage is based on the quantity that each staff member has prepared, or the company will pay on each bag of snack. Therefore, if one is more skillful and professional, she can earn more than others because each bag is paid 1000 LAK. However, in her case, she can earn approximately 150.000 LAK or 10 USD per day, so a month, such income is more than her husband, who serves as government staff. Her friend got less than her, but each staff member got not less than 100.000 LAK per day, and this income is not bad compared with other jobs in Vientiane.

After the operation of the railway, in each station, mainly Vientiane, Vang Vieng and Luangprabang, van drivers have more work to do. For example, in Luangprabang, approximately 50 vans will wait for passengers every day. These van drivers turned their own job from a minivan driver that operated between Luangprabang and Vientiane. However, after arriving on the railway, almost or more than half of the passengers turn to use the railway, which consumes less time and is safer than the minivan. This is because using a minivan takes approximately 8–10 h from Vientiane to Luangprabang, while a railway uses only 2 h. According to discussion with the van driver in Luangprabang, he explained that before the COVID-19 pandemic, he usually goes and back between Vientiane and Luangprabang with his minivan that can contain 10 passengers, and he can earn approximately 500.000 LAK[51] per trip after paid for everything. However, his trip is two times per week. During the COVID-19 pandemic and the lockdown situation, his car was parked in home. Moreover, at the end of 2021, railway operation and the number of passengers traveling from Luangprabang to Vientiane decreased dramatically, even though many drivers park the van in the bus stop but limited the number of passengers using the van for traveling. As a result, he and his friends decided to join the railway van association. This association allows all vans that already registered waiting passengers in stations every day by changing the first to last number of vans to serve and ensure income generation. The same driver also explained further that his income generation is approximately 600.000–900.000 LAK per week. However, he said that the income that can earn each week is enough compared with driving to Vientiane, because here he cans stay with home, no driving hard, and safety drive. Drivers in the Luangprabang railway station are from the inside province and can introduce the places to visits and remember the roads well. Some of them can speak English fluently, and

[51] 500.000 LAK equals approximately 39 USD.

the person who can speak English cans ear more money compared with one who cannot because they can take care of Western tourism of people who cannot speak or understand Lao.

Railways not only generate income for the above-mentioned people but also receive benefits from the local people inside of Luangprabang. For example, local vendors who sell local foods in the night market said that after the arrival of the railway and the government of Lao promoted the "Laos tour Laos Project" during the blocking of the country, many Lao tourists come to Luangprabang, and her foods are selling very well in terms of increasing quantity. One lady local vendor also pointed out that after Laos and Thailand opened the border for both citizens crossing the country, many thousands of Thai people came to Luangprabang for visiting and tourism by using the Laos-Chian Railway. Then, the selling of local food from Luangprabang, for example, *Lam, Khai Phaen, Nang Yum, Sai Oua or Luangprabang* Sausage, dramatically increased. This is because Thai people have the ability to pay more after the Lao currency drops the exchange rate from 2500 to 4500 LAK per Bath (Thai currency) in the beginning of the second quarter of the fiscal year 2022.[52] Most importantly, the railway can save time traveling from Vientiane to Luangprabang. One Thai visitor said that the reason to travel to Luangprabang is because of loving the lifestyle of people here, loving foods, traditional performance of livelihood, being the Luangprabang or special identity of Luangprabang people and would like to try the high-speed train that is not yet available in Thailand. His group of tours comprises six members, and most of them are people from Khon Khaen Province in the northeast part of Thailand.

Tourism guides are another income generation from the Laos-China Railway. This means that after the operation of the railway, the tourism guide is more work to do. This is because more tourists visit Laos, while some of them need a guide for the introduction of places that they would like to visit and make sure of receiving full and correct information. One of the tourism guides in Luangprabang said that he normally works in a famous traveling company; however, after coming to the COVID-19 pandemic, such a company allows a self-sufficient guide, and then he retires from the company and works as a free land guide. However, the previous company or groups of tours as well as the person who has long-term connections with him connecting him as the guide for the introduction of places in Luangprabang and now he already registered the independence guide association. He also mentioned that after railway operation and border opening, his work is dramatically increasing because people from Thailand, Vietnam, and other countries can come to visit Laos. The main reason is that they would like to try rail that links Vientiane to Boten (Laos-China border) because the user of the railway is talking mouth to mouth about the comfort of this travel compared with bus or van, which consumes more time.

In summary, the Laos-China railway project has generated income for local people, namely, local employees of Lao cookies to serve in trains, van drivers in each station, local vendors, restaurants, and tourism guides. However, cion always

[52] See details in Exchange Rate, BANQUE POUR LE COMMERCE EXTERIEUR LAO PUBLIC, https://www.bcel.com.la/bcel/exchange-rate.html?lang=en.

has two sides. On the one hand, the arrival of railways contributes a large amount of income to Laos and local people. On the other hand, the Laos-China railway creates social and environmental impacts that are not avoidable.

6.5 Social and Environmental Concerns from the Laos-China Railway

Social and environmental impacts from the Laos-China railway are another side of the coin compared with economic and income generations. These impacts include the impact on local houses that need relocation to new places, farmlands and other construction, the noise of trains during the early morning and traveling under the tunnel of railways during the rainy season. In terms of the impact on people, there are four villages in three provinces along the railway that require resettlement from their original hometown to new resettlement areas prepared by the compensation and resettlement committee. Those who affected to house and other construction have the rights to receive compensation as provided in the Law on Resettlement and Vocation 2018 and the Decree on Compensation and Resettlement Management in Development Projects No. 84, dated 5 April 2016. However, compensation for the Laos-China railway project is one of the most controversial among the local people, mainly the project's affected people along the railway from Vientiane to Luangnamtha.[53] However, to manage the resettlement and compensation for the development project, Lao PDR has laws and a prime minister decree to address these issues. However, law in paper and law in practice are contested itself. In regard to compensation, the law on the railway provides that whenever the State would like to use the land of individual, legal entity, and organization with the official document to use and customary land use rights for railway activities, the State should compensate the landowner as provided in the law. However, for the land without official documents to use, the state will not compensate for the land, but the buildings, trees and crops will be compensated based on replacement prices.[54]

In the case of resettlement affected people from the railway, there are four villages, one village in Luangnamtha province, namely, Natouay in Luangnamtha district, two villages in Oudomxay province, namely, Namortay of Namor district, Nakok village of Nga district and Bouamor village in Xiengngeun district of Luanprabang province. These four villages have 349 households, which have a total affected population of 1.875 people and require a budget for resettlement of approximately 31 million USD.[55]

The resettlement of the people affected by the railway project in Natouay village of Luangnamtha district, which has total land of 19,6 hectares, and 159 households,

---

[53] Explanation to the Petition of People via hot line 156 of the National Assembly of Lao PDR and hot line 1518 of public works and transportation ministry, (2019).

[54] Law on Railway, article 40, (2019).

[55] LL see, (2022).

while the house divides into three categories, namely, large size has 76 houses, medium size has 45 houses and small size has 38 houses. In Namortay village, there are 60 houses, with a large size of 10 houses, a medium size of 3 houses and a small size of 47 houses. These houses are located on 12.4 hectares of land. The term large size is two story house, medium size is 8×11 m, and small size is 4×8 m. In Nakok village of Nga district, there are 23 houses, while the large size has 5 houses, the medium size has 3 houses and the small size has 15 houses, which are located in 8,7 hectares of total land. There are 107 houses in Bouamor village of Luangprabang province, which has a large size of 13 houses, a medium size of 68 houses and a small size of 26 houses, which are located in 23,76 hectares.[56]

According to the local people's opinion regarding moving to the resettlement village of the Laos-China Railway project, people are happy with the new houses. People from Bouamor village in Xiengngeun district of Luanprabang province said to the public media that people in the village 438 people living in 107 houses are happy to stay in the resettlement village, because the new village far from the original one only 1 km. This means that people can access their original resources, namely, paddy fields, other agricultural land, and natural resources. People can also use basic infrastructure, namely, roads, schools, public health, and piped water. However, there are some concerns that people would like to propose to the Laos-China Railway Company. First, the quality of construction of land slide prevention in some areas is not good because the village is new open-up land that easily slides, and second, landslides can cause damage to some houses in the villages.[57] While village chief of Natouay village in Luangnamtha province said that people are satisfied with the resettlement houses that the Laos-China Railway company offers, this is because new modern houses were built and handover to people as well as people can access public service that is good for them. Meanwhile, the use of lands and natural resources is still in the same places as the original home because such resources are not impacted by the railway. However, the village chief requires the people to protect their houses and infrastructure for sustainable use.[58]

6.6 Conclusion

The Laos-China Railway is one project that links Lao PDR as a landlock country to the world and generates income to the Lao government and Lao people. Trading statistics between Lao PDR and China are increased, goods export and import to Laos are less time consuming compared with trucks, and transportation of both passengers and goods through the railway is also increased. To address the management of railways, the GoL has promulgated the Law on Railways, which contains fifty parts

[56] Ibid.

[57] People satisfy with the new relocation that the Laos-China Railway Company Offering to (2022), https://abclaonews.com/c-163/.

[58] Lao Edaily, (2022), https://laoedaily.com.la/2022/05/30/114670/.

and 167 articles. At the same time, GoL also established an institution to manage railway activities, namely, the Department of Railway under the Ministry of Public Works and Transport and its line agencies at the provincial and district levels and train polices under the Ministry of Public Security and Bureau of Public Security at the provincial and district levels. However, this railway creates some negative impacts on local people. These impacts reflect the unevenness of development, mainly for the local people, whose voices are very soft; however, local people can protect rights and benefits via petitions to the National Assembly of Lao PDR. For example, during the construction of the railway, impacted people have submitted their concerns and impacts to the National Assembly, namely, compensation for losing assets and lands.[59]

The GoL and Laos-China Railway Company would like to solve the main concerns of passengers, mainly outside station facilitation, such as restaurants, toilets and convenient stores, entrance fee collection, safeguarding along the railway, and easy access to tickets.[60] This is because learning by doing on the side of Laos takes more time to gain experience in dealing with and solving issues regarding railway operation. However, speedy responses to the issues that occur from the railway may make all sides happy and bring benefits to all as well. Regarding the service of the Laos-China Railway company, the monthly meeting of the government of Lao in August, the meeting has discussed and agreed as the results of the government meeting that the service of the Laos-China Railway company should be improved mainly ticket selling, facilities inside and outside of the stations.[61] The result of the meeting is the main agreement, which has full power to negotiate companies and will deal with the hope of the passenger in terms of access to ease services, which is more comfortable and convenient for the Laos-China Railway Company.

References

Agreement on Establishment and Activities of the Laos-China Railway Project Management Committee, No. 13481/PWT, article 2, Ministry of Public Works and Transport, July 1, 2020.

Agreement on Establishment and Activity of Department of Railways, No 29259/MPWT, article 3, Ministry of Public Works and Transport, December 8, 2017.

Agreement on Establishment and Activity of the Department of Train Police, No 1701/PS, article 2, Ministry of Public Security, September 22, 2021.

Agreement on Establishment and Activity of the Department of Train Police, No 1701/PS, article 3, Ministry of Public Security, September 22, 2021.

Agreement on Establishment and Activity of the Provincial Division of Train Police and District Unit of Train Police. No 1702/PS, article 2, Ministry of Public Security, September 22, 2021.

[59] Explanation to the Petition of People via hot line 156 of the National Assembly of Lao PDR and hot line 1518 of public works and transportation ministry, (2019).

[60] Laophatthana Newspaper, Laos-China Railway Company Prepare to solve the easy access to ticket, (2022).

[61] Results of the August's government meeting, (2022).

All approved investment project by country in the year 2019, Department of Investment Promotion of Loas, July 7, 2022, https://investlaos.gov.la/wp-content/uploads/formidable/16/rpt_Invest_Summary_Country1A_2019.pdf.

Article 136–145 of the Law on Criminal Procedure, 2017.

ASEAN is abbreviation of the Association of Southeast Asian Nations; more detail please refer to https://asean.org.

Compilation on Hydropower Project in Lao PDR, Vientiane: Department of Energy Policy and Plan, 2015, pp.1–7.

Deputy Minister, head of Laos-China Railway Project Manager "declares about the progressive of the project", 13 December 2018, https://mpwt.gov.la/en/news_page/16.

Exchange Rate, BANQUE POUR LE COMMERCE EXTERIEUR LAO PUBLIC, https://www.bcel.com.la/bcel/exchange-rate.html?lang=en.

Explanation to the Petition of People via hot line 156 of the National Assembly of Lao PDR and hot line 1518 of public works and transportation ministry, No 21918/CO, Cabinet Office of Ministry of Public Works and Transportation, September 4, 2019, p.1.

First Thai rice shipment delivered using Laos-China railway, Bangkok Post, January 20, 2022, https://www.bangkokpost.com/business/2250639/first-thai-rice-shipment-delivered-using-laos-China-railway.

Governmental "Decree on Railway Officer, No 474/PM, article 2, Prime Minister Office, July 16, 2021.

Jasmina Yap, "Everything You Need to Know about the Laos-China Railway", 20 February 2017, https://laotiantimes.com/2017/02/20/everything-you-need-to-know-laos-china-railway/.

Lao Edaily, "Natouay village chief satisfies with the new relocation that the Laos-China Railway Company Offering to", *Laoe Daily*, May 30, 2022, https://laoedaily.com.la/2022/05/30/114670/.

Lao Government and the Laos-China Railway Company Limited, Concession Agreement, 25 December 2016, 21.

Laos-China jointly review economic-commercial and technical work, *Pasaxon Newspaper*, November 20, 2020, https://www.pasaxon.org.la/.

Laos-China Railway Company 'open 600–700 jobs, starting on 27 February 2020, MAUN.LA, February 20, 2020, https://muan.sanook.com/64608/.

Laos-China Railway create more exportation opportunity to China, *Lao National Radio*, September 2, 2022.

Law on Railway, article 1, 2, 3, 9, 10, 11, 40, 149. (2019).

LL see, "handover of four resettlement villages in three provinces which impacts by Laos-China Railway", *Loae Daily,* May 29, 2022, https://laoedaily.com.la/2022/05/29/114640/?fbclid=IwAR2PIHD-I-ZmSNSq-TGYUQdRiEpzE0mlkoGPvhyctoHjVulPcHHHceYBTmo.

Manyphone Vongphachanh, "Laos Exports Sticky Rice to China through Railway System", Laotian Times, June 7, 2022, https://laotiantimes.com/2022/06/07/laos-exports-sticky-rice-to-china-through-railway-system/. Publishing.

Ministry of Public Works and Transport, *report on the draft of the railway law*. (Vientiane Capital, MPWT, 2018), 1.

Not yet a month, goods via the Laos-China Railway reaching more than 100 million Yuan, *Lao Phattana News*, December 16, 2021, https://www.laophattananews.com/archives/120214.

Notice on focusing to solve issues regarding to railway, No 1745/PMO, article 1, Prime Minister Office, December 31, 2021.

People satisfy with the new relocation that the Laos-China Railway Company Offering to, *ABC Lao News*, May 27, 2022, https://abclaonews.com/c-163/.

Phayboune Thanabouasy, "China Remains the Largest Foreign Investor in Laos", *Laotian Times*, August 17, 2021, https://laotiantimes.com/2021/08/17/china-remains-the-largest-foreign-investor-in-laos-2/.

Report of the Six National Socio-Economic Development Plan, Ministry of Investment and Planning, Vientiane Capital: State Printing House, 2011, p. 35.

Report on the draft of the railway law, Vientiane: Ministry of Public Works and Transport, 2018, p.2.

Results of the August's government meeting, Department of Public Relation, Prime's Minister Office, August 25, 2022, http://www.laogov.gov.la/activities/pages/press.aspx?ItemID=162.

See more detail in implementation framework of the ASEAN framework agreement on multimodal transport, https://asean.org/wp-content/uploads/2019/11/Implementation-Framework-AFAMT_FINAL.pdf.

Somsack Pongkhao, "Two heads of state launch historic Laos-China railway", 3 December 2021, https://www.vientianetimes.org.la/freeContent/FreeConten_Two_237_21.php.

Somsack Pongkhao, "More countries using Laos-China Railway for freight transport", *Vientiane Times*, February 1, 2022, https://www.vientianetimes.org.la/freeContent/FreeConten_More_21.php.

Thanouthong, "The Lao-China Railway Company adds EMU trains to accommodate passengers", *Lao News Agency*, September 20, 2023, https://kpl.gov.la/detail.aspx?id=76778.

The Second National Socio-Economic Development Plan, Council of Ministers, Vientiane Capital: State Printing House, 1986, p. 13.

The Seven National Socio-Economic Development Plan, Ministry of Investment and Planning, Vientiane Capital: State Printing House, 2016, p. 107.

The Seven National Socio-Economic Development Plan, Ministry of Investment and Planning, Vientiane Capital: State Printing House, 2011, p. 121.

Tom Wilms, "right on track or off the rails? The Impact of the Laos-China Railway on Lao PDR", Policy Brief, No.14, European Institute for Asian Studies, December 9, 2021, p.2, https://eias.org/policy-briefs/right-on-track-or-off-the-rails-the-impact-of-the-laos-china-railway-on-lao-pdr/.

Yunnan Construction and Investment Holding Group., Co., LTD, Feasibility study of the Vientiane-Boten Expressway Phase 1 Vientiane-Vang Vieng. Yunan, YCIHG, 2017, 31.

Chapter 7
"Debt Trap" in the Philippines?

Alvin Camba, Hunter Willis, Jacob Sorber, and Rongchen Jiang

Abstract This chapter examines to what extent the "debt trap" argument applies to the Philippines. The "debt trap," which is narrowly defined as China's acquisition of geostrategic assets using its loans and investments, has been widely discussed. However, works have yet to examine the degree to which the "debt trap" has empirical support across different contexts. Examining Belt and Road Initiative (BRI) projects during Duterte and Marcos, we argue that the "debt trap" has no empirical backing. Instead, the "debt trap" argument has become a misnomer, a distraction to the broader issues brought about by Chinese development finance and foreign investments in the Philippines. We illustrate this argument through an analysis of international and Filipino writers about China in the Philippines, an examination of the Philippines' macroeconomic data, and a discussion of the BRI projects during the Duterte and Marcos administrations. We conclude this chapter by proposing three recommendations to China and the Philippines to increase the effectiveness of implementing BRI projects.

Keywords Philippines · China · BRI · Duterte · Marcos

A. Camba (✉) · H. Willis · J. Sorber · R. Jiang
Josef Korbel School of International Studies, University of Denver, Denver, CO, USA
e-mail: alvin.camba@du.edu

H. Willis
e-mail: Hunter.Willis@du.edu

J. Sorber
e-mail: Jacob.Sorber@du.edu

R. Jiang
e-mail: Rongchen.Jiang@du.edu

N. Peng and M. Y. Cheng (eds.), *The Reality and Myth of BRI's Debt Trap*, Indo-Pacific Focus, https://doi.org/10.1007/978-981-97-1056-0_7

7.1 Introduction

To what extent does the "debt trap" argument apply to former Philippine President Rodrigo Duterte's (2016–2022) administration? The "debt trap" argument presupposes that China engages in predatory lending by implementing the BRI to acquire strategically important assets. A good number of Western analysts and media organizations have propagated China's "debt trap" diplomacy in the Duterte administration. Both international and foreign analysts hyped up the possibility of a "debt trap" in the Philippines, which unfortunately diverted the attention from more important political and economic effects that the Chinese projects have created.[1] In other words, we suggest that effective opposition against the negative externalities of Chinese projects can only be done when the analysis is rooted in empirically verifiable data.

Our chapter argues that the "debt trap" narrative had no empirical backing. The "debt trap" argument has become a misnomer, a distraction to the broader issues brought about by Chinese development finance and foreign investments in the Philippines. We illustrate this argument in three levels. First, we illustrate that international and Filipino analysts, driven by anxiety around Chinese lending and career-related goals, pushed the narrative across international and local news outlets. Their articles made their way to notable opposition politicians who used the "debt trap" argument to drum up opposition against the Duterte regime. While Chinese projects create numerous political, environmental, and human rights issues, none of these can be accurately described as a "debt trap." Second, we use Philippine government data to show that most Philippine commercial debt was borrowed from domestic or Western lenders. Commercial debt consists of short-term bonds that the Philippine government sells to quickly acquire funds to pay for projects. In this type of finance, Chinese lenders are 5th on the list. In regard to development finance, China is the third largest behind the Japanese and multinational development banks. Finally, we provide a cursory description of Chinese projects in the Philippines. These projects comprise only 5 out of 148 projects during the Duterte administration, illustrating that any "debt trap" to China is highly unlikely. However, these projects also generate numerous problems for the Philippines, which have been ignored by other analysts.

The Philippines is a crucial case for understanding the limits of the "debt trap" narrative on three levels. First, a good number of foreign and domestic analysts have written about the "debt trap" narrative in the country. These writings have reached the ears of key opposition politicians who sounded the alarm on Chinese projects. While scholars have effectively debunked and rebutted the narrative, the narrative persists in some policy and civil society circles. This chapter attempts to, once and for all, nail the coffin on the "debt trap" narrative in the Philippines. Second, the Philippines is a crucial partner of the US and the Western world against China's aggressive activities. A former colony turned a postcolonial ally of the US, and most Philippine presidents and the majority of Philippine institutions look to the US for military protection and economic partnerships. Understanding what the Chinese do and continue to do in the Philippines more accurately helps policy makers in the US

[1] See Punongbayan (2019), Karlan et al. (2019).

shape their responses to the Philippines and China. Third, the Duterte administration provides a critical case to understand the "debt trap" narrative. The prior Benigno Aquino III administration acquired no official development finance from Chinese policy banks. As a result, the about-face of the Duterte administration provides the best conditions for the "debt trap" to be proven true. If the "debt trap" argument holds no water in the Duterte case, it is therefore logical to conclude that in other cases, the "debt trap" argument will likely be false.

The chapter is organized as follows. First, we look at the writings of Filipino and international analysts on the "debt trap" narratives. Second, we examine Philippine government data, illustrating that the Chinese are far from the largest lenders of short-term bonds and development-concessionary and commercial loans-finance. Third, we analyze Chinese projects in the Philippines, illustrating the numerous political, economic, and social issues that Chinese projects have created. The final part is the conclusion.

7.2 "Debt Trap" Narratives in the Philippines

When Duterte came into power in June 2016, he immediately put aside the Philippines' victory in the PCA to acquire favorable political and economic standing with China. Duterte's actions resulted in the greater willingness of Chinese policy banks to finance development projects in the Philippines alongside a higher degree of Chinese state support for Chinese firms to invest in the Philippines. Duterte visited China in 2016, culminating in a Memorandum of Understanding (MoU) that commits China to finance a package of loans and foreign investment projects worth 24 billion USD. Most of the projects were canceled, delayed, or modified due to internal politics in the Philippines, misunderstandings between Chinese and Filipino elites, and cumbersome bureaucratic processes in both countries.[2] Nonetheless, the Chinese government funded five development finance projects with a total value of 2.4 billion USD during Duterte's term.

At that time, both Western and Filipino analysts argued that the proposed projects in the Philippines will significantly increase the foreign debt portfolio in the Philippines, making the country dependent on China. This dependence will result in a "debt trap" that will result in the Philippines ceding geopolitical concessions and strategic assets to China. For instance, prominent Filipino pundit JC Punongbayan, in his weekly op-ed in *Rappler*, an independent online news website in the Philippines, argues that "Duterte himself fell for China's debt trap- hook, line, and sinker-and in the process put at risk the country's natural resources and strategic assets."[3] Punongbayan reasons that the "debt trap diplomacy", which is China's mode of financing and investing in the Global South, has been true in Sri Lanka and other countries.

[2] Camba (2018).

[3] Punongbayan (2018).

The friendship between the Duterte administration and China will likely sink the Philippines in a "debt trap". As he argues in another op-ed, he argues:

> In recent years, China, a strategy now known as "debt-trap diplomacy", has lent billions of dollars to many poor countries worldwide, ostensibly to help finance their infrastructure projects. However, many of these countries, once unable to pay, are forced to give up their natural resources and strategic assets as a form of collateral. This, in turn, promotes China's economic and political interests worldwide. We should heed the experiences of these other borrower countries. Given the actions-rather, inaction-of our current leadership, the Philippines could well be the next victim of this devious scheme.[4]

Apart from Punongbayan, other international analysts have put forth the "debt trap" argument. Writing in *The Forbes*, Anders Corr argues that "the Philippines will have to give political and economic concessions to China in order to repay annual interest, or renegotiate such a large quantity of debt. That could include political concessions, for example, giving up territory or oil rights in the South China Sea…or it could include economic concessions."[5] Corrs reasons are that China will impose high interest rates on Chinese loans, which will be, "at 10% interest the new debt could go to 452 billion USD, bringing Philippines' debt: GDP ratio to 197%, second-to-worst in the world." At the end, Corrs worries that the Philippines will end up like Venezuela, which, in his view, relies on high-interest loans to perpetuate the regime. Venezuela has acquired billions of unpayable Chinese loans in the last 15 years. As a result, the government has become even more repressive to the population, resulting in human rights violations, starvation, and the neglect of human life.

Both perspectives misunderstand the nature of Chinese development finance. In Punongbayan's argument, he cites Antonio Carpio, a former associate justice of the Supreme Court of the Philippines, in making his claim. Carpio points out that in the event of a nonpayment to Chinese loans, the Chinese policy banks will be able to appropriate "patrimonial" assets from the Philippines. However, this view betrays the notion that patrimonial assets have never been interpreted as sovereign territories or maritime boundaries in commercial relations. In commercial law and practice, patrimonial assets refer to the escrow payments made by the borrowing government to China, or at most, a share in the company. This follows a study by *Aid Data*-How China Lends, which analyzes 100 Chinese contracts in dozens of countries. The study finds that the acquisition of patrimonial assets by Chinese or Western institutions has never been used on territories or maritime boundaries.[6]

In Corrs' article, he finds that Chinese banks will impose at least a 10% interest rate, which can go all the way to 15%, on the Philippines. However, there is no basis for that estimate. The *Aid Data* databases place Chinese interest rates at 2–3%, which is higher by a couple of points than that of the World Bank or the Japanese policy banks. On one occasion when Chinese policy banks imposed a 6% interest rate, the Export–Import Bank of China (EIBC) lent to Sri Lanka's Mahinda Rajapaska right before the 2008 financial crisis. During that year, multinational development

---

[4] Ibid.

[5] Corr (2017).

[6] "How China Lends", Aid Data, https://www.aiddata.org/how-China-lends.

banks and commercial banks worldwide refused to lend anything to Global South countries except loans with variable interest rates. The uncertainty of the market and the turbulence created by the US housing market shaped the decision of these government and private institutions to constrain international lending. When the Rajapaskan government asked for a second loan to construct additional phases of the port, EIBC dialed the rates back to 2%. In other words, one wonders where Corrs' conjured the 10%.

Unfortunately, the writings of these analysts made their way to the offices of Philippine opposition leaders. For instance, former Vice President Leni Robredo said, "first of all, it's debt. Very enormous, (Philippine Pesos) 171 billion. That's very enormous… Our fear is we might get stuck in a debt trap like the one experienced by Sri Lanka.[7]" While other opposition party members did not express similar concerns, Robredo was the highest ranked member of the Liberal Party with an actual government position. As such, her views represent party beliefs on the issue. To be fair, not all Robredo's claims on and about Chinese financing were wrong. In a 2019 interview, she argued that "the first step is for the government to inform the public what the terms of agreement are. The Philippines incurs debts not just from China but from other foreign countries as well."[8] While this call for transparency is the correct move, the opposition's strategy was to capitalize on the debt trap rather than other issues that emanate from Chinese development finance.

The Marcos administration has yet to mention the Chinese debt trap in any way. This signals a greater understanding among the appointed and career officials on Marcos' own team. However, there are currently no new BRI projects proposed by Marcos, indicating that acquiring BRI projects is not a priority to the Marcoses. This has happened for several reasons. First, despite Marcos' visit to China, there have been no new Chinese development finance projects in the administration. All the large-scale BRI projects were either started or finished during the Duterte administration. Marcos canceled the three railway projects that Duterte started in the Philippines due to the lack of commitment on the Chinese side, the difficulties of land redistribution in the affected railway areas, and the lack of due diligence on the Philippines' end. There is ongoing construction of the Kaliwa Dam project, which has made little progress since the COVID-19 pandemic. There were several joint ventures between major Philippine and Chinese firms. Some Engineering Procurement and Construction (EPC) projects have also commenced, but these are not considered BRI projects. Second, BRI projects during the Duterte administration did not yield any meaningful positive contribution to the lives of most Filipinos, at least not yet. The two bridge projects, which were finished in Manila and Mandaluyong in theory, helped reduce the traffic situation in Metro Manila. However, traffic in Metro Manila is a larger structural problem that will need multiple other solutions. The Chico River Pump Irrigation project, which helped Cagayan elites transfer water away from the Kalinga population toward their own lands, theoretically resulted in a more competitive fruit export sector. However, Philippine agriculture has long suffered from insufficient

[7] Robredo Warns of China Debt Trap, Cites Sri Lanka|Inquirer News (2017).

[8] Robredo: Gov't Must Be Transparent on China Loans (2019).

infrastructure and the frequency of typhoons. Finally, Philippine involvement with the BRI has become unpopular due to South China Sea disputes and Chinese migrants in the Philippine online gambling sector. Filipinos are constantly bombarded by negative news about Philippine and Chinese disputes. In addition, the surge of Chinese workers in the online gambling sector has generated a largely negative response among those living in major Philippine cities. Marcos is wary of making decisions that might damage his family's political fortunes.

In sum, Filipino and international analysts misunderstand the nature of Chinese financing in the Global South. This lack of discernment on their part is compounded by the occurrence that the Duterte administration, which can be rightly described as pro-China along the way, only acquired five Chinese development finance projects throughout its term. Most of the Philippine projects were funded by Japanese policy banks or financed by Western multinational development banks.

7.3 Philippine Debt Profile

7.3.1 Bonds and Development Finance

The Philippine government's debt can be found mostly in bonds and long-term development finance. On the former, Japanese entities still hold Philippine bonds. Japan holds almost four times as much Philippine debt as the second highest bilateral creditor, the United States. By the end of FY 2021, Japan owned approximately 14.5 billion USD of Philippine bonds. The vast majority (over 92%) of this was held in medium- and long-term structures, with an approximately 60–40% split between public and private institutions, respectively. Three traditional Western lenders (United States, United Kingdom, Netherlands) are second, third, and fourth in total volume of Philippine bonds held by states. However, these three nations combined still only hold approximately two-thirds of the amount of Philippine debt as Japan. Over 80% of Philippine bonds to the U.S. are short-term loans. In contrast, the United Kingdom and Netherlands hold medium- and long-term loans. China is the sixth-largest state holder of Philippine bonds, controlling approximately 2.3 billion USD, less than one-sixth of the debt volume controlled by Japan. When comparing the structure of Chinese bond ownership to traditional Western lenders, Chinese debt is more concentrated in short-term, private loans. Approximately 40% of Philippine debt to China and Hong Kong is classified as private and short-term; only Taiwan has a comparable ratio. Debt owed to Western lenders such as Japan, the U.S., and South Korea is concentrated in long-term structures; over 90% of Philippine debt to these nations is classified as such.[9] This trend continues across the board, as over 85% of all Philippine debt is held in medium- and long-term loans.

[9] Total Philippine External Debt by Creditor Type (2022).

Regarding development finance, China has developed only 5 projects in the Philippines. Japan (45), the Asian Development Bank (ADB) (52) and the World Bank (29) still dominate this space, together accounting for 85.93% of ODA in the Philippines.[10] When including multilateral lending institutions, China's role becomes even more diminished. The ADB is the second leading creditor of the Philippines by volume (state or multilateral), holding approximately 13 billion USD. The International Bank for Reconstruction and Development (IBRD), the lending arm of the World Bank, is the Philippines' third largest creditor, holding $10.6 billion in Philippine debt. While the International Monetary Fund (IMF) has played a reduced role over the years, they are still a prominent lender and are owed 3.7 billion USD. Despite raising concerns among analysts as China's predatory alternative to the World Bank or ADB, the Asian Infrastructure Investment Bank (AIIB) has only minimally entered the scene, holding just over 1 billion USD in Philippine debt (good for 13th on the total list by volume).[11] It should be noted that Chinese loans differ from Western overseas development assistance (ODA), which is defined by the Organization for Economic Co-operation and Development (OECD) as foreign loans with concessional rates that often have extended grace periods. Three out of five Chinese projects can be considered commercial loans, while two can be put in the ODA category.

Overall, it appears that concerns about China's role in Philippine national debt have been overblown. China is still only ninth in volume of debt held on the overall list of creditors that includes both states and multilateral institutions, despite the Duterte administration's efforts to bring in Chinese funding through the Belt and Road Initiative (BRI) and integrate it with the domestic "Build Build Build" program. It is important to note that Hong Kong holds just over 2 billion USD in Philippine debt; the links to China remain unclear as their relationship with Hong Kong tightens. However, Japan still dwarfs any other nation in the sheer volume of debt held due to its geopolitical status as a strong Western lender in the region and its advanced, stable economy.

7.3.2 Debt-to-GDP Ratio

Much has been made of the supposed Chinese practice of 'debt-trap diplomacy', and some argue that the Philippines has gone down this path under the Duterte administration. A debt trap occurs when a country's debt obligations become too high and overwhelm the country's gross domestic product (GDP). A high debt-to-GDP ratio hampers economic growth, and much of the output produced is used to cover increasingly unsustainable debt payments. The spread of COVID-19 forced governments around the world to increase domestic spending to offset the economic impacts of lockdowns and to sustain and improve public health measures aimed at containing the pandemic. The Philippines saw a sharp decrease in activity in the tourism and

[10] Official Development Assistance Portfolio Review Report (2021).

[11] Total Philippine External Debt by Creditor Type (2022).

travel sectors due to international travel restrictions, and strict domestic lockdowns hampered the retail and services industries of the country. The national government provided direct financial assistance to citizens in need, enacted fiscal measures to help small businesses, and improved funding for workers in the healthcare sector to improve the nation's response against the pandemic.[12] This combination of economic retraction and increased government spending is reflected in the national debt figures. Figure 1 (refer footnote 13) highlights this shift; debt as a percentage of GDP saw a 15% increase from 39.6% in CY 2019 to 54.6% in CY 2020. In 2021, this figure reached a 16-year high of 60.4%.[13]

Under the Duterte administration, the volume of external debt has increased, yet the sharp increase in total government debt has largely been driven by an uptick in domestic borrowing. External debt grew by 65% from 2016–2021, while domestic debt more than doubled in the same time span. This growth in domestic debt was largely fuelled by the issuance of treasury bonds; the volume of bonds issued doubled from P3.6 trillion in 2016 to P7.3 trillion in 2021. During this same time period, the volume of treasury bills increased from P287.9 billion to P796.1 billion. These shifts marked a change from the domestic borrowing approach of the previous president Aquino III. During Aquino's administration (2010–2016), there was a focus on shifting the sources of domestic debt, as the volume of treasury bills decreased from P527.4 billion to P287.9 billion (19.4% of the total distribution down to 7.3%), while bond issuance increased from P2.8 trillion to P3.6 trillion (80.3% of the debt distribution to 92.7%). As expected, a large amount of the debt growth in both internal and external categories was driven by responses to the COVID-19 pandemic; domestic debt saw a 30.6% increase from FY 2019 to FY 2020, and external debt grew by 19.1%.[14] In the first four years of the Duterte government prior to the coronavirus pandemic, national debt continued to decline as a percent of GDP. This follows a decade-long pattern after the national debt reached its peak of 71.6% of GDP in FY 2004. The preceding Aquino administration aimed to reduce external debt exposure and was successful in lowering the total amount owed externally for three consecutive years (2011–2014). However, the Duterte administration broke this trend and has steadily increased the volume of external debt.[15] Prior to the pandemic, the increase in both domestic and external debt was in large part driven by Duterte's signature "Build Build Build" program, aimed at overhauling the country's infrastructure through over 70 different projects.[16]

[12] "Policy Responses to COVID-19", International Monetary Fund, https://www.imf.org/en/Topics/imf-and-covid19/Policy-Responses-to-COVID-19#P.

[13] "NG Debt Indicator 1986–2021", Philippines Bureau of the Treasury, https://www.treasury.gov.ph/wp-content/uploads/2022/09/DEBT-INDICATOR-ANNUAL-1986-2021.pdf.

[14] Ibid.

[15] Ibid.

[16] Heydarian (2018).

7.4 Chinese Projects in the Philippines Since Duterte

Chinese projects focused on building and improving much-needed domestic infrastructure but also rewarded political and economic elites to consolidate the power of the Duterte administration.[17] Many of the projects also created political, economic, and social problems in their own ways. The acquisition and implementation of Chinese capital is not top down; the winning and losing stakeholders are determined by the actions of the leader in power, as well as the influence of local elites. There is a clear focus on domestic infrastructure, and the costs range from tens of millions to billions. Projects can be broadly split into two categories: those focusing on resources or investments needed to accommodate the growing Philippine economy and those focusing on the transportation of citizens and goods. Both categories of development are expected to have generally positive impacts on Philippine GDP, although localized effects will be more variable, with some groups becoming marginalized and losing out.

The Kaliwa Dam and the Chico River Pump were considered flagship projects of Duterte's 'Build Build Build' program from its inception. While the Kaliwa Dam will provide much-needed water to the growing population in metro Manila, this benefit will come at the expense of indigenous communities and rural farmers in the area.[18] Similarly, the Chico River Pump Irrigation project will benefit the fruit export economy at the expense of indigenous peoples[19] while producing economic returns for those who benefit. Both projects were placed in the hands of Chinese construction companies, but local elites provided inputs and workers to the ventures. Both projects also stood to benefit two important elites to the Duterte administration: the military elites who will be able to justify troop relocation through the dam and the provincial elites of Northern Cagayan who will acquire cheap water to increase irrigation. Thousands of indigenous groups have been relocated because of both dams.[20]

Apart from dams, the Chinese also funded a telecommunication foreign investment. Dito Telecommunity, a joint venture between China Telecommunications, the largest state-owned telecommunications company, and Mislatel, a private Philippine firm by Duterte-crony Dennis Uy, was a flagship project of the Duterte administration. While the project appears to be a foreign direct investment, the Dito Telecommunity is actually a special purpose vehicle funded by EIBC. A special Dennis Uy neither has the capital nor the assets to fund the project. However, EIBC loaned out billions to Dito Telecommunity.[21] As such, this creates informal pressure on the Philippine government to bail out and ensure that Dito Telecommunity succeeds because of Uy's close connection to the Duterte administration. The money loaned to Dito came in

---

[17] Camba (2019a).

[18] Chavez (2019).

[19] Garcia (2021).

[20] Camba (2021).

[21] From Investor to Suppliers to Creditors, Cash-Strapped Dennis Uy Rolls the Dice with China: DITO Racks up P58B in Loans from Chinese Banks-Bilyonaryo Business News (2022).

the form of a special purpose vehicle, masking this deal from the total amount of Chinese development finance to the Philippines.

Both the Binondo Friendship Bridge and Estrella-Pantaleon Bridge projects are located in metro Manila and aim to ease traffic congestion in their respective areas. The Estrella-Pantaleon bridge underwent an expansion and upgrade, improving its earthquake resistance and increasing the volume of cars and pedestrians it could handle. While the bridges were constructed by Chinese firms, the initial construction processes were performed by local elites with links to the administrations.[22] In other words, bridge projects were also launched to reward local elites.

The PNR South Long-Haul rail is an extremely ambitious project aiming to eventually link Manila to the southeastern city of Matnog via high-speed rail and a freight line. Likewise, the Mindanao Railway project aims to link major cities on the island of Mindanao and improve transport for citizens.[23] On the same island, the potential Davao-Samal Island bridge aims to better connect Davao City with the island attraction of Samal.[24] The Subic-Clark railway is a strict freight line set to link Subic port and Clark city airport, upgrading logistics possibilities and the transport of goods between two strong economic zones.[25] While the three projects aim to increase mobility and efficiency in moving people, goods, and services, the three projects intended to reward local elites who will provide the inputs and labor to the Chinese projects. In addition, the successful construction of a railway stop in a specific province or municipality will greatly strengthen and embed the local elites in their respective areas, cementing their political power for generations to come. This political gain led to inter-elite fighting among local elites for railway stops on the PNR South Long-Haul railway. The three Chinese-funded railways, which were initially planned but canceled, fit the profile.[26]

All three projects were canceled by Marcos and are now being reconsidered to be funded by other financiers. The interest rates of the three projects were put at 2%,[27] and China was hesitant to finance all of them without proper Philippine government procedures on land reclamation and reform. As such, China's own hesitance to finance the project and interest rates that cohere to Chinese financing elsewhere illustrate the hollowness of the "debt trap" narrative.

The current projects under the Marcos administration are ongoing commitments from the previous government. The Chinese companies and their Filipino partners finished the construction process of the Chico River Pump Irrigation project, the Binondo Friendship Bridge, and the Estrella-Pantaleon Bridge during Duterte. The Chico River Pump Irrigation began operation in October 2022, making irrigation cheaper for landowners in Cagayan. A good number of these landowners are exporters of fruit and foodstuff. In the 20th China–ASEAN Expo held at Nanjing, Philippine

[22] Rey (2021).
[23] Clark (2020).
[24] Zuasola (2022).
[25] Venzon (2022).
[26] Camba (2019b).
[27] Vera (2022).

officials and fruit exporters across the country, including those in Cagayan, showcased the country's products to would-be purchasers from China.[28] The Cagayan fruit exporters wanted to increase their exports of banana and tomato chips to the Chinese market.[29] However, despite having access to cheaper water due to the Chico River Pump Irrigation Project, Cagayan fruit exporters have had a difficult time increasing their export capacity. Constant typhoons and disasters that ravage Cagayan and the whole of Luzon have often hindered increasing fruit production.[30] Furthermore, Cagayan alongside many other Philippine provinces suffer from a lack of competitive public infrastructure, making it more difficult to decrease the cost of production for fruit or any other exports.

In a broader context, President Bongbong Marcos has moved to increase Philippine fruit exports to China. President and General Secretary Xi Jinping agreed to purchase 2.08 billion USD worth of fruit imports to the Philippines.[31] These purchases will come in the form of credits to Chinese importers of Philippine fruits. While these officials found success from Chinese fruit importers, the Philippines has been unable to increase its capacity to export more durian to China. Current Philippine durian exports are worth 1.88 million USD annually. This amount is far smaller than Vietnam's 828 million and Thailand's 3 billion USD.[32] Like Cagayan, fruit exporters across the Philippines have had a difficult time increasing their exports to China.

There are several Engineering, Procurement, and Construction projects, such as the reclamation projects in Metro Manila and a proposed road construction project in Laog. The China Communications Construction Co. LDT (CCCC) has been involved in 3 ongoing EPC projects in the Philippines.[33] First, the China Harbor Engineering Company (CHEC), a subsidiary of the CCCC, has been contracted by the Pasay Harbor City Corporation to be part of the 655-acre Pasay Harbor City Reclamation Project. This project will feature commercial buildings, residential condominiums, tourism facilities, cruise ship docks, and theme parks, raising the profile of Pasay City for foreign investors, tourists, and retirees. Second, CHEC has been contracted to build artificial islands for SM Prime Holdings, a company owned by one of the wealthiest Filipino business groups in the country. Third, China First Highway Engineering Co. LTD, a CCCC subsidiary, is also involved in a 785-reclamation project. CCCC has spoken to the Marcos administration about constructing a 270-km highway linking Ilocos Norte's Laoag City to La Union Province's Rosario City.[34] Manila has yet to take substantial steps toward this deal. None of these are BRI projects. However, these commercial transactions are emblematic of increasing commercial relations between state and private firms between the two countries.

[28] Crismundo (2023).

[29] Garcia (2023).

[30] Magramo (2023).

[31] PBBM opens door for more PH fruit exports to China (2022).

[32] Ibid.

[33] Elemia (2022).

[34] Ibid.

7.5 Conclusion

Our chapter examined the degree to which the "debt trap" argument applied to former Philippine President Rodrigo Duterte's (2016–2022) administration. We found that the debt trap argument does not have any empirical backing at all. Rather, a good number of Western and Filipino analysts hyped up the narrative due to their own anxiety and enacted their career-related goals. In our analysis of the evidence, we found that analysts misinterpreted the statements made by Philippine officials and misunderstood how laws on overseas finance were interpreted. We additionally found that most Philippine bonds and development finance were owned by either Japanese or Western entities. In addition, the Philippine GDP-to-debt ratio, while slowly shrinking, remains healthy despite the crisis brought about by the pandemic. Finally, through an analysis of Chinese projects in the Philippines, we found that these projects were deployed to reward local elites and increase the political power of the Duterte administration. In sum, the Philippine case illustrates the absence of the debt trap in any way. Our structure of analyzing the writings of other scholars, data on bonds and development finance, and projects can be replicated in other countries.

We end this chapter with several policy recommendations that will help Philippine China relations and improve the implementation of BRI projects. First, there is a need to increase the transparency of Chinese projects to the Filipino public. To do so, China will need to dispense the confidentiality clauses that were found in most of its BRI projects. To some degree, it is understandable why the Chinese government will choose to place these clauses. However, confidentiality clauses arouse suspicion from the Philippine population, making it difficult for Filipinos to trust China and the BRI projects. Second, apart from increasing transparency, there is a need to expand the participation of civil society actors and outside observers in many of these projects. Construction contracts or development finance projects are often deals made and implemented by firms and governments. Civil society actors, who are outside the formal relationship between China and the Philippines, do not have a say in the process. This lack of say generates further mistrusts and opens opportunities for Filipino elites to take advantage of the projects for their own personal goals. If China wants to win over the Philippine public, there is a need to involve others in the process apart from just the government and the firms. For China to take this seriously, the Philippines should start demanding this not only from China but also from all the other foreign financiers and construction companies. Finally, the development impact of BRI projects should be made explicit. This could come in the form of increasing local employment, involving Filipino firms at different stages of production, and increasing the livelihood aspects of the major projects.

References

"From Investor to Suppliers to Creditors, Cash-Strapped Dennis Uy Rolls the Dice with China: DITO Racks up P58B in Loans from Chinese Banks-Bilyonaryo Business News", Bilyonaryo.com, May 30, 2022, https://bilyonaryo.com/2022/05/30/from-investor-to-suppliers-to-creditors-cash-strapped-dennis-uy-rolls-the-dice-with-China-dito-racks-up-p58b-in-loans-from-chinese-banks/business/.

"How China Lends", Aid Data, https://www.aiddata.org/how-China-lends.

"NG Debt Indicator 1986–2021", Philippines Bureau of the Treasury, https://www.treasury.gov.ph/wp-content/uploads/2022/09/DEBT-INDICATOR-ANNUAL-1986-2021.pdf.

"Official Development Assistance Portfolio Review Report", National Economic and Development Authority of The Philippines, 2021, https://neda.gov.ph/wp-content/uploads/2021/08/92321_2020_ODA.pdf.

"PBBM opens door for more PH fruit exports to China", *Philippine Information Agency,* January 5, 2022, https://pia.gov.ph/press-releases/2023/01/05/pbbm-opens-door-for-more-ph-fruit-exports-to-China.

"Policy Responses to COVID-19", International Monetary Fund, https://www.imf.org/en/Topics/imf-and-covid19/Policy-Responses-to-COVID-19#P.

"Robredo Warns of China Debt Trap, Cites Sri Lanka | Inquirer News", *Philippine Daily Inquirer*, October 22, 2017, https://newsinfo.inquirer.net/939735/leni-robredo-China-debt-trap-rodrigo-duterte.

"Robredo: Gov't Must Be Transparent on China Loans", *Panay News*, March 13, 2019, https://www.panaynews.net/robredo-govt-must-be-transparent-on-China-loans/.

"Total Philippine External Debt by Creditor Type", International Operations Department of The Philippines, June 30, 2022, https://www.bsp.gov.ph/statistics/external/Table%2005.2.pdf.

Camba, Alvin, "Claims about China's 'Missing' US$24 Billion Border on Yellow Journalism," East Asia Forum, August 21, 2018. https://www.eastasiaforum.org/2018/08/21/claims-about-chinas-missing-us24-billion-border-on-yellow-journalism/.

Camba, Alvin, "Examining Belt and Road 'Debt Trap' Controversies in the Philippines." *Jamestown*, January 18, 2019, https://jamestown.org/program/examining-belt-and-road-debt-trap-controversies-in-the-philippines/.

Camba, Alvin, "ANALYSIS: Inside Belt and Road 'Debt Trap' Projects in the Philippines", The News Lens International Edition, February 1, 2019, https://international.thenewslens.com/article/112937.

Camba, Alvin, "How Duterte Strong-Armed Chinese Dam-Builders However, Weakened Philippine Institutions", Carnegie Endowment for International Peace, June 15, 2021, https://carnegieendowment.org/2021/06/15/how-duterte-strong-armed-chinese-dam-builders-but-weakened-philippine-institutions-pub-84764.

Chavez, Leilani, "A Philippine Tribe That Defeated a Dam Prepares to Fight Its Reincarnation," Mongabay Environmental News, November 5, 2019, https://news.mongabay.com/2019/11/a-philippine-tribe-that-defeated-a-dam-prepares-to-fight-its-reincarnation/.

Clark, James, "Mindanao Railway Project-The Proposed 2000 km Railway on the Second-Largest Island in the Philippines", Future Southeast Asia, July 21, 2020, https://futuresoutheastasia.com/mindanao-railway/.

Corr, Anders, "New Philippine Debt of $167 Billion Could Balloon To $452 Billion: China Will Benefit." *Forbes*, May 13, 2017. https://www.forbes.com/sites/anderscorr/2017/05/13/new-philippine-debt-of-167-billion-could-balloon-to-452-billion-china-will-benefit/?sh=333f4db62fb6.

Crismundo, Kris, "Supply constraints limit PH fruit exports to China", *The Philippine News Agency,* September 20, 2023, https://www.pna.gov.ph/articles/1210200.

Elemia, Camille, "US issues environmental warning about Chinese firm's Manila Bay reclamation projects", *Radio Free Asia,* August 8, 2022, https://www.rfa.org/english/news/China/philippines-usa-08022023151117.html.

Garcia, Geela, "China-Funded Water Project Meets Stiff Opposition in the Philippines," *China Dialog*, March 4, 2021, https://chinadialogue.net/en/nature/China-funded-water-project-meets-stiff-opposition-in-the-philippines/.

Garcia, Jenica, "Cagayan MSME goods showcased in China", *Manila Times*, October 19, 2023, https://www.manilatimes.net/2023/09/19/regions/cagayan-msme-goods-showcased-in-China/1910662.

Heydarian, Richard, "Duterte's Ambitious 'Build, Build, Build' Project To Transform The Philippines Could Become His Legacy", *Forbes*, February 28, 2018, https://www.forbes.com/sites/outofasia/2018/02/28/dutertes-ambitious-build-build-build-project-to-transform-the-philippines-could-become-his-legacy/?sh=586ac08f1a7f.

Magramo, Kathleen, "Typhoon Doksuri kills at least five as Philippines battles floods and landslides", *CNN*, July 26, 2023, https://www.cnn.com/2023/07/25/asia/philippines-typhoon-doksuri-egay-landfall-intl-hnk/index.html.

Other official flows (OOF) (indicator), OECD, 2023, https://doi.org/10.1787/6afef3df-en.

Punongbayan, JC, "[OPINION] What Scares Me the Most about China's New, 'Friendly' Loans." *Rappler*, March 2, 2018. https://www.rappler.com/voices/thought-leaders/197207-china-loans-philippines-fears/.

JC Punongbayan, "[Analysis] How the Philippines fell for China's infamous debt trap", *Rappler*, March 27, 2019, https://www.rappler.com/voices/thought-leaders/226745-analysis-how-philippines-fell-china-debt-trap/.

Karlan, Dean, Sendhil Mullainathan, and Benjamin N. Roth. 2019, "Debt Traps? Market Vendors and Moneylender Debt in India and the Philippines", American Economic Review: Insights, Vol. 1, No. 1, pp. 27–42.

Rey, Aika, "China-Funded Estrella-Pantaleon Bridge Now Open", *Rappler*, July 30, 2021, https://www.rappler.com/business/estrella-pantaleon-bridge-now-open-July2021/.

Singh, A., The myth of 'debt-trap diplomacy' and realities of Chinese development finance. *Third World Quarterly*, Vol. 42, No. 2, 2021, pp. 239–253.

Venzon, Cliff, "China to Fund $940 m Philippine Railway Linking Former US Bases", *Nikkei Asia*, November 20, 2022, https://asia.nikkei.com/Politics/International-relations/China-to-fund-940m-Philippine-railway-linking-former-US-bases.

Vera, Ben O. de, "PH Gets P17.4B Chinese Loan for Bridge Days before Duterte Gone", *INQUIRER*, June 14, 2022, https://business.inquirer.net/350437/ph-gets-p17-4b-chinese-loan-for-bridge-days-before-duterte-gone.

Zuasola, Ferdinand, "Marcos Leads P23-B Davao-Samal Bridge Project Groundbreaking amid Protests", *Rappler*, October 27, 2022, https://www.rappler.com/nation/mindanao/marcos-jr-leads-davao-samal-bridge-project-groundbreaking-environmental-protests/.

Chapter 8
BRI in Malaysia: Debt Trap or Leapfrogging Opportunity?

Ming Yu Cheng and Kuk Fai Fok

Abstract This chapter analyzes Malaysia's participation in the Belt and Road Initiative (BRI), focusing on the types of BRI projects, financing mechanisms, and economic implications for Malaysia. The BRI, initiated in 2013, has significantly broadened the horizons of trade and investment between China and Malaysia. Nevertheless, there are various concerns, criticisms, and reservations about BRI projects among participating countries, largely stemming from the controversial nature of BRI-linked projects. These controversies primarily stem from a lack of transparency in project implementation, the scale and risks associated with mega projects, funding mechanisms, and uncertain impacts on host countries. Issues such as project viability, debt sustainability, control over strategic assets, socioeconomic and environmental impacts, and operational effectiveness are central to the discourse on BRI investments. The impact of the BRI on Malaysia's debt sustainability is contingent on the commitment and approaches of both the lender and recipient. Malaysia's manageable external debts, predominantly denominated in its currency, coupled with strong export earnings and economic growth prospects, create a positive outlook. In addition, Malaysia's exposure to Chinese debt is manageable and comparatively low. However, to ensure the long-term sustainability of BRI projects, close collaboration between the governments of Malaysia and China is essential to enhance transparency in loan negotiations, mitigate potential risks, and channel financial resources toward viable projects to ensure sustainable BRI development in Malaysia.

Keywords BRI · Financing · Debts · Risks · Sustainability

M. Y. Cheng (✉) · K. F. Fok
Faculty of Accountancy and Management, Universiti Tunku Abdul Rahman, Kampar, Malaysia
e-mail: chengmy@utar.edu.my

K. F. Fok
e-mail: fokkf@utar.edu.my

N. Peng and M. Y. Cheng (eds.), *The Reality and Myth of BRI's Debt Trap*, Indo-Pacific Focus, https://doi.org/10.1007/978-981-97-1056-0_8

8.1 Introduction

The Belt and Road Initiative (BRI), which aims to connect China with the rest of the world, has been under the spotlight since its launch in 2013. Generally, described as large-scale interconnectivity projects to improve economic cooperation and stimulate economic growth, BRI-linked projects initiated by China have attracted much attention. Although China has envisaged developing BRI as an initiative that would benefit all participating countries, particularly developing countries, by accelerating their development progress, BRI projects are frequently portrayed as having the characteristics of "debt-trap diplomacy" or "Chinese-colonialism".[1]

Analyzing the data provided by the American Enterprise Institute (AEI) and the Heritage Foundation Database, a database that tracks China's global investment and construction since 2005, revealed that projects related to the BRI have contributed substantially to China's overseas investments and constructions since the BRI was introduced in 2013. As shown in Fig. 8.1, both non-BRI and BRI investments grew significantly from 2013 to 2017, where approximately half of the investments from China after 2013 were classified as BRI investments and constructions. These investments are largely concentrated in sectors that require massive financing, such as telecommunications and transport, as well as real estate and the energy sector.[2] The BRI engagement increased from 32,450 million USD in 2013 to its peak amount of 121,420 million USD in 2018. As the construction of infrastructure projects is at the heart of the BRI, approximately 60% of BRI engagements were allocated to construction, and 40% were allocated to investment projects in various sectors. China's overseas expansion has slowed since 2018. Tighter control of capital outflows by the Chinese government to curb speculative investments, as well as more stringent regulatory requirements imposed by host countries' cumulative trade tensions between China and the United States (US), have contributed to the steady drop in Chinese outbound foreign direct investment (FDI) and financing for BRI projects in recent years. The outbreak of the COVID-19 pandemic in 2020 disrupted global economic development and pushed a pause button to global activities due to the lockdown measures implemented by almost all governments around the world. Although China recorded relatively good performance in 2020 compared to other large economies, the pace of foreign investments worldwide slowed significantly in 2020. When the world recovers slowly from the fragile economy, outward investment from China rebounded slightly in 2021.

Many of the BRI-linked infrastructure projects involved China's large companies or state-owned enterprises supported through loans provided by Chinese financial institutions or contracts backed by the loan repayment guarantees of the host country's government institutions.[3] Due to the divisive nature of BRI-linked projects, there were reservations among participating countries concerning the risks associated with the BRI. The BRI projects were framed within a "winner versus loser" context rather

[1] Tritto (2019).

[2] McKenzie (2022).

[3] Nedopil (2022).

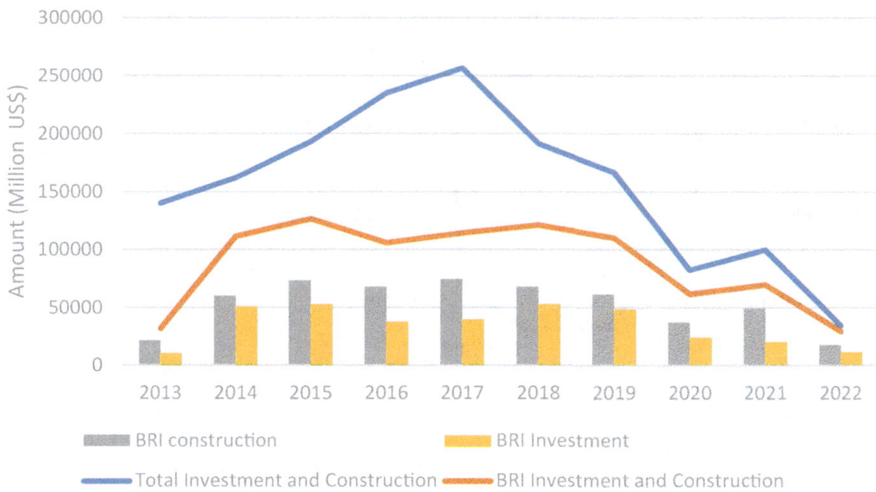

Fig. 8.1 China's global investment and BRI engagements (2013–2022). *Source* American Enterprise Institute (2022) *The China Global Investment Tracker* (updated on December 25, 2022)

than the "win–win" and "shared development" frameworks promoted by China. In general, the controversies or "discomfort" with the BRI stem mainly from the lack of clarity of the BRI and transparency in the implementation of BRI projects. In addition, the complications associated with the BRI are also due to the scale of the BRI projects and risks involved in these mega projects, in addition to the controversial funding mechanisms and the uncertain impacts of BRI projects on the host countries, resulting in misperception and mismatch of expectations from multiple stakeholders. Generally, project viability, debt sustainability, ownership and control over strategic assets, socioeconomic as well as environmental impacts and operational effectiveness of BRI projects are the issues at the center of discussion related to BRI projects.[4]

In this chapter, we will first look at the types of BRI projects in Malaysia and the financing mechanisms of BRI projects, in particular, BRI debts and related issues, such as the differentiation between loan management and "debt-trap diplomacy". It is followed by a discussion to examine the economic potential and implications of BRI development in Malaysia.

[4] Khor (2018).

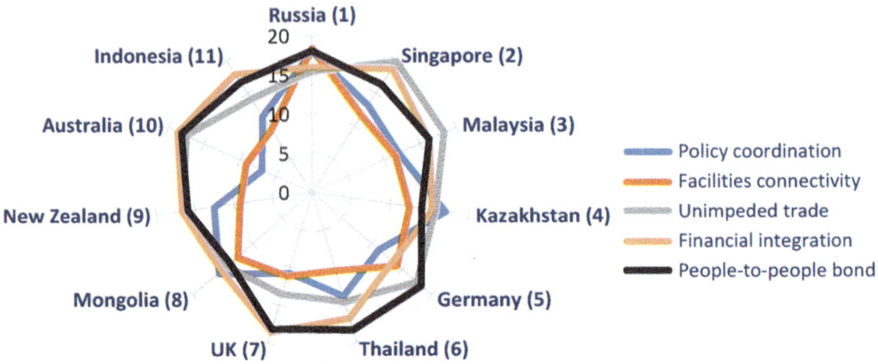

Fig. 8.2 Five connectivity indexes of nations along BRI in 2018 (Smooth Cooperation Nations). *Source* The Belt and Road Initiative: Annual Report on Five Connectivity Indexes (2018). * The number in the bracket shows the ranking position of the country

8.2 The Development of BRI in Malaysia

Malaysia is one of the countries that participated actively in BRI development and ranked highly in the Five Connectivity Indexes.[5] The Indexes assess the level of cooperation and overall development of BRI in 94 countries and rank these countries into one of the eight categories, namely, (1) nations of generally smooth cooperation; (2) nations with great potential; (3) nations with enormous strength in a single area; (4) nations of equal potential in all areas; (5) nations of financial weakness; (6) nation of facilities weakness; (7) nation of policy weakness; and (8) nations to be strengthened in cooperation. Malaysia was ranked in the 3rd position after Russia and Singapore in the category of "Smooth Cooperation Nations", together with the other ten countries, as shown in Fig. 8.2. The Indexes cover five core elements of connectivity between China and BRI participating countries, namely, policy coordination, facilities connectivity, unimpeded trade, financial integration, and people-to-people bond. These five dimensions of connectivity are also the five priority areas of the cooperative framework of the BRI. According to this measurement, Malaysia ranked relatively high in trade and financial integration as well as people-to-people bonds, if compared with facilities (transport, communications, and energy facilities) connectivity and policy coordination.

As an open economy, Malaysia welcomes foreign investments and trade with other countries. The rapid development of the economy since the 1960s has largely relied on its strategy to integrate the economy with global markets through trade and investment. Malaysia is one of the most open economies in the world. For the period between 1970 and 2022, Malaysia's average share of total trade (exports + imports)

[5] [Press Release] (2018).

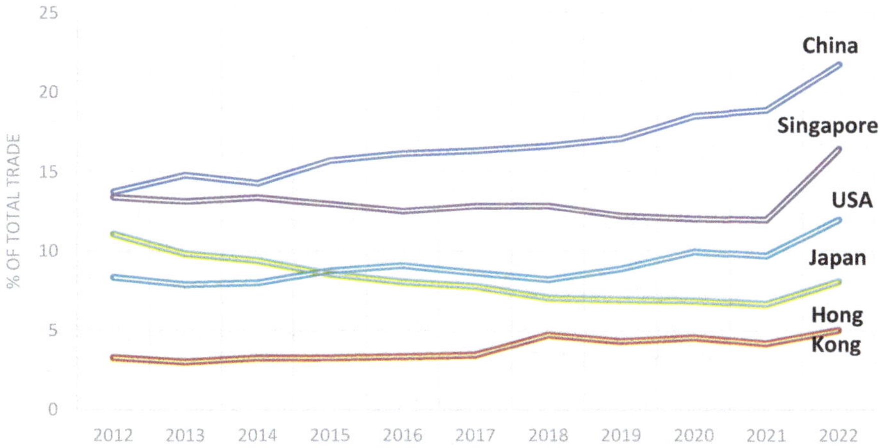

Fig. 8.3 Malaysia's top trading partner (2012–2022). *Source* Department of Statistics, Malaysia (DOSM)

to gross domestic product (GDP) was 142%, a ratio that is well above other ASEAN member states, except for Singapore, with a trade-to-GDP ratio of 340%.[6]

Malaysia and China have developed a strong bilateral trade relationship since 2009. China has been Malaysia's main trading partner since 2008, while Malaysia has been China's main trading partner among the Association of Southeast Asian Nations (ASEAN) member states since 2009.[7] Through BRI connectivity, the potential for trade between China and Malaysia expanded, and the share of total trade with China increased progressively from 13.8% in 2012 to 21.8% in 2022 (Fig. 8.3).

In terms of investment, although China's international development finance has intensified in recent years, especially after 2013 for BRI-linked projects, the amount of China's investment in Malaysia is rather small compared with the investments originating from the United States, the European Union (EU), Japan, and other ASEAN member states. Nonetheless, China has steadily emerged as one of the major sources of FDI after 2015, as shown in Fig. 8.4. In particular, China has consistently held the position as one of Malaysia's primary foreign investors in the manufacturing sector since 2016. China maintained its leading status in foreign direct investment (FDI) for Malaysia's manufacturing sector even throughout the challenges posed by the COVID-19 pandemic.[8]

China's BRI activities are typically associated with mega projects for building infrastructure facilities. Hence, there is a general perception that China's engagement in Malaysia primarily centers around large-scale construction and infrastructure endeavors. However, beyond these infrastructure projects, Chinese state-owned enterprises (SOEs) and private companies have also made investments in diverse

[6] World Development Indicators (2022).

[7] Cheng (2021).

[8] "China remains Malaysia's largest foreign partner for manufacturing sector (2021).

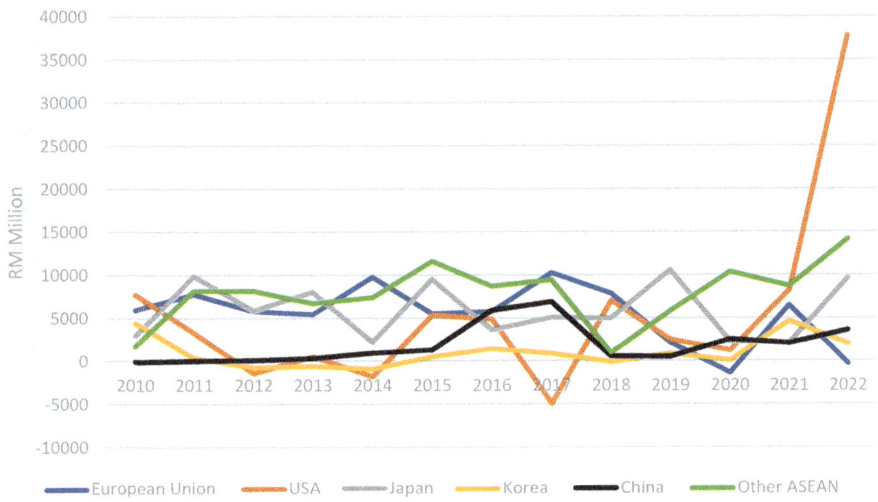

Fig. 8.4 Net FDI inflows in Malaysia (2010–2022). *Source* Department of Statistics, Malaysia (DOSM)

industrial sectors within Malaysia. These include manufacturing, logistics, automobile production and maintenance, energy, finance, education, and various other areas.[9]

The AEI Database classified China's global investments into two main categories, i.e., investment and construction. The categorization has the advantage of differentiating the construction projects undertaken by Chinese contracting companies from Chinese investments in other various sectors, including greenfield investments. Most studies tend to assess BRI projects in host countries without making a clear distinction between the two. This often leads to an oversight of China's potential impact on driving the economic upgrading and diversification of the host country. Specifically, enhancement through the advancement of production capacities and production networks; the development of industrial parks, integrated residential townships, ports and railway infrastructure; and the construction of power generation plants and manufacturing facilities.

Tables 8.1 and 8.2 show the types of BRI projects in various sectors in Malaysia. The BRI engagements in Malaysia for the period between 2013 and 2022 amounted to 30,060 million USD. Slightly more than half of the financing was classified as investments, with a cumulative amount of 15,530 million USD. Energy and real estate are the two main sectors that attracted most of the investments from China, occupying 40% and 26% of the total investment, respectively. On the other hand, 14,530 million USD were allocated to projects related to construction, whereby approximately half of the allocations in construction went to the transport sector where the two key contractors are China Communications Construction Company (CCCC) and China

[9] Gomez (2020).

Table 8.1 BRI projects by sector in Malaysia (Investment Category)

Year	Investment (Million US$)								
	Agriculture	Energy	Finance	Metals	Real Estate	Technology	Tourism	Transport	Others
2013					1370				
2014					380				200 (Textiles)
2015		5360			660	370		280	
2016		340		140	210		1680		
2017	280	140	120		280			110	
2018					840	440			
2019		140			340				880 (Timber)
2020		320							140 (Education)
2021									300 (Timber)
2022				210					
Grand Total	280	6300	120	350	4080	810	1680	390	1520

Table 8.2 BRI projects by sector in Malaysia (Construction Category)

Year	Construction (Million USD)						
	Chemical	Energy	Metals	Real Estate	Tourism	Transport	Utilities
2013						1190	
2014		1570					
2015	180			530		550	
2016	300		110	470	210	620	160
2017	100	620	1660		550	110	
2018				350		4480	140
2019		110	310	110			
2020							
2021							
2022			100				
Grand total	580	2300	2180	1460	760	6950	300

Source American Enterprise Institute (2022), *The China Global Investment Tracker* (updated on December 25, 2022)

Railway Construction Corporation Limited (CRCC). Major ongoing construction projects include the East Coast Rail Link (ECRL), Malaysia-China Kuantan Industrial Park (MCKIP), Kuantan Port Expansion, Penang Second Bridge, and Tun Razak Exchange (TRX).

8.3 The Financial Management of BRI Projects

Although the "debt-trap diplomacy" narrative has received considerable attention in the media, such a narrative has been challenged by others as a myth. Commentators and researchers such as Rana and Ji (2020),[10] Hutchinson and Tham (2020),[11] and Brautigam and Rithmire (2021)[12] argued that there is a lack of factual support for the "debt-trap diplomacy" narrative, while Jones and Hameiri (2020)[13] contended that the "debt-trap diplomacy" narrative is motivated by geostrategic considerations to reverse the declining Western influence in global affairs against rising China power. The counterarguments of the "debt-trap diplomacy" claim that BRI investments are fragmented and decentralized by nature, driven mainly by economic factors rather than the conspiracy theory of a top-down scheme to design a series of unsustainable debts to achieve China's geopolitical ambition or acquisition of strategy resources in recipient countries. The projects involved are primarily business-oriented and are

[10] See footnote no. 13.

[11] Hutchinson (2020).

[12] Brautigam (2021).

[13] Jones (2020).

motivated by profit-making decisions. In contrast to the "debt-trap narrative," China's noninterventionist approach in managing BRI projects offers developing countries an alternative and valuable financing resource.[14] Instead of placing all the blame on China for enticing countries into the "debt trap", recipient countries should also bear the responsibility to uphold governance and accountability to ensure that the projects fulfil their national interests and are financially sustainable as well as economically viable. In other words, whether the BRI is a "debt trap" or leapfrogging opportunity relies on the commitment and approaches taken by both the giver and recipient sides.

Like the World Bank (WB)'s bifurcated structure, China's overseas development finance program also consists of aid-financed grants and debt-financed loans, generally labeled "Official Development Assistance" (ODA) and "Other Official Flows" (OOF), following the definition given by the Organization for Economic Co-operation and Development (OECD).[15] In the case of the WB, ODA is the financial contribution from donor governments to promote the welfare and economic development of developing countries. ODA is concessional, and the fund will only be disbursed if certain eligibility requirements and criteria are fulfilled, whereas OOF is the loan arranged or mediated by the WB through international financial markets, which charges higher interest rates and imposes shorter maturity periods than ODA.[16]

Compared with the lending terms offered by multilateral financial institutions such as the WB, global financial markets and Paris Club's lenders, the average lending terms of China's aid-financed and debt-financed loans tend to be less favorable, and the rates offered are near or higher than market interest rates. Based on Aid Data, which documents and tracks the activities of global development finance, Malik et al. (2021) studied the structure, scope, types of lenders and evolution of China's overseas development finance program before and after 2013, spanning until 2017. They highlighted some observations about the characteristics of Chinese loans to low- and middle-income countries (LMICs), as stated below:

- From 2013 to 2017, within the first five years of the launch of the BRI, China's overseas lending underwent a profound expansion to an accumulated sum of USD 425 billion, which is more than double the amount provided by the USA during the same period.
- Only approximately 12% of China's overseas development finance program was ODA, whereas the ODA level for the USA was 73%, approximately 40% for Japan and almost 100% for the United Kingdom and Canada.
- Before the 2010s, China's overseas development finance program was primarily provided to the governments of recipient countries. However, in the era of BRI, there was a dramatic shift in the allocation, which skewed toward government-linked companies, private business entities and the partnership between Chinese and local companies.

---

[14] Singh (2021).

[15] Other official flows (OOF) (indicator), OECD, 2023, http://doi.org/10.1787/6afef3df-en.

[16] Ibid.

- China's financing of BRI megaprojects in energy, industry, mining, construction, and transport and storage has become increasingly dependent on co-financing. Such co-financing is usually in the form of large and syndicated loans backed by a few Chinese state-owned banks and, in some cases, also involves foreign banks and multilateral development finance institutions.
- One way for Chinese state-owned banks to manage default risks is to issue loans to special purpose vehicles (SPVs), which are set up for specific activities or projects. Such loans are issued with some types of repayment guarantees, such as collateralization, government guarantees and credit insurance. In the case of collateralization, the government borrowers will offer either part of the assets, future flows of revenues or export of resources as collateral to secure financing from Chinese state-owned banks.[17]

Generally, China's approach to financing BRI projects is primarily commercial-led, which is aligned with the high-risk, high-reward principle. Some distinguishing characteristics of China's financial commitments in BRI projects include the use of debt rather than aid, and loans rather than grants in BRI projects, the use of collateralization, a lack of transparency in the loan negotiation process and poor governance.[18]

The financing of BRI projects encounters potential risks and challenges of financial sustainability. On the one hand, borrower countries that rely heavily on the development finance provided by China are subjected to heavy debt burdens.[19] On the other hand, Chinese state-owned banks and development banks, such as the China Development Bank (CDB) and the Export–Import Bank of China (EIBC), are exposed to default risks that may entail, especially when the economic or political situations in the recipient countries become unstable. To manage and counteract the high risks involved, Chinese lenders have introduced countermeasures such as cofinancing, collateralization, credit insurance and government or third-party repayment guarantees as default risk management measures.[20] As suggested by Cheong (2022), these risk mitigation measures undertaken by China's overseas lending activities are not suspicious; rather, they serve as methods to prevent the occurrence of undesired nonperforming loans. Hence, the use of the "debt-trap" connotation needs further analysis.

When depicting "debt-trap diplomacy", very often the advocators have sidelined the mechanisms through which China's development finance system is guided and implemented, as well as the responsibilities of the recipient governments in securing BRI financing. Although the Ministry of Foreign Affairs (MFA), the Ministry of Commerce (MOFCOM) and the National Development and Reform Committee (NDRC) of China are jointly responsible for the policy formulation and promotion of the BRI, the MFA has the least role to play in BRI financing due to the

---

[17] Malik 2021.

[18] Ibid.

[19] Horn (2022).

[20] Custer (2021).

economic nature and commercial orientation of BRI activities. The criteria established by the MOFCOM and NDRC for SOEs, development banks and state-owned commercial banks involved in overseas BRI projects are predominantly driven by economic considerations, and the procedures are loosely guided or regulated by the central government. Generally, the approval and decision-making process for BRI projects is made on a case-by-case basis. It lacks coordination between central and provincial agencies and hence lacks strategic intent in BRI projects. Multilateral financial institutions such as the International Monetary Fund (IMF) and the World Bank (WB) have also been involved in some BRI development financing initiatives to mobilize international capital and resources for better development.[21] On this basis, the IMF has acknowledged the significant role played by China's BRI in global economic development.[22]

Jones and Hameiri (2020) underlined that many BRI projects in recipient countries were initiated by politicians or ruling elites for their domestic political agendas or business interests. As such, the negotiation and approval process of BRI loans by Chinese state-owned banks and syndicated co-finance always lacks transparency and spawns all kinds of disputes and controversies. However, due to the noninterventionist approach and loose governance of financial management both in China and the recipient countries, there could be asymmetric information between China as the lender and recipient countries as the borrowers. The existence of asymmetric information between lenders and borrowers provides opportunities for borrowers to conceal information about the true nature of the projects or businesses, repayment commitment and capacity. In this case, a *moral hazard* problem will occur when the borrowers, who are the BRI host country's ruling elites, and their business interests abstain from the full disclosure of investment risks and default risks. The lenders, i.e., the Chinese state-owned banks or co-finance syndicate, may have to overcome the *adverse selection* problem by imposing higher interest rates than the Paris Club and demanding collateral or the government's repayment guarantee. The problem has become prevalent in emerging economies and developing countries as they increasingly seek non-Paris Club lending. Based on the findings of Guler, Onder and Taskin (2022), one of the solutions for the BRI debt governance problem could be a shift from asymmetrical information to full disclosure of information by borrower governments. The increased transparency would enable the borrower governments to negotiate for more favorable terms from a larger source of potential lenders.

8.4 The Debt Issue in Malaysia

The discussion on whether Malaysia is haunted by nonperforming BRI debts or even the "debt-trap diplomacy" of China's BRI project should be looked at in two aspects. First, whether the external debts of Malaysia have reached an unmanageable level.

[21] Belt and Road Initiative (2019).

[22] IMF official: BRI an 'important contribution' to global economy (2019).

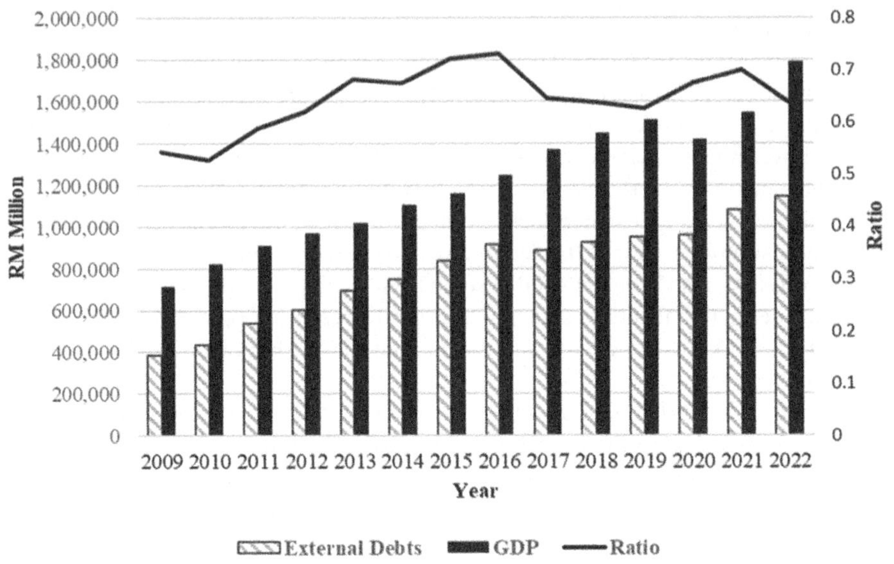

Fig. 8.5 External Debt-GDP ratio of Malaysia. *Source* Bank Negara Malaysia (BNM)

Second, has the exposure of Malaysia's sovereign debts to China been plagued by default risks?

8.4.1 External Debts of Malaysia

Malaysia's ratio of external debt to GDP has caught the attention of social media and political debates in recent years.[23] The external debts of Malaysia have been rising due to expansionary fiscal policy in the past few years. Figure 8.5 shows that the external debts of Malaysia increased from RM 388,345 million in 2009 to RM 1,144,663 million in 2022, a 194.8% rise in 13 years or an annual increment of 15.0% on average. Hence, the external debt-to-GDP ratio has also increased from 54.4% in 2009 to 63.9% in 2022. The rising debt level may increase the vulnerability of Malaysia to external shocks, such as the depreciation of the Ringgit Malaysia and sluggish economic development. However, the International Monetary Fund (IMF) contends that Malaysia's external debts are manageable, as more than one-third of them are denominated in Ringgit Malaysia.[24] The IMF even projected that the external debt-to-GDP ratio of Malaysia would stabilize to a steady downward path as a result of better economic growth prospects after the COVID-19 pandemic.[25]

[23] Yeap (2022).

[24] Malaysia: 2022 Article (2022).

[25] Ibid.

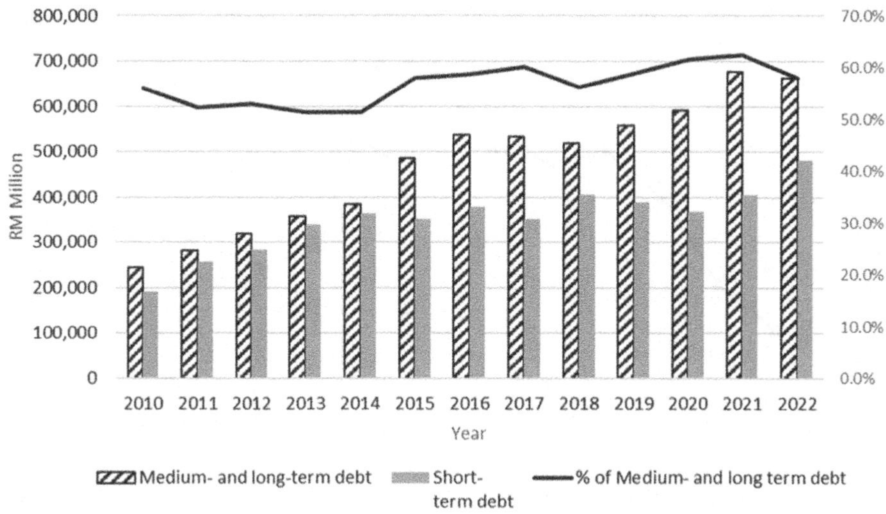

Fig. 8.6 Tenures of Malaysia's external debts. *Source* Bank Negara Malaysia (BNM)

Figure 8.6 exhibits the proportion of the medium- and long-term debt to the total external debts of Malaysia from 2009 to 2022. The medium- and long-term debt accounts for less than 60% of the external debts before 2020 and reached 62.5% in 2021 but returned to below 60%, i.e., 57.9% in 2022. A higher medium- and long-term debt implies a reduction in short-term financial obligations, such as higher interest rates, debt redemption and the risks associated with debt rollovers.[26] The rise in the ratio of short-term debts posed some concerns about the rollover risks of Malaysia's external debt obligations. Figure 8.7 demonstrates the debt service ratio for Malaysia's external debt from 2009 to 2022. The ratio is calculated by the central bank of Malaysia, the Bank Negara Malaysia, to measure the principal repayment and interest payment of the total external debts as a proportion of the gross export of goods and services. The debt service ratio is also used as one of the indicators of external debt sustainability to assess a country's debt sustainability. After increasing from 11.6% in 2018 to 13.8% in 2020, the debt service ratio reverted to 11.0% in 2021 and then marginally increased to 11.4% in 2022, which is far below the 22.5% in 2015 and 2016. Thus, contrary to the common perception that Malaysia is going to face bankruptcy or default risk crises, Malaysia's debt servicing commitments as a whole are sustained by strong export earnings and the optimistic prospect of economic growth.

[26] Bank Negara Malaysia (2022).

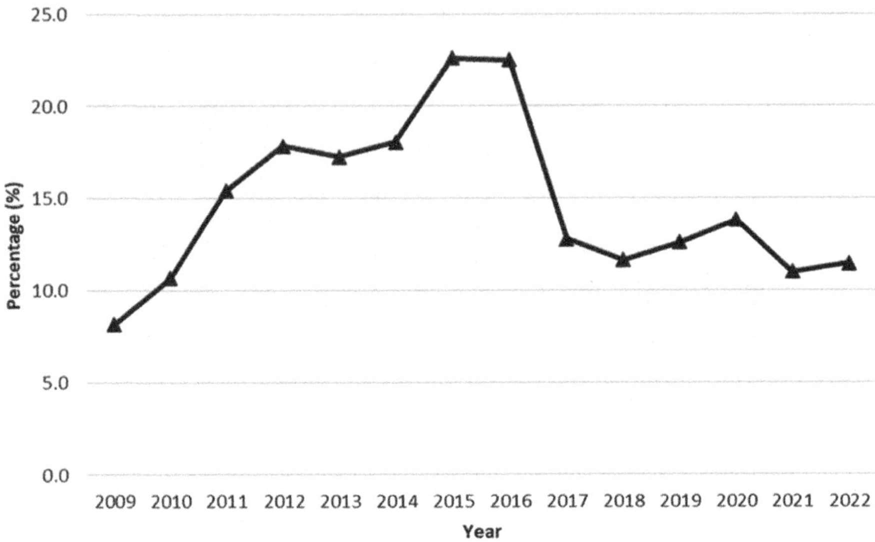

Fig. 8.7 Debt service ratio (%) of Malaysia's external debts. *Source* Bank Negara Malaysia (BNM)

8.4.2 Malaysia's Exposure to BRI's "Debt-Trap Diplomacy"

The growing presence of Chinese companies in Malaysia, from both private firms and SOEs, has provoked criticism and suspicions about "debt-trap diplomacy". In Malaysia, the "debt-trap diplomacy" narrative concerning BRI projects in the country is closely associated with the 1Malaysia Development Berhad (1MDB) scandal. In short, 1MDB is a state investment fund, wholly owned by the government of Malaysia and launched by the then Prime Minister and Finance Minister of Malaysia, Najib, in 2009.[27] Originally set up as a strategic development fund envisioned to promote long-term economic development and transform Malaysia into a newly industrialized nation, the 1MDB funds, which were supposedly allocated to finance strategic development projects in the areas of energy, real estate, tourism, agribusiness and other new industries, were allegedly misused.[28] The 1MDB quickly evolved into a troublesome entity, debts were accumulated, and negative news related to suspicious money transactions, bribery, corruption, or fund diversions were piling up at the same time, leading to the so-called 1MDB scandal. The 1MDB scandal has been described by *BBC News* as "*one of the world's greatest financial scandals*".[29] High-profile projects funded by the 1MDB include the Tun Razak Exchange, Bandar Malaysia,[30] and the problematic projects cancelled by the Pakatan Harapan government in 2018

[27] Explainer: Malaysia's ex-PM (2022).

[28] Malaysia says recovered 1MDB (2022).

[29] 1MDB: The playboys (2019).

[30] Ali (2018).

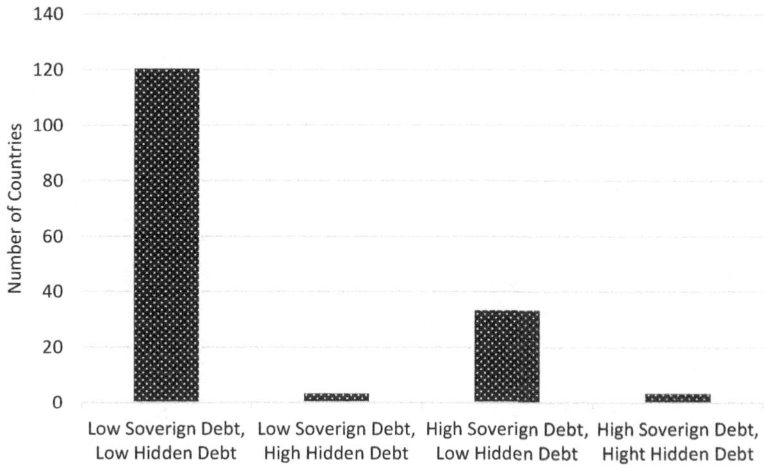

Fig. 8.8 BRI debt stress of Borrower Countries. *Source* Malik et al. (2021)

include the Trans Sabah Gas Pipeline and Multi Product Pipeline projects. Another project being scrutinized is the East Coast Rail Link (ERCL), where the cost of construction is said to have been inflated to cover the 1MDB's debts.[31]

Therefore, is Malaysia at significant risk of BRI-related debt strain? The key question here is whether the government or sovereign debt linked to China has an adverse impact on Malaysia's fiscal stability. One potential measure for assessing BRI debt stress is debt exposure to China as a percentage of GDP. If the proportion of a country's sovereign debts or hidden debts to China is more than 10%, it could be classified as high exposure to BRI debt stress. Hidden debts refer to debts that are not sovereign debts, but their repayments are guaranteed by the government of borrower countries. Based on this calibration, out of the 165 countries traced by the Aid DATA, 121 countries or 73.3% have both a low sovereign and hidden debt exposure to China (Fig. 8.8), while only 6 countries or 3.6% have risky exposure to China in both sovereign and hidden debts. Malaysia is one of those with low sovereign debt and hidden debt exposure.

Figure 8.9 further exhibits the sovereign debt exposure to China as a percentage of GDP by various borrower countries from 2000–2017, reproduced from Aid Data. The debt exposure ratios range from 53% for Congo to 0% for countries such as Brunei, Columbia and Israel. Malaysia's sovereign debt exposure to China is 2%, which is lower than the mean of 6.1% but slightly higher than the median of 1.0%. Malaysia's relatively low debt exposure to China contravenes the prevailing opinion that Malaysia is facing a debt crisis caused by involvement in BRI activities.[32] In other words, Malaysia has some exposure to debt from the BRI, but it is not considered to be highly exposed compared to some other countries.

---

[31] China's Belt and Road (2018).

[32] Yeap (2022).

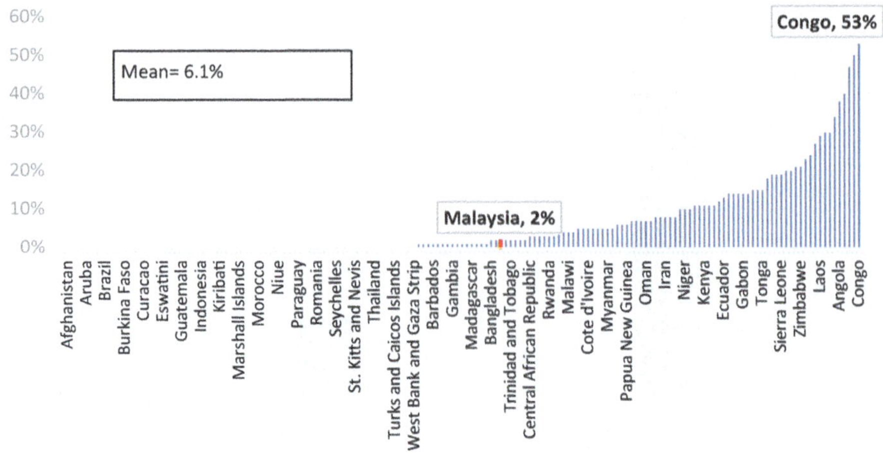

Fig. 8.9 Sovereign debt exposure to China as a percentage of GDP (2000–2017). *Source* Aid Data's Global Chinese Development Finance Dataset, Version 2.0

8.4.3 The Chinese Lenders and Borrowers

Figure 8.10 exhibits major Chinese lenders according to their loans for BRI activities in Malaysia. The information is extracted from Aid DATA after removing lendings that were subsequently canceled or suspended during the period. The lending amounts are adjusted to the constant US dollar in 2017.[33] The Export–Import Bank of China (EIBC), one of the policy banks of China, is the most active Chinese lender in Malaysia, accounting for 11.8 billion USD or 79.5% of the total 14.8 billion USD loans disbursed or pledged by Chinese banks. The EIBC focuses on promoting international trade and overseas investment in Chinese companies. It has a long history of providing loans to infrastructure construction projects and financial institutions, as well as local and foreign investments in Malaysia. Figure 8.10 shows that EIBC had also participated in the syndicated loans jointly provided by the Chinese state-owned commercial banks such as the Agricultural Bank of China (ABC), Chinese Construction Bank (CCB) and Industrial and Commercial Bank of China (ICBC). The China Development Bank (CDB) is also a policy bank of China, but it only accounts for 3.3% of the total Chinese lending to Malaysia.

Figure 8.11 exhibits the composition of the borrowers of Chinese loans in Malaysia. Joint ventures/special purpose vehicles (JV/SPV), mainly owned by Malaysian shareholders, form the largest group of receivers of Chinese loans, constituting 52% of the total amount. The borrowers include the Malaysia Rail Link

[33] According to the definition of AidData, "AidData first converts the financial commitment (or pledge) amount in its original currency of denomination to nominal U.S. dollars at the average exchange rate in effect during the commitment (or pledge) year, and then converts this amount to constant 2017 U.S. dollars using the OECD's deflation methodology to adjust for inflation and ensure comparability over time and space." (Custer et al., 2021).

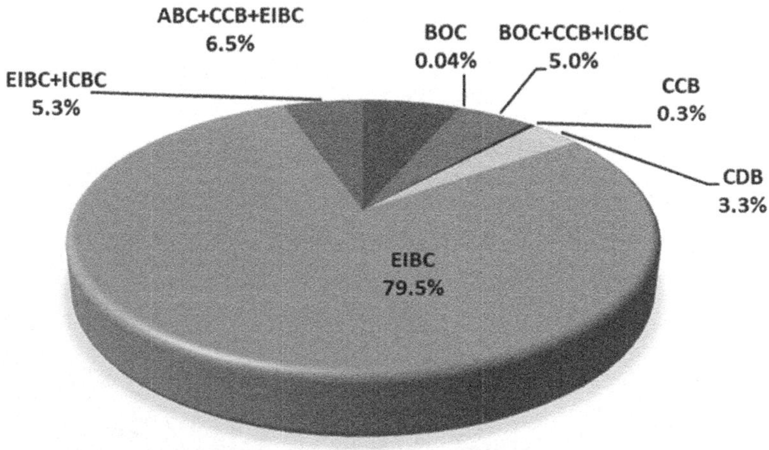

Fig. 8.10 The Major Chinese lenders to BRI Projects in Malaysia, 2000–2017. *Source* Aid Data's Global Chinese Development Finance Dataset, Version 2.0 *Note ABC = Agriculture Bank of China, BOC = Bank of China, CCB = China Constructon Bank Corporation, CDB = China Development Bank, EIBC = Export–Import Bank of China, ICBC = Industrial and Commercial Bank of China*

Sdn Bhd (MRL) for the ECRL project, the Trans-Sabah gas pipeline and multi-product pipeline construction projects, MCKIP Sdn Bhd for the development of Malaysia-China Kuantan Industrial Park, Jambatan Kedua Sdn Bhd for the Second Penang Bridge Construction project, and the IWH-CREC Sdn Bhd (ICSB), which was the previous developer of the Bandar Malaysia in Kuala Lumpur.[34] The other loan receivers include the Sarawak aluminum smelter construction project, which was a joint venture between Malaysian and Chinese companies, Bank Pembangunan Malaysia Berhad, Export–Import Bank of Malaysia, solar cell and solar module production line projects by Jinko Solar Holding Co. Ltd. of China, Malaysian government agencies, Malaysia state-owned banks, and JV/SPV with Chinese companies as major stakeholders.

Chinese lending activities in Malaysia are channeled through a highly concentrated lending source. The high concentration of loans from one or two policy banks is possibly the outcome of the "Go Global" policy of the Chinese government since 1999, which was then further enhanced by the BRI.[35] The policy banks of China, especially EIBC, played a proactive role in fostering joint ventures between China and Malaysia's companies, particularly between China's SOEs and Malaysia's government-linked companies (GLCs).

---

[34] IWH-CREC Sdn Bhd (ICSB) (2021).

[35] Chow (2022).

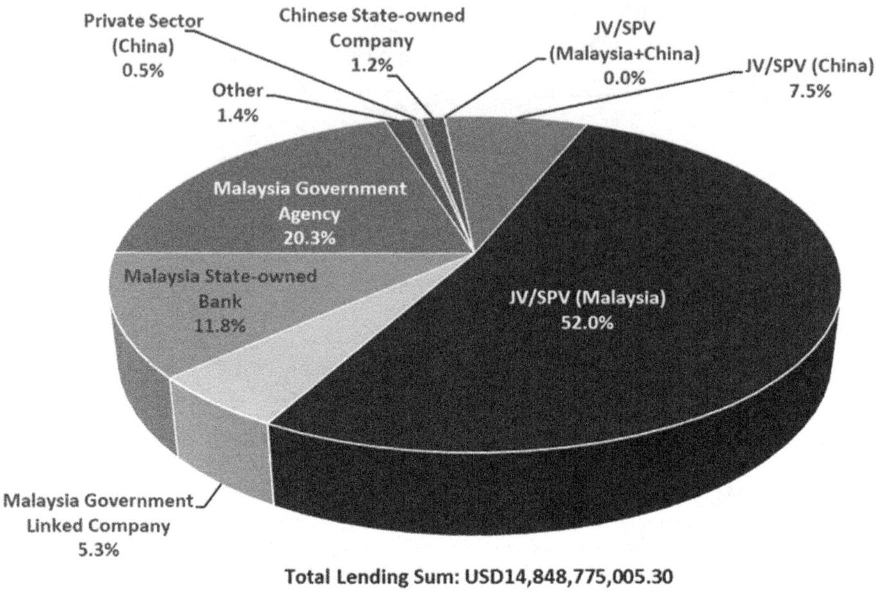

Fig. 8.11 The Types of borrower agencies for Chinese loans in Malaysia, 2000–2017. *Source* Aid Data's Global Chinese Development Finance Dataset, Version 2.0. *Note JV = Joint venture; SPV = Special purpose vehicles*

8.5 BRI's Benefits to Malaysia

Malaysia, a country that relied heavily on agricultural commodities such as rubber and tin as the basis of economic growth before the 1970s, underwent a series of successful transformations to develop into an industrial-based economy in the 1980s and 1990s. Various initiatives were introduced to build the economy. Among the efforts taken include import-substitution strategy, export-oriented industrialization and liberalization in trade and investment policies.[36] The outward-oriented growth strategy adopted by the country to benefit from trade, foreign direct investment and globalization has spawned favorable outcomes for Malaysia to achieve a decade of impressive growth after the 1985 economic recession. The economy grew at an average annual rate of nearly 10% from 1988 to 1997. The impressive growth performance before the 1997–98 Asian Financial Crisis helped Malaysia transit successfully from the lower middle-income country category to an upper middle-income economy in 1992, based on the World Bank income classification.[37] However, the 1997–98 Asian Financial Crisis has derailed the growth trajectory of the economy.

---

[36] Cheng (2021).

[37] World Bank classification is based on Gross National Income (GNI) per capita using the World Bank Atlas method. The World Bank divides the world's economies into four income groups: high, upper-middle, lower-middle, and low income countries. The threshold and countries classification will be adjusted every year on July 1. As of 1992, upper middle income economies are defined as

After 1998, although the GDP was still achieving an average growth rate of approximately 4.5% annually, the growth momentum slowed down thereafter. As a result, Malaysia failed to achieve its Vision 2020, which was launched in 1991 to transform Malaysia from a developing nation to a fully developed and industrialized society by 2020. Additionally, the country is at risk of falling into the "Middle-income Trap".

The main factor that contributed to the deteriorating competitiveness of the Malaysian economy was the lack of effective policies to support the industrialization process to move the manufacturing sector up the value chain and to cultivate a highly skilled labor force to compete in high value-added production. Due to a lack of investment in local innovation and R&D efforts and overreliance on imported technology or FDI for technological transfer, there is a lack of local technology creation and weak industrial linkages, as well as low absorptive capacity among local firms, especially SMEs. Hence, firms are competing primarily in the low-skill sectors and occupy the lower end of the value chain to take advantage of their labor cost comparative advantage. When there was a shortage of Malaysian workers, foreign workers were imported from neighboring countries. When other emerging countries in the region, such as Vietnam and Cambodia, started their industrialization process and offered similar or better cost advantages, Malaysia lost its competitiveness to neighboring countries in trade and foreign investment. Malaysia would need to transform and improve its capability to compete in the increasingly competitive global economy.

The strong economic ties between Malaysia and China are considered a mutually beneficial relationship for both sides. Malaysia needs foreign direct investment from China, more so expertise in advanced technology, which is instrumental in transforming the Malaysian economy, strengthening backward and forward industrial linkages, and creating employment opportunities.[38] In recent years, China has emerged as the trendsetter in new technology and business models,[39] particularly in the development of the digital economy. Companies such as Huawei, Alibaba, and Tencent are leading the way in 5G, mobile payments, e-commerce, fintech and other cutting-edge technologies. The strong support given by the Chinese government for innovation and technological development has made China a technology leader and innovation country. In 2019, according to the World Intellectual Property Organization (WIPO), China surpassed the US to become the top filer of international patent applications with WIPO.[40]

To revitalize the growth momentum, there is an urgent need for Malaysia to identify new sources of growth and undergo structural economic transformation to catch up in the new economy characterized as Industry 4.0, strengthen Malaysia's competitiveness, and restore the economy from the pandemic. Malaysia launched the National Policy on Industry 4.0 on 31 October 2018 and the Malaysia Digital

---

those with a GNI per capita range from US$2,696 to US$8,355. https://datahelpdesk.worldbank.org/knowledgebase/articles/378834-how-does-the-world-bank-classify-countries.

[38] Tham (2018).

[39] Dychtwald (2021).

[40] China Becomes Top Filer of International (2020).

Economy Blueprint on February 19, 2021 to drive Malaysia toward digital transformation and foster the adoption of digital technologies across various sectors, including commerce, industry, education, and government services.[41]

From an economic development perspective, the BRI is perceived to provide not only advantages in infrastructure connectivity, trade, and investment linkages but also a catching-up opportunity for Malaysia. For instance, the establishment of the Malaysia-China Kuantan Industrial Park (MCKIP) at Kuantan in 2013, as the sister park of the "Two Countries Twin Parks",[42] is expected to serve as a platform to promote cross-border investment and trade cooperation between China and Malaysia. Industrial parks act as catalysts of growth to foster the innovation and development of high-value-added industries in Malaysia.[43] With the implementation of the Regional Comprehensive Economic Partnership (RCEP) in 2022, the "Two Countries Twin Parks" could play a more important role in utilizing its unique cross-country coordination mechanisms and industry linkages that have already been created to deepen the bilateral cooperation between China and Malaysia as well as with other RCEP members.[44]

The surveys conducted by Cheng et al. (2022) in 2019 and 2020 also revealed that the BRI received a positive response in Malaysia.[45] A majority of the respondents who participated in the surveys conducted for two consecutive years in 2019 and 2020 (597 and 608 respondents, respectively) viewed the BRI as beneficial for generating positive impacts on economic, cultural, and educational development in Malaysia. The creation of jobs, business, and investment opportunities are recognized as the most important outcomes for Malaysia to participate in the BRI. Additionally, the BRI is perceived as an effective platform for Malaysia to participate in international economic cooperation, facilitate technology transfer, and promote cultural and educational exchange and interaction. Having said so, there are concerns about potential risks arising from BRI activities. In particular, there is increasing competition in the local labor market due to the influx of foreign workers from China, brain drain, and the growing influence of China in Malaysia. The creation of enormous debt is one of the worrying issues but is not highlighted as the top issue of concern. The studies concluded that while Malaysians are optimistic about the impacts of BRI development in Malaysia, they are also aware of the potential negative implications associated with BRI projects; hence, Malaysia should participate in BRI but cautiously.

---

[41] Malaysia digital economy blueprint (2021).

[42] The "Two Countries Twin Parks" refers to the sister parks of the China-Malaysia Qinzhou Industrial Park (CMQIP) located in Qinzhou, China and the Malaysia-China Kuantan Industrial Park (MCKIP) in Kuantan, Malaysia.

[43] Cheng (2022).

[44] Cheng (2022).

[45] Cheng (2022).

8.6 Conclusion

China's BRI presents numerous benefits for economic growth, particularly for developing countries such as Malaysia. The BRI opens up significant opportunities for host nations to expand their markets, access resources, mobilize capital and financing for development projects, and integrate more effectively with the global economy, thereby increasing their competitiveness in the international arena. However, to fully reap the benefits of the BRI, both China and the host countries must fulfill their joint responsibility to ensure that the projects are executed in a sustainable, transparent, and inclusive manner, taking into account any potential impacts on local communities and the environment.

This chapter presents a thorough analysis of the debt situation in Malaysia. The analysis of available evidence and data reveals that Malaysia's exposure to Chinese debt is manageable and comparatively low. Nevertheless, to ensure the long-term sustainability of BRI projects, the governments of Malaysia and China must collaborate closely to improve the transparency of loan negotiations and disbursements. It is imperative to address the issue of asymmetrical information between Chinese lenders and Malaysian borrowers to ensure that financial resources are directed toward economically viable projects and to mitigate potential risks for sustainable BRI development in Malaysia.

References

Ali, A. M., 1MDB: corporate governance going berserk? Part I, *International Journal of Academic Research in Business and Social Sciences*, Vol.8, No.12, 2018, pp.1861–1946.

According to the definition of AidData, "AidData first converts the financial commitment (or pledge) amount in its original currency of denomination to nominal U.S. dollars at the average exchange rate in effect during the commitment (or pledge) year, and then converts this amount to constant 2017 U.S. dollars using the OECD's deflation methodology to adjust for inflation and ensure comparability over time and space." (Custer et al., 2021)

Bank Negara Malaysia, BNM quarterly Bulletin: Fourth Quarter 2021, In Bank Negara Malaysia, Vol.36, No.4, 2022

Brautigam, D., & Rithmire, M., "The Chinese 'debt trap' Is a myth", *The Atlantic,* February 6, 2021, https://www.theatlantic.com/international/archive/2021/02/China-debt-trap-diplomacy/617953/

Belt and Road Initiative: two key channels to achieving financial connectivity, International Monetary Fund, 2019, https://www.imf.org/en/News/Articles/2019/04/24/sp042519-belt-and-road-initiative-two-key-channels-to-achieving-financial-connectivity

Custer, S. et al., *Tracking Chinese development finance: an Application of AidData's TUFF 2.0 methodology,* 2021, https://docs.aiddata.org/ad4/pdfs/AidData_TUFF_methodology_2_0.pdf

Cheng, M. Y., Cham, T. H., Ng, K. Y. & Tai, S. Y., The "Twin Industrial Parks": a study on the development of MCKIP and Its perceived impacts on local communities. In H. N. Au Yong, X. C. Yuan & L. Low (Eds). *China's Belt and Road initiative: going global and transformation in the global Arena,* Singapore: World Scientific, 2021, pp. 31–56

Chow, Y. P., "Internationalization of Chinese firms and its impact on Malaysia", *The Star,* February 14, 2022, https://www.thestar.com.my/opinion/columnists/search-scholar-series/2022/02/14/internationalization

China Becomes Top Filer of International Patents in 2019 Amid Robust Growth for WIPO's IP Services, Treaties and Finances, WIPO, 2020, https://www.wipo.int/pressroom/en/articles/2020/article_0005.html

"China remains Malaysia's largest foreign partner for manufacturing sector, says MIDA", Malaysian Investment Development Authority, 2021, https://www.mida.gov.my/mida-news/China-remains-malaysias-largest-foreign-partner-for-manufacturing-sector-says-mida/

"China's Belt and Road builder finds itself embroiled in a scandal in Malaysian Coastal Railway Link", *South China Morning Post*, June 12, 2018, https://www.scmp.com/business/companies/article/2150411/chinas-belt-and-road-builder-finds-itself-embroiled-scandal

Cheng, M. Y., Cham, T. H., Ng, K. Y., & Tai, S. Y., The "Twin Industrial Parks": a study on the development of MCKIP and Its perceived impacts on local communities. In H. N. Au Yong, X. C. Yuan & L. Low (Eds). *China's Belt and Road Initiative: Going global and transformation in the global Arena*, Singapore: World Scientific, 2021, pp.31–56

Cheng, M. Y., "RCEP and the "Two Countries, Twin Parks", *China-ASEAN Business,* May, 2022, pp. 32–37

Cheng, M. Y., Lim Y. W., & Low, S. C., The development of Belt and Road Initiative in Malaysia: a perception Analysis. In C. K. Choong, L. S. Lau & F. M. Liew (Eds). *Belt and Road Initiative: paving the way to mutual respect, sincerity and sustainable development,* Kuala Lumpur: Pustak Prinsip Sdn Bhd, 2022

Cheng, M. Y., Malaysia at the Crossroads toward Vision 2020. In L. Ashish (Ed.), Facets of Competitiveness: Narratives from ASEAN, Singapore: World Scientific, 2021, pp. 223–255.

Dychtwald, Z., China's new innovation advantage, *Harvard Business Review*, May–June, 2021, https://hbr.org/2021/05/chinas-new-innovation-advantage

"Explainer: Malaysia's ex-PM Najib and the multibillion dollar 1MDB scandal", *Reuters*, 2022, https://www.reuters.com/world/asia-pacific/malaysias-ex-pm-najib-multibillion-dollar-1mdb-scandal-2022-08-23/

Gomez, E. T., Tham, S. Y., Li, R., & Cheong, K. C., *China in Malaysia: state-business relations and the new order of investment flows,* Malaysia: Palgrave Macmillan, 2020, pp.12–14.

Hutchinson, F. E., & Tham, S. Y., The BRI in Malaysia's Port Sector: Drivers of Success and Failure, ISEAS Economics Working Paper, No.10, 2020, https://www.iseas.edu.sg/wp-content/uploads/2020/11/ISEAS_EWP_2020-10_Hutchinson_Tham.pdf

Horn, S., Reinhart, C. M., & Trebesch, C., Hidden Defaults, Policy Research Working Paper, No.9925, 2022, https://documents1.worldbank.org/curated/en/773311643912553263/pdf/Hidden-Defaults.pdf

"IMF official: BRI an 'important contribution' to global economy", *China Daily,* 2019, https://www.chinadailyhk.com/articles/202/244/103/1555052219582.html

IWH-CREC Sdn Bhd (ICSB) had quitted the Bandar Malaysia development project in July 2021. See Aziz, A., & Fong, K., *"IWH-CREC's RM7.4 billion deal to buy 60% stake in Bandar Malaysia falls through", The Edge Markets*, July 2021, pp.1–9, https://www.theedgemarkets.com/article/iwhcrecs-rm74-billion-deal-buy-60-stake-bandar-malaysia-falls-through

Jones, L., & Hameiri S., Debunking the myth: How recipient countries shape China's Belt and Road Initiative, Chatham House Research Paper, 2020, https://www.chathamhouse.org/2020/08/debunking-myth-debt-trap-diplomacy

Khor, H.E., Poonpatpibul, C. & Foo, S. Y., Belt and Road Initiative: A Framework to Address Challenges and Unlock Potential for High-Quality and Inclusive Growth, *Singapore Economic Review*, Vol. 66, No.1, 2021, pp.21–58; Wheeler, A., "Far from a 'debt trap', China's Belt and Road Allows Countries like Myanmar to Leapfrog Poverty", *South China Morning Post*, 2018, https://www.scmp.com/comment/insight-opinion/China/article/2154839/far-debt-trap-chinas-belt-and-road-allows-countries

Malaysia: 2022 Article IV consultation staff report, International Monetary Fund, 2022, https://0-doi-org.library.svsu.edu/10.5089/9798400206696.002

Malik, A., Parks, B., Russell, B., Lin, J., Walsh, K., Solomon, K., Zhang, S., Elston, T., & S. Goodman, *Banking on the Belt and Road: Insights from a new global dataset of 13,427 Chinese development projects*. Williamsburg, VA: AidData at William & Mary, 2021

McKenzie, B, Trends and Spotlights of the Chinese Investment Landscape, *bakermckenzie.com*, 2022, https://www.bakermckenzie.com/-/media/files/insight/publications/2022/02/fdi-China-report-2022-english.pdf?sc_lang=en&hash=054A2FD520CD9CB19224E661D8A777E8#:~:text=In%202021%2C%20Chinese%20outbound%20investment,USD%20117%20billion%20in%20 2019

"Malaysia says recovered 1MDB funds only enough to pay debt principal for 2022", *Reuters*, 2022, https://www.reuters.com/world/asia-pacific/malaysia-has-received-817-mln-kpmg-1mdb-settlement-2022-01-13/

Malaysia digital economy blueprint, Economic Planning Unit, Prime Minister's Department, 2021, https://www.epu.gov.my/sites/default/files/2021-02/malaysia-digital-economy-blueprint.pdf

Nedopil, C, "China Belt and Road Initiative (BRI) Investment Report H1 2022", Green Finance&Development Center, FISF Fudan University, Shanghai, July 2022, https://greenfdc.org/China-belt-and-road-initiative-bri-investment-report-h1-2022/

"[Press Release] World Premier of The Belt and Road Initiative: 2018 Report on Five Connectivity Indexes", Institute for Ocean Research of Peking University, September 15, 2018, https://ocean.pku.edu.cn/info/1165/3077.htm

Tritto, A., & Camba, A, "The Belt and Road: the good, the bad, and the mixed-demystifying China's Belt and Road Initiative through 3 case studies", *The Diplomat*, April 4, 2019, https://thediplomat.com/2019/04/the-belt-and-road-the-good-the-bad-and-the-mixed/

Singh, A., The myth of 'debt-trap diplomacy' and realities of Chinese development finance. *Third World Quarterly,* Vol.42, No.2, 2021, pp. 239–253

Tham, S. Y., Chinese investment in Malaysia: five years into the BRI, ISEAS-Yusof Ishak Institute, No.11, 2018, https://www.iseas.edu.sg/images/pdf/ISEAS_Perspective_2018_11@50.pdf

The "Two Countries Twin Parks" refers to the sister parks of the China-Malaysia Qinzhou Industrial Park (CMQIP) located in Qinzhou, China and the Malaysia-China Kuantan Industrial Park (MCKIP) in Kuantan, Malaysia

World Development Indicators, World Bank, 2022, https://databank.worldbank.org/source/world-development-indicators/

World Bank classification is based on Gross National Income (GNI) per capita using the World Bank Atlas method. The World Bank divides the world's economies into four income groups: high, upper-middle, lower-middle, and low income countries. The threshold and countries classification will be adjusted every year on July 1. As of 1992, upper middle income economies are defined as those with a GNI per capita range from US$2,696 to US$8,355. https://datahelpdesk.worldbank.org/knowledgebase/articles/378834-how-does-the-world-bank-classify-countries

Yeap, C., "The state of the nation: why Malaysia is unlikely to go bankrupt like Sri Lanka but cannot afford debt like Singapore", *The Edge Markets*, 2022, pp.1–8, https://www.theedgemarkets.com/article/state-nation-why-malaysia-unlikelygo-bankrupt-sri-lanka-cannot-afford-debt-singapore

1MDB: The playboys, PMs and partygoers around a global financial scandal", *BBC News*, August 9, 2019, https://www.bbc.com/news/world-asia-46341603

Chapter 9
The BRI: Debt Management and Narrative of Debt Risk in Indonesia

Candra Fajri Ananda and Risyaf Fahreza

Abstract This chapter discusses the narrative of debt risk in Belt and Road Initiative (BRI) projects in Indonesia, linked to government debt management, fiscal sustainability, and development agendas. China's BRI, led by the Chinese government, offers opportunities for many developing countries, including Indonesia, to improve their infrastructure. Most BRI projects in Indonesia have brought economic benefits to local areas and the whole country. However, there is a growing narrative in society that there is a potential debt risk from these BRI projects. Debt stands as a perennial concern in Indonesia, encompassing not only economic dimensions but also a social and political issue. Currently, the Indonesian government is in a strong financial position, can handle different economic situations and manage debt wisely to achieve development goals. Therefore, the idea that China's BRI projects will lead to a debt risk in Indonesia seems more like a myth than reality. However, the Indonesian government still needs to remain vigilant and take several policy measures to mitigate debt risks. One challenge faced in Indonesian BRI projects is the Jakarta-Bandung high-speed rail project. This has been delayed and costs more than expected.

Keywords BRI · Debt management · Debt risk · Infrastructure · Fiscal sustainability

9.1 Introduction

Debt has always been a prominent issue in Indonesia, not only in the economic context but also as a social and political concern. The public perceives that the government's increasing debt will have negative repercussions on the lives of its citizens. On the other hand, the Indonesian government still relies on debt as a fiscal instrument to

---

C. F. Ananda (✉)
Faculty of Economics and Business, Universitas Brawijaya, Malang, Indonesia
e-mail: candra064@gmail.com

R. Fahreza
Ministry of Finance, Jakarta, Indonesia

N. Peng and M. Y. Cheng (eds.), *The Reality and Myth of BRI's Debt Trap*, Indo-Pacific Focus, https://doi.org/10.1007/978-981-97-1056-0_9

support sustainable development. The critical nature of debt as a primary issue in Indonesia compels the government to exercise caution in managing this issue.

The dilemma surrounding Indonesia's debt position underscores the importance of prudent debt management. Debt management must be conducted with utmost care to effectively address the concerns that have arisen in society while maintaining fiscal sustainability. This, in turn, ensures that future development agendas can progress as anticipated.

Compared to many peer countries, Indonesia's debt management is considered one of the most effective. There are three factors contributing to this assessment. First, the debt-to-Gross Domestic Product (GDP) ratio has consistently declined over the past two decades. In 1999, Indonesia's debt ratio reached 100% of GDP,[1] but it currently stands at approximately 39.6% of GDP. Second, Indonesia has successfully shifted its debt structure to be more domestically oriented. Presently, approximately 85% of government debt is sourced from the issuance of domestic government securities, predominantly dominated by domestic securities. This reduces exposure to exchange rate fluctuations and foreign interventions. Third, 90% of government debt consists of long-term loans.[2]

However, despite Indonesia's relatively sound debt management, debt-related issues have not completely subsided. One of the hotly debated topics currently is the potential debt risk with China. Many believe that the numerous cooperation projects between Indonesia and China may lead to a debt risk. In conceptual terms, a debt risk refers to the inability of the borrower to repay debts, resulting in the lender taking over assets. Although not empirically proven, the public perceives that China's loans could create a debt risk for Indonesia, especially through Belt and Road Initiative projects.

Therefore, this chapter will engage in a comprehensive discourse on debt management in Indonesia with the overarching aim of bolstering its development agenda. It will specifically address the intricacies of facilitating the implementation of Belt and Road Initiative (BRI) projects in Indonesia, which present opportunities for accelerating development. Furthermore, it will scrutinize the narrative surrounding the potential debt risks associated with these projects.

9.2 Debt Management to Support Economic Development in Indonesia

Debt constitutes a pivotal element in the context of national development. As a developing nation with substantial developmental requirements, Indonesia must inevitably employ debt as a crucial means to finance its developmental endeavors. According to the Directorate General of Budget Financing and Risk Management, as of the first quarter of 2022, the total debt incurred by the Government of Indonesia amounted

[1] Makmun (2009).

[2] Nurmillah (2021).

to IDR7,123.6 trillion, which is approximately equivalent to 491.3 billion USD.[3] This cumulative debt load stands at 39.6% of the country's GDP. This increase in the debt-to-GDP ratio aligns with the escalated budgetary demands necessitated by the pandemic response. Over the past five years, the average debt-to-GDP ratio has remained at 32.5%.

From the perspective of debt sustainability, Indonesia's current debt ratio remains within manageable bounds. In accordance with the State Finance Law (Law No. 17/2003), which adopts a debt ratio benchmark akin to the Maastricht Treaty, the maximum permissible public debt ratio to GDP stands at 60%.[4] Given the present ratio, Indonesia's debt remains relatively sustainable for the foreseeable future. Furthermore, in comparison to other nations, Indonesia's debt ratio is comparatively lower. Among the G20 nations, Japan, Italy, and the United States exhibit the highest debt-to-GDP ratios, standing at 266%, 150%, and 137%, respectively.[5]

Moreover, as per the Ministry of Finance, Indonesia's debt vulnerability has shown consistent improvement. In 2022, the ratio of debt interest to government revenue stood at 14.13%, marking a decline from the previous year's 18%.[6] This figure is also lower than the five-year average of 16.52%. Similarly, the debt service ratio, encompassing both interest and installment payments, has demonstrated a decreasing trend. In 2022, the debt service ratio registered at 42.79%, lower than the previous year's 51.27% and the five-year average of 50.57%. This amelioration in the government's debt vulnerability is underpinned by a significant upswing in state revenues.

Regarding the currency denomination of this debt, a predominant 71% of the Indonesian Government's debt is denominated in Rupiah, with the remaining portion denominated in foreign currencies. In terms of currency composition, 69% of the debt is held in the USD, followed by the Japanese yen and the Euro, each representing 5 and 6%, respectively. Concerning creditors, Singapore emerges as the primary creditor, holding 28.37% of the total external debt, trailed by the United States and Japan with shares of 16.63 and 11.78%, respectively (Fig. 9.1).

China has emerged as a significant lender to Indonesia, with the country's debt to China experiencing a remarkable 461% increase over the past decade. This debt surged from 3.7 billion USD in 2011 to 20.8 billion USD in 2022. In terms of lending institutions, the International Bank for Reconstruction and Development (IBRD) holds the position of the primary creditor, particularly in support of infrastructure projects and poverty alleviation, aligning with the IBRD's core objectives. Subsequently, the Asian Development Bank (ADB) and the International Monetary Fund (IMF) also rank among the most substantial creditors.

---

[3] Directorate General of Budget Financing and Risk Management (2022).

[4] Five things you need to know about the Maastricht Treaty (2020).

[5] Debt/GDP (2022).

[6] Dataset APBN (2022).

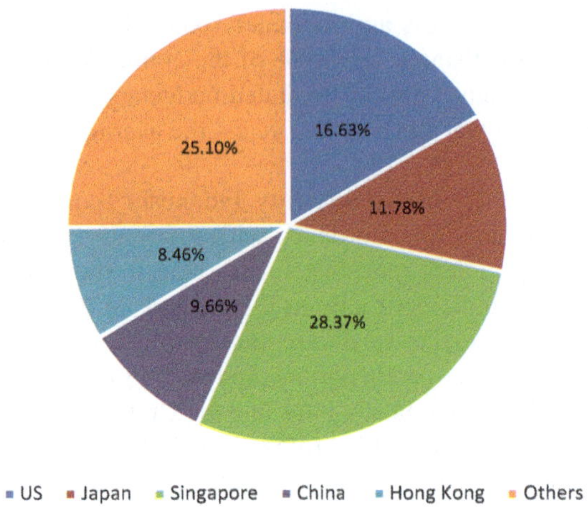

Fig. 9.1 External debt position by creditor (%). *Source* Ministry of Finance, 2022 and Bank of Indonesia, 2022[7]

Examining the economic sectors that have received loans, financial and insurance activities, human health and social work activities, and the electricity, gas, steam, and air conditioning supply sector have emerged as the largest beneficiaries, with respective allocations of 18.4%, 11.5%, and 10.8% (Fig. 9.2). Notably, the construction sector stands out as one of the sectors with the highest growth in external debt, experiencing a remarkable increase of 142.7% over the past decade. This trend aligns with the Indonesian government's focus on bolstering infrastructure development in recent years.

Regarding the types of debt, the Indonesian government's debt portfolio is predominantly composed of debt securities, specifically Government Bonds/Surat Berharga Negara (SBN). As of the first quarter of 2022, the nominal value of the Indonesian government's debt securities stood at IDR6,222 trillion, equivalent to 429 billion USD. This nominal value constitutes approximately 87% of the total government debt, with the remaining 12% originating from loans, primarily geared toward promoting infrastructure development. In terms of lender composition, the proportion between government and private sector lenders is nearly evenly split, with government lenders accounting for 49% and private sector lenders comprising the remaining 51%.

According to data sourced from the Directorate General of Budget Financing and Risk Management within the Ministry of Finance, the ownership landscape of Indonesia's government bonds is predominantly influenced by domestic factors, with national banks being the dominant owners, accounting for approximately 33.56%

[7] External debt statistics of Indonesia", Bank of Indonesia (2022).

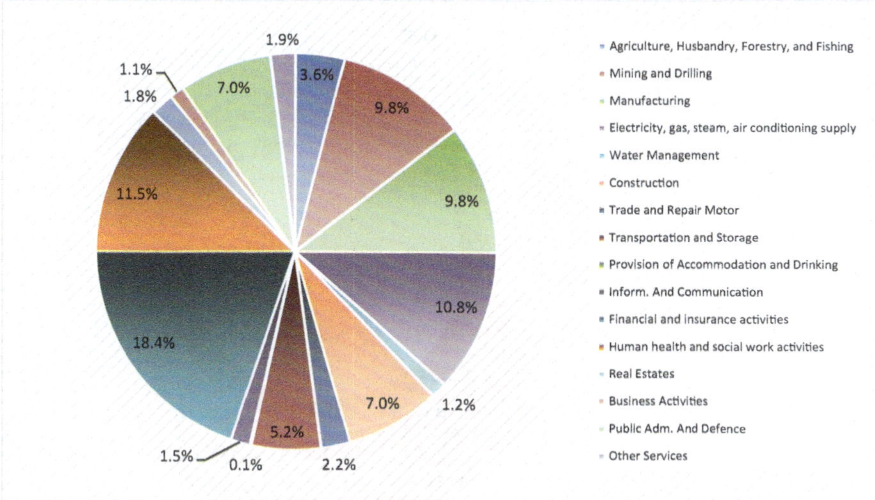

Fig. 9.2 External debt position by economic sector. *Source* Bank of Indonesia, 2022[8]

of the total tradeable Surat Berharga Negara (SBN) in the market (Fig. 9.3).[9] Following closely in second place is the Bank of Indonesia, the central bank, with a 16.7% ownership stake. In the third position, we find insurance institutions and pension funds, collectively owning 16.37% of government bonds. Meanwhile, foreign ownership of SBN as of August 2022 stands at 15.51%.

Foreign ownership in Indonesian government bonds has witnessed a continuous decline. In 2019, foreign ownership reached a peak of 38.57% of the total tradeable SBN. This figure gradually receded to 25.16% in 2020, coinciding with the initial period of the COVID-19 pandemic. Furthermore, in 2021, foreign ownership continued its descent to 19.05%. The diminishing foreign ownership of Indonesian government bonds can be attributed to the escalating risks in global financial markets. The pandemic-induced crisis, coupled with heightened inflation and tighter monetary policies in developed nations, prompted capital outflows from the securities markets of developing countries, including Indonesia.

Indonesia has been fortunate in this context. The exodus of foreign capital from the state securities market was offset by increased participation from domestic investors, notably banking, insurance, and pension fund institutions. This phenomenon contributed significantly to the stability of yields on Indonesian debt securities amidst substantial foreign capital outflows. As of August 2022, the foreign capital outflow from the government bond market reached approximately IDR120 trillion, marking one of the highest records in history. Meanwhile, the yield on Indonesian government securities increased by 79 basis points (bps). In fact, the majority of emerging market countries witnessed a surge in yields due to capital outflows in their respective state

[8] Ibid.

[9] Directorate General of Budget Financing and Risk Management (2022).

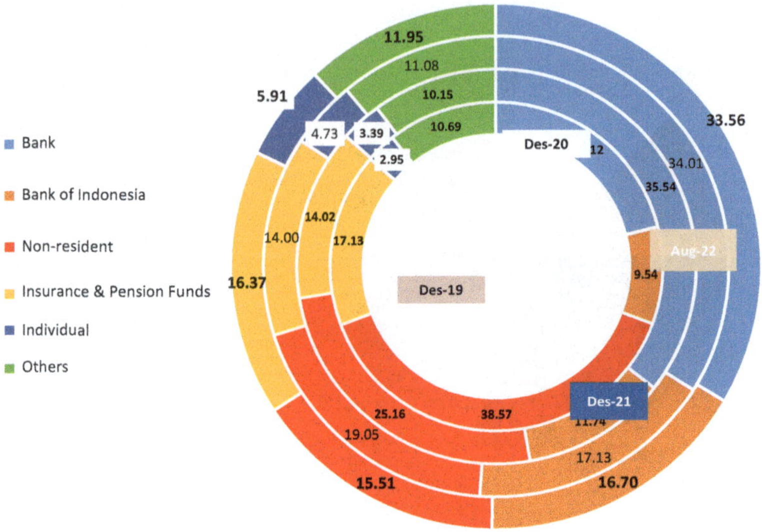

Fig. 9.3 Indonesian government bond ownership. *Source* Directorate General of Budget Financing and Risk Management, Ministry of Finance, 2022

securities markets. For instance, Turkey's government bond yields increased by 265 bps.

The decrease in nonresident ownership of government bonds (and the increased participation of domestic investors) will increase the stability of the national financial system in the future. On the other hand, the Government of Indonesia still needs the participation of foreign investors to increase financial market depth. For this reason, the government of Indonesia will continue to maintain the yield level of government bonds at an attractive level and affordable level in terms of the cost of funds. In addition, the Government of Indonesia will continue to strengthen the individual investor base, considering that the role of individual investors in the sovereign debt market also continues to increase from time to time.

Government debt is one source of fiscal risk that has a significant effect. To that end, the Government of Indonesia will continue to maintain the debt within safe limits. In addition to outstanding debt, the Government of Indonesia also continues to pay close attention to several variables related to debt sustainability. First, the variable rate ratio (VR) represents interest rate risk in the medium term, which is still within safe limits, which is 16.29% from 20% (March 2022). The increase in the VR ratio in the last two years was due to the issuance of SBN to Bank of Indonesia in accordance with the 2020 SKB II (Burden Sharing II) for Public Goods and the 2021 SKB III (Burden Sharing III) for handling health and protecting Indonesian people, as well as the withdrawal of program loans that were large enough for the needs of handling the impact of COVID-19 and the national economic recovery program. Second, refinancing risk is considered to be under control. This is reflected in the debt maturity ratio in 1 year, which has been maintained below a maximum of 12.5%, from 2017 (9.9%) to March 2022 (5.3%).

In the future, the Government of Indonesia will continue to maintain debt sustainability through various policies and strategies as follows[10]: (1) Optimizing funding potential from domestic sources of debt and foreign debt sources as a complement, (2) Increasing coordination with BI in fulfilling debt financing both BI as a backstop (SKB I in 2020) as well as the implementation of SKB III in 2021, (3) developing the SBN market through instrument diversification to encourage cost and risk efficiency, as well as market needs, (4) expanding the investor base, (5) managing portfolios by utilizing hedging instruments and other liabilities management mechanisms, and (6) controlling the debt-to-GDP ratio at a safe limit taking into account the post-COVID-19 economic and financial market conditions.

Accordingly, Indonesia financing policy is directed at (1) closing the budget deficit as a consequence of expansionary and consolidative fiscal policy; (2) performing prudent and sustainable debt management; (3) controlling the level of debt risk at a safe and credible level; (4) supporting financial market deepening (financial deepening); (5) utilizing SAL to maintain economic stability and anticipate uncertainty and enhancing the effectiveness of investment financing to support economic transformation; (6) encouraging financing innovation (among others strengthening the role of BUMN, BLU, SWF and SMV as well as encouraging more massive PPP schemes); and (7) improving integrated cash management management to maintain a reliable and efficient fiscal buffer.

9.3 BRI in Indonesia: Development Breakthrough

The BRI, inaugurated by the Chinese Government in 2013, represents a novel endeavor in the realm of regional economic development. China, as a prominent global economic powerhouse, aspires to rekindle the legacy of the Silk Road, an ancient trade route that historically linked Asia, Africa, the Middle East, and Europe. The BRI, serving as a contemporary global economic corridor, is designed to establish connections with 71 nations, including Indonesia. Furthermore, the BRI encapsulates a vision of fostering cross-continental connectivity, encompassing both land and maritime routes. Within this initiative, the Chinese government asserts that the BRI presents an opportunity for countries across Asia, Africa, and Europe to collectively finance the development of various sectors, particularly infrastructure and industrial facilities. To be more precise, the Chinese government has delineated five priority areas of cooperation, namely, (1) policy coordination, (2) facility connectivity, (3) unimpeded trade, (4) financial integration, and (5) cooperation at the grass root level.[11]

---

[10] Kerangka Ekonomi Makro dan Pokok-Pokok Kebijakan Fiskal (2022).

[11] Kurniawan (2018).

The BRI program initiated by China is expected to bring broad benefits to Indonesia, especially as an alternative source of financing in the context of accelerating infrastructure development. According to the World Bank (WB) quoted by Yakti,[12] BRI can provide benefits for countries that are members of it, including reducing mileage by 12%, increasing trading capacity between 2.7% and 9.7%, and reducing extreme poverty to 7.6 million people. Moreover, the BRI can also increase country revenue by 3.4%. This claim needs to be explored further. Several BRI projects in Indonesia can prove whether BRI is an alternative financing for infrastructure development in developing countries in Asia, Africa, and Europe, or whether BRI has a debt risk as the narrative that is developing in the West Countries.

In Indonesia, the BRI project was agreed upon in 2013 during the administration of President Susilo Bambang Yudhoyono. In the agreement, the two countries have agreed on at least six aspects, namely, industry, economy, trade, maritime, tourism, meteorology and climatology, and aerospace.[13] In its development, the BRI China project in Indonesia has begun to be implemented. The project that the public is most familiar with is the construction of a high-speed train connecting Jakarta (DKI Jakarta) and Bandung (West Java). Megaproject undertaken by PT. Kereta Cepat Indonesia-China (PT. KCIC) aims to improve the ease of regional access and encourage economic development in the area traversed. The Indonesia-China consortium was built in 2015 to carry out construction on the USD6.9 billion Jakarta-Bandung high-speed rail project.[14] After completion of the construction phase, this project will operate and can save travel time of approximately 2 h 15 min, from a normal travel time of 3 h to approximately 45 min.

From an economic point of view, the high-speed train project appears to have good prospects to accelerate the domestic economy. This project is currently under construction and is capable of absorbing 39 thousand workers in the construction sector. In the future, when this project starts operating, it will provide positive benefits such as accelerating regional development in the area, regional economic growth and facilitating the flow of goods and services. In terms of technology, this project will also be followed by the process of technology transfer in the railway and construction sectors from China to Indonesia. For the second-round benefit, this high-speed train project also provides an opportunity for Indonesia to build a high-speed train carriage factory in West Java. The factory will stand on an area of 500 ha and open up job opportunities for thousands of people in the future.

The next BRI project in Indonesia is the Morowali Industrial Park development project undertaken by PT. Indonesia Morowali Industrial Park (PT. IMIP). This project is an industrial area with main products based on nickel, stainless steel and carbon steel. Moreover, the industrial area also runs a business in the field of coal power plants, silicon, chrome, lime, coke, and others, to ocean ports and airports. Thus, the Morowali industrial area has a very long industrial chain. PT. IMIP, which started work on the Morowali Industrial Park project in 2014, has invested 10.2

[12] Yakti (2020).

[13] Pashya (2021).

[14] Rahayu and Sukmana (2022).

billion USD in funds from a joint venture company, Shanghai Decent Investment (Group) China, PT Sulawesi Mining Investment, and PT Bintang Eight Investama, with ownership of 49.69%, 25%, and 25.31%, respectively.[15]

This project provides many economic benefits. The presence of the Morowali Industrial Area has opened up opportunities for local communities to develop, such as knowledge, absorption of technology, and job opportunities for the surrounding community. In addition, the Morowali Industrial Area project also encourages economic growth, both regionally and nationally. Through the development of supporting infrastructure, a number of new economic growth areas have emerged around the Morowali Industrial Area. This indirectly also improves the welfare of the surrounding community.

From an economic perspective, the Morowali Industrial Area contributed 6.38 billion USD in export value in 2020. This figure increased significantly compared to 2015, which was 203 million USD. Increasing production and investment capacity also have a positive impact on state revenues. Throughout 2020, PT. IMIP has contributed to the country's revenue of IDR5.4 trillion. This number increased significantly compared to 2015, which amounted to IDR306 billion. PT. IMIP states that deposits to the state are expected to increase by approximately 10% to 15% annually. In terms of manpower, the Morowali Industrial Area can absorb as many as 20 thousand direct workers and 86 thousand workers related to industrial activities. Another benefit derived from the Morowali Industrial Area is the development of energy sources through a steam power plant with a capacity of 2 × 350 MW whose benefits can be felt by the surrounding population.

Another project included in the BRI is the construction of the Weda Bay Industrial Park. The industrial area located in Halmahera has the main product in the form of nickel. Initially, Weda Bay Industrial Park was a joint venture between a Canadian company and PT. Antam Indonesia. Later, China's Tsingshan Group took over 57% ownership in 2017, while the rest was taken over by the French mining and metallurgy company Eramet.[16] The investment value in the project reached 10 billionUSD.[17]

This project benefits the local and national economy. In 2020, Weda Bay Industrial Park contributed 5.47% to the GRDP growth of the manufacturing sector in North Maluku Province. In addition, this park is also able to contribute to increasing the income of the surrounding community because more than 90% of the workers at Weda Bay Industrial Park are local residents. The project is able to absorb a workforce of 32 thousand people. Another benefit obtained is the existence of a 750 MW power plant that can be utilized by the community around the area.

The next project is the construction of the Probolinggo-Banyuwangi toll road connecting Probolinggo City and Banyuwangi Regency in East Java. The project is a collaborative project between PTs. Jasa Marga (Indonesia) with China Communications Construction Indonesia. For this project, China Communications Construction

[15] Tuwo (2020).

[16] Tsingshan and Eramet's Indonesia Weda Bay nickel project starts production (2020).

[17] Chinese company PT IWIP's investment in Halmahera reaches USD 10 billion (2020).

Table 9.1 BRI projects in Indonesia

Project	Economic benefits	Employment benefits	Other benefits
High Speed Train Jakarta Bandung	1. Acceleration of travel time from Jakarta to Bandung 2. Regional economic development of the area being passed	39 thousand (only construction)	Build a Carriage Factory 500 ha
Morowali Industrial Area	1. New source of economic growth 2. Increase exports by USD6.38 billion (2020) 3. Improve CAD 4. Increase taxes by IDR5.4 trillion	106 thousand	Electric powerplant with a capacity of 2 × 350 MW
Weda Bay Industrial Park	1. Mobilize the local economy and promote national recovery. (GDP of the North Maluku manufacturing sector grows 5.47% in 2020) 2. Encouraging an increase in the income of local residents 3. Increase Exports by USD4 billion	32 thousand	Electric powerplant with a capacity of 750 MW
Probolinggo Banyuwangi Toll Road	1. Save travel time approximately 2 h 2. Encouraging the flow of goods and services	N/a	N/a

Sources Multiple sources

Indonesia invested 1.61 billion USD to build a 172-km toll road.[18] Generally, this project brings benefits for Indonesia, especially connecting some regions in East Java Province. With the toll road, people can save approximately 2 h of travel time (Table 9.1).

With such great benefits, Chinese investment in Indonesia through the BRI program opens up enormous opportunities for accelerating Indonesia's infrastructure development in the future. It has been stated that Indonesia has a greater investment need than the accumulation of domestic savings. For this reason, Indonesia needs FDI from abroad to meet its investment needs.

[18] Rini (2019).

9.4 BRI in Indonesia: Narrative of Debt Risk

The BRI holds the potential to contribute to the transformation of Indonesia's economic landscape. However, it also introduces certain challenges that warrant a comprehensive examination. Currently, two main issues are under discussion in the public domain, namely, concerns related to debt risk and the dominance of Chinese labor in the BRI's project in Indonesia.

One recurring criticism of Chinese investment projects under the BRI in Indonesia pertains to the potential debt risk. It is essential to note, however, that not all BRI projects in Indonesia carry this risk. Debt sustainability is a paramount consideration for Indonesia, as it actively engages in the BRI. To finance ambitious infrastructure projects, the nation requires substantial financial resources. Consequently, the government, through state-owned enterprises (BUMN), promotes collaboration with the private sector to undertake these strategic projects. In Indonesia, BRI projects primarily follow a business-to-business model. Nevertheless, the government does provide debt guarantees for certain specific projects.

Jakarta-Bandung High-Speed Rail Project: One of the projects often cited in discussions about debt risk is the Jakarta-Bandung High-Speed Rail Project. This ambitious endeavor aims to connect the capital city of Jakarta with the city of Bandung in West Java through a high-speed railway network. While the project holds the promise of significantly reducing travel time between these two major urban centers, it has raised concerns due to several factors.

The Jakarta-Bandung High-Speed Rail Project involves substantial construction costs, including the development of tunnels and bridges across challenging terrains. The sheer magnitude of investment needed has raised eyebrows, as it can strain the financial resources of the Indonesian government. Another point of contention is the profitability of the project. Questions have been raised about whether the revenue generated from ticket sales and other related services will be sufficient to cover the project's operational and maintenance costs in the long run.

Concerns also revolve around the long-term financial viability of the high-speed rail. If the project does not generate the expected returns or faces operational challenges, it could lead Indonesia into a debt spiral. While the Jakarta-Bandung High-Speed Rail Project has been a focal point of debate due to these concerns, it is important to note that the Indonesian government has been actively working on financial arrangements and risk mitigation strategies to address these challenges. Properly managed, this project has the potential to enhance transportation infrastructure and connectivity between two major urban areas.

Despite bringing significant positive impacts, the Jakarta-Bandung high-speed railway project also carries potential risks, especially in terms of debt risk. With a construction cost of 7.2 billion USD, a substantial 75% of this funding originates from loans provided by PT. KCIC, the consortium responsible for the project, from the China Development Bank.[19] Given the magnitude of this debt, there are concerns

[19] Lestarini (2023).

that PT. KCIC may struggle to repay it, as the project is expected to generate profits below initial expectations.

Bhima Yudistira, an economist and the director of the Center of Economics and Law Studies, has expressed his concerns that the Jakarta-Bandung high-speed railway project may turn into a debt trap.[20] A sentiment echoing this concern has also been expressed by Yusuf Rendi, an economist at the Center of Reform on Economics Indonesia in 2023. He has stated that the Jakarta-Bandung high-speed railway project could become a debt trap if the project management does not promptly generate the expected revenue.[21]

While these investments hold the promise of economic growth and development, the looming risk of accumulating unsustainable levels of debt is a cause for concern, especially when projects do not yield the expected returns. Drawing from cautionary tales in Africa, where countries such as Zimbabwe, Cameroon, and Djibouti struggled to repay BRI-related debts, we find valuable lessons.[22] Mismanaging these debts could undermine Indonesia's economic sovereignty, leaving it vulnerable to external pressures and compromises.

Despite the prevalence of narratives expressing concerns about debt risks associated with the high-speed train project, the Indonesian government assures that the project is relatively secure and unlikely to result in uncontrollable debt risks. Wahyu Utomo,[23] the director of the Center for the State Budget Policy at the Ministry of Finance, articulated that the default risk associated with the high-speed train project is highly quantifiable. Consequently, the government provides assurance through the National Budget (APBN). Furthermore, the scale of the debt is relatively modest when compared to the fiscal capacity of the government, thereby minimizing potential risks.

Indonesia's experience with the BRI has also generated a narrative that suggests that Chinese workers dominate the nation's labor market, particularly in projects backed by Chinese investments. However, a closer examination of official data from the Ministry of Manpower in 2022 reveals a more nuanced reality. While it is true that Chinese workers constitute a significant portion of foreign laborers in Indonesia, comprising 42% of this demographic, their presence diminishes when considered within the context of Indonesia's vast workforce. When we calculate the percentage of Chinese workers relative to the entire Indonesian population working in the country, their presence is minimal, accounting for only 0.03%.

Moreover, the growth rate of Chinese workers in Indonesia over the past four years has been relatively modest. From 2018 to 2021, the number of Chinese workers in Indonesia increased by just 17%. In 2018, the number stood at 32.2 thousand, indicating that the overall trajectory of Chinese labor migration to Indonesia has been gradual rather than explosive. These data-driven insights challenge the prevailing narrative of Chinese workers dominating the Indonesian labor market. While they

[20] Idris (2023).

[21] Rachman (2023).

[22] Al-Fadhat and Prasetio (2022).

[23] Praditya (2023).

constitute a notable segment of foreign labor, they represent only a fraction of the broader Indonesian workforce. The perception of dominance may stem from specific high-profile projects where Chinese labor is more visible, but this does not necessarily reflect the broader reality.

It is imperative to acknowledge that foreign labor, including Chinese workers, plays a significant role in various sectors of the Indonesian economy, contributing notably to infrastructure development, manufacturing, and various other industries. These foreign workers are subject to regulations and policies established by the Indonesian government aimed at ensuring equitable competition and safeguarding labor rights.

Yusuf Wibisono, an economist and the director of IDEAS Indonesia in 2003, has asserted that Chinese investments consistently come accompanied by Chinese labor.[24] This phenomenon is largely due to the substantial size of China's labor force, leading its government to have a policy of exporting its labor force in conjunction with its investments. This practice can potentially impact the absorption of local labor in the Indonesian workforce.

Another significant challenge associated with the BRI is the readiness of Indonesia's workforce to embrace technology transfers. While these transfers have the potential to foster skill development and technological advancement, it is crucial for Indonesia to ensure that its labor force is adequately prepared to absorb and apply these new technologies. The consequences of a lack of readiness in this regard are multifaceted. First, it impedes the full realization of the benefits offered by technology transfers. Indonesian companies may struggle to adopt and adapt to these advanced technologies, limiting their competitiveness on the global stage. This, in turn, hinders the full potential of the BRI's promise of economic growth and technological advancement.

Moreover, a lack of workforce readiness perpetuates the technological gap between Indonesia and more advanced economies. While the BRI aims to bridge infrastructure gaps, a workforce unprepared to leverage modern technologies may impede the country's long-term economic development. This technological lag could have cascading effects on various sectors, hindering innovation and productivity.

Furthermore, the failure to adequately prepare Indonesia's workforce can exacerbate social inequality. As technology-driven industries flourish, those lacking the necessary skills may find themselves marginalized in the job market, further deepening income disparities. This social divide can contribute to social unrest and political instability, posing additional challenges to the successful implementation of the BRI in Indonesia.

The BRI holds the promise of significant economic growth for Indonesia but is fraught with complexities. By addressing issues of debt sustainability, workforce readiness, misconceptions about Chinese labor dominance, and the potential of debt risk through strategic and transparent approaches, Indonesia can effectively navigate its BRI journey. In doing so, the nation can harness the benefits while safeguarding its economic sovereignty and societal well-being. Indonesia's path within the BRI is

---

[24] Alfarizi and Hidayat (2023).

intricate, but with the right strategies and policies in place, it can lead to a brighter economic future.

9.5 Conclusion

In summary, China's BRI, initiated by the Chinese government, offers opportunities for many developing countries to fund their development, particularly in infrastructure. BRI projects in Indonesia have generally yielded economic benefits at local and national levels. However, concerns regarding the rumored debt risk associated with the BRI program require ongoing vigilance.

Financially, the Indonesian government maintains a robust fiscal position capable of addressing various economic dynamics, including those related to debt risk. Prudent debt management in Indonesia supports numerous development initiatives. Consequently, the notion of a Chinese debt risk stemming from BRI projects remains more of a myth than a reality.

Thus far, the primary challenge faced in BRI projects in Indonesia pertains to the Jakarta-Bandung high-speed rail project. Delays and cost overruns have been attributed to factors beyond the project implementers' control, such as escalating land acquisition costs. The central government has stepped in by providing state capital participation to address these issues. From the perspective of fiscal sustainability, this intervention is deemed secure, given that the expenses related to the high-speed rail project problems remain relatively low compared to the fiscal capacity of the Indonesian government.

To conclude, Indonesia's participation in the BRI offers a wealth of opportunities, but it also comes with its share of challenges. To fully harness the potential benefits while effectively addressing these challenges, Indonesia can adopt a set of strategic approaches and policy recommendations. In this section, we delve into these strategies in more detail.

First, ensuring transparent and sustainable financing for BRI projects is paramount. Indonesia should prioritize conducting comprehensive cost–benefit analyses for long-term financial viability. This involves a thorough evaluation of the economic, social, and environmental impacts of each project. Transparent financing mechanisms can help in several ways: risk assessment, debt management, and public accountability.

Second, investing in workforce development and education is crucial to bridge the skills gap and prepare the labor force for technology transfers, a central aspect of many BRI projects. Collaborating with Chinese institutions can be particularly beneficial in this regard. Here is why capacity building is essential:

- Skills Enhancement: Offering training programs and educational initiatives can enhance the skills of Indonesian workers. This includes not only technical skills but also soft skills such as adaptability and cross-cultural communication, which are valuable in international collaborations.

- Technology Transfer: Collaborating with Chinese institutions can facilitate technology transfer and knowledge sharing. Joint research and development initiatives can accelerate the adoption of advanced technologies in Indonesian industries.
- Competitiveness: A well-prepared workforce contributes to the competitiveness of Indonesian firms on the global stage. This is essential for maximizing the benefits of BRI-related trade and investments.

Third, establishing robust risk assessment and management frameworks is essential to navigate the complexities of BRI projects. These frameworks should be designed to evaluate the financial implications of debt guarantees and other potential risks. Key considerations include:

- Project-Specific Risk Assessment: Each BRI project should undergo a detailed risk assessment, considering factors such as political stability, market demand, and potential cost overruns. This information can inform decision-making and help prioritize projects with the most favorable risk profiles.
- Contingency Planning: Indonesia should develop contingency plans to mitigate risks effectively. This could involve setting aside financial reserves for unforeseen challenges or establishing mechanisms for renegotiating terms with project partners.
- Regular Monitoring and Evaluation: Continuous monitoring and evaluation of ongoing projects are crucial to identify emerging risks and take corrective actions promptly. This proactive approach can prevent minor issues from escalating into major challenges.

References

Alfarizi, M. K. & Hidayat, A. A. N., "Banjir pekerja China di proyek kereta cepat Jakarta Bandung", *Tempo*, 2023, https://fokus.tempo.co/read/1763362/banjir-pekerja-cina-di-proyek-kereta-cepat-jakarta-bandung.

Al-Fadhat, F., & Prasetio, H., How China's Debt-trap diplomacy works in African countries: evidence from Zimbabwe, Cameroon, and Djibouti, *Journal of Asian and African Studies*, 2022,doc.00219096221137673.

"Chinese company PT IWIP's investment in Halmahera reaches USD 10 billion", *Asiatoday*, 2020, https://asiatoday.id/read/investasi-perusahaan-China-pt-iwip-di-halmahera-capai-usd10-milia.

"Debt/GDP", Tradingeconomics, 2022, https://tradingeconomics.com/matrix.

"Dataset APBN", Ministry of Finance of Indonesia, 2022, http://www.data-apbn.kemenkeu.go.id/Dataset/Topics/1.

"Directorate General of Budget Financing and Risk Management", Ministry of Finance of Indonesia, 2022, https://www.djppr.kemenkeu.go.id/page/load/785.

"Directorate General of Budget Financing and Risk Management", the Ministry of Finance of Indonesia, 2022, https://www.djppr.kemenkeu.go.id/page/load/29.

"External debt statistics of Indonesia", Bank of Indonesia, 2022, https://www.bi.go.id/en/statistik/ekonomi-keuangan/sulni/PublishingImages/Pages/SULNI-Agustus-2022/SULNI_August_2022.pdf.

"Five things you need to know about the Maastricht Treaty", European Central Bank, 2020, https://www.ecb.europa.eu/ecb/educational/explainers/tell-me-more/html/25_years_maastricht.en.html.

Idris, M., "Disebut jebakan China, berapa utang kereta cepat?", Kompas, September 24, 2023, https://money.kompas.com/read/2023/09/24/121023026/disebut-jebakan-china-berapa-bunga-utang-kereta-cepat?page=all.

"Kerangka Ekonomi Makro dan Pokok-Pokok Kebijakan Fiskal", *Fiscal Policy Agency*, 2022,https://fiskal.kemenkeu.go.id/publikasi/kem-ppkf#:~:text=Dokumen%20KEM%20PPKF%20Tahun%202023,meningkatnya%20aktivitas%20sosial%20ekonomi%20serta.

Kurniawan, Y., One Belt One Road (OBOR): Agenda Keamanan Liberal Tiongkok?, Jurnal Politica Dinamika Masalah Politik Dalam Negeri dan Hubungan Internasional, Vol.7, No.2, 2018.

Lestarini, A. H., "Terjebak utang Tiongkok di proyek kereta cepat Jakarta-Bandung", *Metro TV*, 2023, https://www.metrotvnews.com/read/bD2C1rpy-terjebak-utang-tiongkok-di-proyek-kereta-cepat-jakarta-bandung.

Makmun, "Debat kusir seputar utang Pemerintah", 2009, https://fiskal.kemenkeu.go.id/kajian/2009/07/13/125252-debat-kusir-seputar-utang-pemerintah.

Nurmillah, A., "Memahami utang Pemerintah", 2021, https://www.djkn.kemenkeu.go.id/artikel/baca/14049/Memahami-Utang-Pemerintah.html.

Pashya, M, H., "Belt and Road Initiative di Indonesia: Perkembangan, kritik, dan alternatif", *kumparan.com*, 2021, https://kumparan.com/introvert-note/belt-and-road-initiative-di-indonesia-perkembangan-kriik-dan-alternatif-1vRtw7nbzLo/3.

Praditya, I. I., "Proyek kereta cepat dijamin APBN, Kemenkeu: tenang, Cuma Rp824 miliar", liputan6.com, 2023, https://www.liputan6.com/bisnis/read/5407563/proyek-kereta-cepat-dijamin-apbn-kemenkeutenang-cuma-rp-824-miliar?page=2.

Rahayu, I. R. S. & Sukmana, Y., "5 penyebab biaya proyek kereta cepat Jakarta Bandung bengkak", *Kompas*, 2022, https://money.kompas.com/read/2022/04/09/043000926/5-penyebab-biaya-proyek-kereta-cepat-jakarta-bandung-bengkak?page=all.

Rini, A. S., "Jasa Marga (JSMR) gandeng China bangun jalan tol Probolinggo-Banyuwangi. Bisnis Indonesia", 2019, https://market.bisnis.com/read/20191106/192/1167351/jasa-marga-jsmr-gandeng-investor-China-bikin-jalan-tol-probolinggo-banyuwangi.

Rachman, A., "Proyek kereta cepat bukti RI masuk jebakan utang China?", CNBC Indonesia, April 14, 2023, https://www.cnbcindonesia.com/news/20230414163523-4-430086/proyek-kereta-cepat-bukti-ri-masuk-jebakan-utang-China.

Tuwo, A. G & Hidayati, N., "China: PT IMIP Ubah Morowali dari Desa Terpencil Jadi Kota Industri", *Kumparan,* 2020, https://kumparan.com/kumparannews/china-pt-imip-ubah-morowali-dari-desa-terpencil-jadi-kota-industri-1tXAlnTrFiZ/1.

"Tsingshan and Eramet's Indonesia Weda Bay nickel project starts production", *Reuters*, 2020, https://www.reuters.com/article/us-indonesia-nickel-idUSKBN22C1UK.

Yakti, P. D., *Belt and Road Initiative RRT: Kemunculan dan Perluasan Orde Developmentalisme Di Indo-Asia-Pasifik sebagai Tandingan Liberalisme AS,* Doctoral dissertation, UNIVERSITAS AIRLANGGA, 2020.

Chapter 10
Bangladesh's Debt Management and BRI

Kazi Mahmudur Rahman

Abstract Bangladesh is set to graduate from the category of least developed countries (LDCs) and has undertaken various infrastructural development projects to expedite the country's economic growth. China has been a significant investor in this initiative through its Belt and Road Initiative (BRI), a massive infrastructure project, and is providing a substantial amount of funding for Bangladesh's numerous development projects. By building an economic corridor, the BRI accord seeks to provide a chance for Bangladesh to grow in financial markets and expand its infrastructure. However, China is facing significant charges for its lending known as "debt trap diplomacy", which refers to its policy of lending to developing nations and the consequences for borrowing countries if they fail to repay. The goal of this chapter is to assess Bangladesh's worries over the goals and repercussions of the Chinese BRI program while keeping Bangladesh's debt repayment commitments in mind by analyzing the larger economic effects and implications. This study suggests that Bangladesh must apply more vigilance in areas of governance, foreign exchange movements, debt repayment strategy, effective execution of projects, corruption concerns, transparency and so on to avoid falling into a "debt trap". Before establishing debt repayment agreements, Bangladesh should review the realities of the debt position, gauge honest projections, and estimate the expected risks. As a result, before engaging in debt repayment agreements, this chapter provided an avenue for Bangladesh to review the realities of its debt position, analyze accurate forecasts, and quantify the potential risks.

Keywords BRI · China · Bangladesh · Debt · Infrastructure

K. M. Rahman (✉)
Department of Social Sciences and Humanities, Independent University, Dhaka, Bangladesh
e-mail: mahmudur.rahman@iub.edu.bd

N. Peng and M. Y. Cheng (eds.), *The Reality and Myth of BRI's Debt Trap*, Indo-Pacific Focus, https://doi.org/10.1007/978-981-97-1056-0_10

10.1 Introduction

Bangladesh has set some very high ambitions for itself, as it has boasted a steady trajectory toward economic growth and development: to establish itself as an upper middle-income country (UMIC) by 2031; to become a higher income country (HIC) by 2041; to attain major sustainable development goals (SDGs) by 2030 as a UN member state; and to graduate from the status of least developed country (LDC), among others. To accelerate economic growth, the country has embarked upon several development projects and increased investment in the development sector. At present, infrastructural development is one of the key development activities of Bangladesh. In its 8th Five-Year Plan, the National Development Strategy claims to make noteworthy progress in transforming Bangladesh' agrarian economy into a more urban and modern economy, with a focus on manufacturing and services. Some of the successful and ongoing infrastructural development projects that are predicted to assist the country in achieving these desired goals are the multipurpose Padma Bridge, which has now increased connectivity of the southwestern parts of Bangladesh to the rest of the country; the metro rail and elevated expressway in the capital in an effort to combat traffic congestion in Dhaka; the two deep-sea ports at Payra and Matarbari, which are expected to enhance trade; and the Rooppur Nuclear Power Plant, which is expected to meet the increasing demands for power in this rapidly developing country.

In addition, in its endeavors for increased infrastructural development and trade, China has been an important partner for Bangladesh. Bangladesh and China have maintained a close relationship for four decades. While trade relationships remain a higher priority, infrastructure development has also perhaps emerged as a significant activity among several other bilateral relations between these two countries. When China decided to extend support for the construction of the Padma Bridge, especially on the occasion that other partners had withdrawn their support, a display of China's new and emergent role as an important development partner of Bangladesh garnered attention. Such an event is also representative of Bangladesh's own determination and agency in negotiating partnerships, and it must be noted that the negotiations of this relationship are guided by significant political, economic and geographical contexts.

One such important context that is found at the crux of this paper's discussions is China's efforts to become the economic giant of Asia and a global superpower. The Belt and Road Initiative (BRI) is one such ambitious infrastructure project that stretches from East Asia to Europe with goals for economic and geopolitical expansion. It is in this ever-expanding list of expenditures and investments that China's interest in funding Bangladesh's development agenda comes to the fore and presents itself for some important debates about the future of Bangladesh's economy and "debt diplomacy".

China is interested in Bangladesh for the fruition of the last economic corridor in the project, the China-Bangladesh-India-Myanmar Economic Corridor (BCIM). Bangladesh's geographical positioning in South Asia makes it a strategic maritime nation because of its important entrance to the Bay of Bengal and the Indian Ocean, and Chinese policymakers take this strategic benefit into important consideration for its trade and infrastructural development in the region. When the President of China visited Bangladesh in October 2016, the implementation of various government-to-government (G2G) and business-to-business (B2B) projects was discussed, at the end of which China became Bangladesh's largest trading partner of present time upon assuring investments of approximately 40 billion USD in Bangladesh.[1] China committed to spending 24.45 billion USD on the improvement of bilateral assistance to support infrastructure projects and a further 13.6 billion USD on joint ventures. In addition, 20 billion USD in loan agreements was also committed.[2] The two countries signed eight projects for which China will finance more than 9.45 billion USD.[3] These projects include the Padma Bridge rail link valued at 3.3 billion USD; the power plant in Payra valued at 1.9 billion USD; the power grid network strengthening project valued at 1.32 billion USD; and the development of digital connectivity valued at 1 billion USD. Additionally, a contract was ratified with a China-Bangladesh consortium in 2018 after Bangladesh signed a toll road project for the first time.[4] The goal of the project is to upgrade the 48-km-long Dhaka Bypass Road to a dual carriageway so that the northern and northwestern parts of Bangladesh are better connected to Chittagong Port.

Twenty-seven projects will be financed by China, all of which have been signed by both parties.[5] Bangladeshi experts believe that China is continuing to divest from all out-label industries and instead move further up the manufacturing chain and beyond.[6] The BRI accord hopes to serve as an opportunity through which Bangladesh may advance in financial subdivisions and expand its capital market infrastructure by establishing an economic corridor. While the main goal of the BRI is the betterment of infrastructure and transport (road and railway connections, usage of ports, thermal and hydropower projects), the financial facet and the execution of these various projects to completion remains a major concern that must be taken into consideration when decisions are made for these projects.

While the interests and need to maintain relations between the countries are evident, it is not as simple as it seems. The power dynamics and tensions related to the development of infrastructure and construction with the West have posed several challenges for China. One of the biggest allegations that China now faces is that of "debt trap diplomacy", that is, its policy to lend to developing nations and the consequences that are thereafter faced by borrowing nations in case of failure to repay.

The government of Bangladesh is also concerned about this issue, and many analysts believe that Bangladesh will be able to avoid the "debt trap diplomacy"

[1] Bangladesh-China (2016).

[2] Ibid.

[3] Khatun and Saadat (2020).

[4] Chinese consortium (2018).

[5] Datta (2021).

[6] Ibid.

if these projects are managed well and completed in time. However, the dynamics of the BRI should not be assessed with simple explanations of either the China-Bangladesh relations or that of the individual but interrelated interests and needs of the two countries. The BRI must also be embedded in Bangladesh's relations with India and understood in relation to the Indo-Pacific strategy. India is an important neighboring country, and its relationship with Bangladesh carries great value for the country. Since India has not joined China in the BRI scheme, this adds even more pressure and concerns for Bangladesh. These are matters to be monitored and analyzed thoroughly, and this chapter will discuss the evidence on hand to analyze and provide a critical opinion on Bangladesh's debt management, the BRI and the concerns of China's "debt trap diplomacy".

The objective of this paper is to evaluate Bangladesh's concerns in terms of the Chinese BRI initiative's intentions and consequences, keeping in mind Bangladesh's debt repayment obligations. It will also assess the broader economy-wide ramifications and implications. This article attempts to identify three issues: (i) salient features of Bangladesh's overseas borrowings, debt servicing obligations and trends, and BRI; (ii) an evaluation of whether Bangladesh has motives to trail an instructive stance in view of attaining global and national challenges; and (iii) an avenue to be followed to overcome any anticipated risks. This paper will contribute to the debate surrounding Bangladesh's involvement with the BRI and engage in a critical discussion of China's 'debt trap diplomacy'. A desk review was conducted on various articles, news reports, media coverage and academic literature on Bangladesh's debts and progress in infrastructural development, so the country's position on debt management could be analyzed. Although the issue at hand is a concern for many economies and borrowing nations, including Bangladesh itself, the subject has not yet gathered substantial academic attention or research. Thus, the literature available on the issue is very limited. There is also a dearth of comprehensive information on China's loans, which poses a limitation for this paper as well.

10.2 Criticisms of China's BRI

The BRI is a tool for China, where it uses its enormous funds as a tactic to acquire geopolitical footholds in several regions. It connects all three continents in a network of roads and sea routes with more than 120 countries as signatories of the BRI.[7] The magnitude of the scheme is massive, and thus, China's President Xi Jinping calls BRI its project of the century. Bangladesh is also a signatory country of the BRI and a geopolitically important strategic member in China's agenda.[8] The positive response received by Bangladesh upon joining the BRI is an indication of the continual present trends in its international relationships, which are motivated to satisfy its demand for large international funding on easy terms for the construction of roads, railways,

[7] Emran (2019).

[8] Ibid.

telecom services, power plants, ports, etc.[9] The BRI also provided China with a new opportunity for its state-owned firms to escalate its infrastructure projects, specifically in energy and transport areas. Additionally, it allowed us to pave the way for arrangements with the Chinese education sector, private and civil sectors, and think tanks. Bangladesh scholars explained that China's motivation for the BRI is to strengthen its place and engagement in the global economy mainly via investments in infrastructure. The Chinese aim to restore the road system used to connect China to Europe along Central Asia ("One Belt") as well as the marine passage used to connect China to Southeast Asia, the Middle East, and Eastern Africa ("One Road"). Indeed, China persuaded 153 countries with 32 international organizations to sign more than 200 cooperation proposals by 2023.[10]

Another aspect of the BRI to note is China's infrastructure war with the Western world. Shazzad states that "the debt-trap diplomacy" narrative against China is thought to have originated from the "infrastructure war" between China and the Western world.[11] Brautigam and Rithmire remarked that the Chinese have learned over the last two decades how to fare in the international construction market.[12] Twenty-seven of the 100 leading global contractors are now Chinese firms, whereas this number was only 9 in 2000. In comparison, Europe now has 37 firms in the list, where it had 41 in 2000, and the number of U.S. firms in the list has sharply fallen to 7 from its previous count of 19 firms since 2000.

The main difference between China and Western countries in regard to lending to developing nations is that the Western world's loans are conditional. They often set preconditions for policy reforms and macroeconomic stability and debt relief if preconditions in the policy reforms are met. China does not follow this strategy. Green has presented the main differences between the lending principles of China and the common patron states called the Paris Club.[13] The members of the Paris Club are a community of 22 countries that act as autonomous creditors and are devoted to sustainable payment solutions for poorer borrower countries, with also offers of debt relief on the table on the condition that a debtor launches reforms to repair its macroeconomic and financial state. Conversely, where the Paris Club offers such clarity and economic sustainability, China abstains from such globally standard sustainable and clear loan practices. China prefers to trade loans for a country's critical resources. They do not follow the norms that the International Monetary Fund (IMF) and World Bank (WB) generally endorse to ensure transparency, which in turn aids policy-making, thwarts debt crises, and deters corruption.[14]

---

[9] Datta (2021).

[10] Yan Fujing and Chen Weiwei. *Wo Guo Yi Yu 152 Ge Guo Jia, 32 Ge Guo Ji Zu Zhi Qian Shu Gong Jian 'Yi Dai Yi Lu' He Zuo Wen Jian* [China has singed cooperation agreements on jointly building BRI with 152 countries and 32 international organizations], *Ri Min Ri.* Bao (2023).

[11] Hussain (2021).

[12] Brautigam and Rithmire (2021).

[13] Green (2019).

[14] OECD (2012).

However, China's lending policy differs on these principles. Chellaney states that China is not concerned with evaluating a borrower country's creditworthiness and its ability to repay.[15] This motivates developing nations to borrow from China so that they may retain their sovereignty. However, when developing countries fail to return these Chinese loans for multibillion-dollar projects, it results in a loss of strategic assets along with increased vulnerability in their respective economic development as well as loss of sovereignty.[16] As the debt burden on the borrower increases, China's own leverage also becomes greater. He also elaborates on a new international study that has shed light on the vigorous and exploitative loan practices of China by investigating 100 contracts with 24 countries, many of which are part of the BRI. The analysis deduced that China gains great leverage through these contracts and agreements, which surpass global lending contracts. Furthermore, China's loan agreements require collateral arrangements, such as lender-controlled revenue accounts. These proceedings ensure loan reimbursements through revenue inflow from goods exportation, which allows debt-for-equity trade and relinquishes critical resources to the Chinese.[17]

Another concern is the lack of transparency in Chinese lending data, loans and reporting of lending in the government system. Wang cites from a study conducted by Aid Data, an international development body at William & Mary University in the US, that records of at least half of China's lending to developing countries cannot be found in official debt statistics.[18] The data are not recorded in the government balance sheets but rather recorded in state-owned companies, banks, joint ventures and private institutions. As we know, the majority of China's BRI debt has been disbursed to be invested in large infrastructure projects such as roads, railways and ports and even in infrastructure projects pertaining to the energy and mining industries. However, Wang explains that China does not publish records of its foreign loans.[19] In fact, most of its contracts contain nondisclosure clauses, which creates a lack of transparency regarding the terms and agreements of the deals and limits borrowers from disclosing any information related to the loan. China's argument for such nondisclosure is that such a type of confidentiality is a common practice is in the field of international loan contracts. In contrast, the major industrialized nations share information on lending activities.

Green further points out that, "according to a study by IMF, China's contribution to the public debt of heavily indebted poor countries nearly doubled from 6.2 to 11.6% from 2013 to 2016".[20] While BRI has boosted China's lending, many observers express their doubts about the financial usefulness of some BRI projects, suspecting that the action is in part driven by the Chinese desire to boost its own economy by attaining strategic assets. The economic entry to these resources could then be

[15] Chellaney (2021).
[16] Green (2019).
[17] Gelpern et al. (2021).
[18] Wang (2022).
[19] Ibid.
[20] Green (2019).

used in political and strategic domination in the beneficiary states. Wang depicts China as one of the world's largest single-creditor nations and notes that there has been a threefold rise over the span of a decade in the amount of loans that China has disbursed to lower- and middle-income countries, reaching a total of 170 billion USD by the end of 2020.[21]

Moreover, China has a higher rate of interest than Western governments. Wang rightly points out that with interest rates at approximately 4%, these debts are nearer to the rates found in commercial markets but are quadruple that of a conventional loan given by the likes of the WB or an autonomous country such as France or Germany.[22] In contrast, Japan's interest rates for its infrastructure loans to developing countries mostly run below half a percent. Additionally, the needed repayment period for a loan from China is quite short, just under 10 years, in comparison to other lending countries' time limit for loan repayment of approximately 28 years for developing countries. It is also important to note, however, that as Bangladesh's position has shifted from a low-income country (LIC) to an LMIC (low-middle income country), opportunities for low-cost borrowing are rapidly shrinking. It is no longer eligible for borrowing from the World Bank on soft terms, where the interest and service charges of the loans are very low.[23] In contrast, Bangladesh will only be able to borrow from WB on commercial International Bank for Reconstruction and Development (IBRD) terms. As recent events have shown, when financiers such as WB refused to fund the construction of the Padma Bridge, China swooped in with an alternative financing option.

10.3 Bangladesh's Debt Management

Bangladesh's outstanding foreign debt amounted to 68.25 billion USD as of March 2022, which is a 16.9% share of its GDP and 91.3% share of its foreign exchange earnings from exports and remittances. These figures are rather impressive, as they are much lower than the thresholds used by the IMF and WB to assess a country's debt-carrying strengths, which are currently at 55% share of GDP and 240% share of earnings from exports and remittances for Bangladesh.

10.3.1 External Debt Management

The amount of foreign debt that Bangladesh has borrowed has steadily increased over the last decade. A study by a foreign source of the state's debt reparation statistics shows that the net flow of foreign debt has increased remittances in FY2022-23

[21] Oloruntade (2022).

[22] Wang (2022).

[23] Rahman (2021).

in contrast to the earlier fiscal year because principal payments rose by 7.61%. According to Rahman, this is set to rise furthermore to take into account higher foreign borrowings to underwrite fiscal deficits and service development needs.[24] Bangladesh's foreign debt is projected to be more than USD 12 billion in the current FY2023. Indeed, there has been a 22.1% rise in public sector debt between June FY2020 and June FY2021.

It is also important to note that as foreign debt has increased steadily for Bangladesh, the proportion of grants in its loan portfolio has also been on a steady decline. According to Rahman, where the shares of loans and grants in total disbursed borrowing were 49.3% and 50.7%, respectively, in FY1992, the same rose to 66.8% and 33.2% in FY2002 and then to 93.6% and 6.4%, respectively, in FY2021.[25]

The Economic Relations Division (ERD) manages Bangladesh's foreign debts and has the ability to manage it at a global standard. The division has been managing its debt for the last 30 years using the internationally standardized software 'Debt Management Financial Analysis System' (DMFAS). At present, the foreign loans accepted by the Bangladeshi government are medium- and long-term debts, all of which are concessional.

10.3.2 Debt Servicing

The ERD also manages foreign debt repayment and boasts to have never failed to make foreign loan repayments in due time since independence. Similarly, the ERD has also never needed rescheduling repayment installments either. In FY 2021–22, the division paid a total amount of 2017.7 million USD against foreign debts to development partners. Of this, the principal amount was 1526.72 million USD, and the remaining 490.98 million USD was paid in interest. The budget allocation for foreign loan repayments in 2023–2024 FY is 1.78 billion USD. This is a good indicator for Bangladesh, and if this trend continues, the country can avoid falling into any debt trap, be it of China or any other foreign lender. However, it must also be noted that foreign debt servicing liabilities are predicted to be on the rise in the future, especially in the cases of strict term loans such as those received from China, India and Russia, where repayments will have to be made in the next couple of years. These loans are semi and nonconcessional in nature and incur service charges, and the cost of delays in the implementation of the projects contribute to additional financial burdens on the debt repayment.

---

[24] Ibid.

[25] Rahman (2019).

Table 10.1 Bangladesh's foreign obligation sustainability indicators (2016–2022)

Financial year indicators	Foreign debt to		Debt service to	
	GDP (%)	Export plus remittance (%)	Revenue (%)	Export plus remittance (%)
2016–17	12.8	63.6	7.9	4.0
2017–18	13.9	68.6	8.3	3.9
2018–19	14.7	69.78	9.4	4.4
2019–20	15.5	88.45	10.2	5.5
2020–21	16.9	85.87	8.4	4.7
2021–22	13.78	79.14	9.22	4.59
Threshold level	40	180	18	15

Source Economic Relations Division https://erd.gov.bd/site/page/a2035999-b8c0-4e37-8067-b05c0b7e7482/2F--Debt-sustainability-indicators-for-public-sector

10.3.3 Debt Sustainability

According to the IMF, debt sustainability is the state at which a "government is able to meet all its current and future payment obligations without exceptional financial assistance or going into default." Foreign debt sustainability is determined using various indicators worldwide.[26] A very common indicator to determine foreign loan sustainability is the foreign debt status coupled with the relative analysis of the GDP of the country, earnings from exports, and revenue proceeds with principals and interest reimbursements. Until now, the WB and IMF have resolved the borderline risk of debt sustainability indicators for developing countries. A relative graph of Bangladesh's foreign obligation sustainability indicators from 2016 to 2022 is shown in Table 10.1.

A close examination of the above evidence shows that the offshore debt sustainability of Bangladesh is far lower than the highest risk limit. From this, it can be affirmed that the country's risk limit is at an acceptable degree. It is also important to note that an overwhelming 93.9% of Bangladesh's foreign debt is of long-term nature, which allows the country to strategize adequately with regard to debt repayment and debt sustainability. The following tables will make the debt sustainability issue of Bangladesh clearer (Graph 10.1 and Table 10.2).

[26] Flow of External Resources into Bangladesh, 2020–2021, Golden Jubilee Special Edition. Economics Relations Division, Ministry of Finance, Government of Bangladesh. https://erd.portal.gov.bd/site/page/7f192f96-1442-48b4-a947-2e09ce30ec54/Flow-of-Exter.

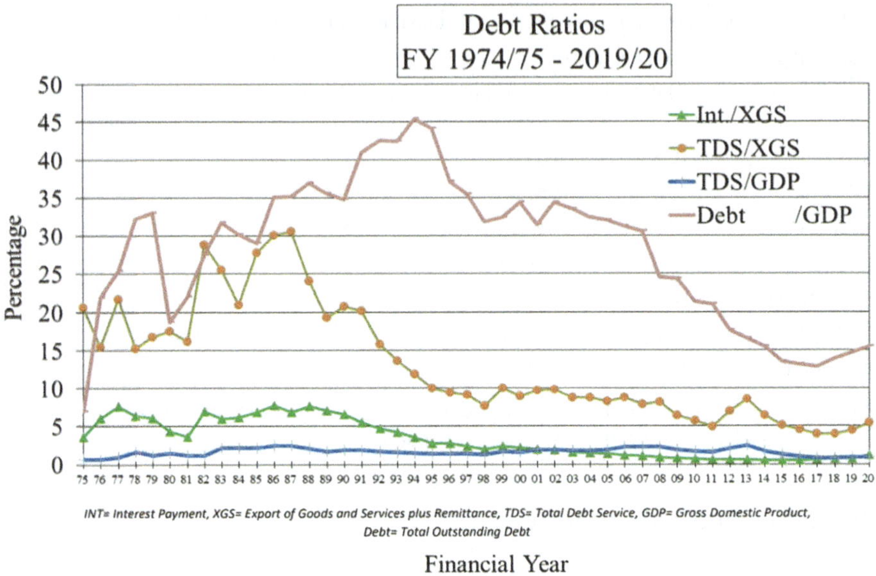

Graph 10.1 Historical debt sustainability analysis within DSA. *Source* FABA and the ICT Wing, ERD

Table 10.2 Debt sustainability indicators for the public sector

Indicator	2018–19 (%)	2019–20 (%)	2020–21 (%)	2021–22 (provisional)	Threshold (%)
Debt stock					
Debt to GDP	14.7	15.5	16.9		40
Debt to goods and service plus remittance	69.78	88.45	85.87		180
Debt service liquidity (DSL)					
Debt service to goods and service plus remittance	4.4	5.5	4.7		15
Debt service to revenue	9.4	10.2	8.4		18

Source FABA and ICT Wing, ERD

10.4 BRI's Benefits to Bangladesh

The BRI offers expectations of economic growth for the country. As part of the Indo-Pacific Strategy and BRI, Bangladesh is strategically important for both the US and China. The BRI project, however, offers more to Bangladesh's economy. Dhaka's cautious engagement with the BRI could create a fruitful situation that offers benefits to either party via a concrete bilateral partnership between the countries. The BRI also offers increased connectivity and opportunities for benefits in areas such as trade, infrastructure, investment, education, and tourism, among other countries in South Asia along its corridors. For example, the Kunming to Kolkata corridor has the potential to reduce costs of transport in trade for Bangladesh. The BRI projects can better embed Bangladesh in the region and offer better integration with the global economy. To do so, trade facilitation reforms are necessary, and a project such as the BRI can act as a catalyst for that. According to Khatun and Saadat, examples of such reforms are "standardization and harmonization of procedures and regulations across countries, improvement of trade facilitation and logistics at the border, cross-border electronic data exchange, speedy customs clearance, customs cooperation, and measures to ensure security of people, vehicles, and cargo on the move.[27]

Bangladesh is the second highest recipient of Chinese investment in South Asia, just after Pakistan. Bangladesh is also its largest trading partner because it imports the highest volume of goods from China. The data also demonstrate that China has historically maintained strong affiliations with South Asian countries to participate in the region's "big bazaar". Shazzad highlights that it is a contentious argument to make in alleging that China truly has any "Machiavellian strategy" because "Chinese projects in Bangladesh are too fragmented to achieve such cunning strategic objectives".[28] China is especially keen to take advantage of Bangladesh's profiteering market ventures due to its geopolitical eminence and commercial noteworthiness.

Furthermore, Bangladesh is motivated to become an "economic hub" of South Asia[29] and needs external funding for its flagship development projects, the financing of which goes beyond domestic affordability.[30] Thus, Bangladesh seeks external funding options under conducive conditions. Bangladesh lost out on international financiers such as the WB when the latter backed out of its commitment to fund the construction of the Padma Bridge. In that instance, China found an easy passage to enter and invest in Bangladesh's economy. Some security analysts believe that BRI offers Bangladesh an opportunity to be connected beyond its region, making it easier for Bangladesh to integrate further with the international market.[31] Meanwhile, China, as a part of its foreign strategy, has found its means to build partnerships with Bangladesh by associating the country with various Chinese provincial platforms, e.g., the Asian Infrastructure Investment Bank (AIIB) and BRI (Table 10.3).

It is also important to note that China's principle of nonintervention in the domestic affairs of its partners attracts Bangladesh. Conversely, Bangladesh plays a major role in China's bureaucratic calculations because it hopes to connect the enclosed southeastern territory of China through Bangladesh. Bangladesh also offers cheap labor, which attracts the Chinese to move its sunset industries.

[27] Khatun and Saadat (2020).

[28] Hussain (2021).

[29] Agarwal (2019).

[30] Hossain (2018).

[31] Khatun and Saadat (2020).

Table 10.3 Detailed Commitments by Development Partners (July 2020–June 2021) (million USD)

Partner	Grant/loan	Agreement title	Signing date	Commitment amount
AIIB	Loan	Dhaka Sanitation Improvement Project	1-Sep-20	170.000
	Loan	Improvement of Sylhet-Tamabil Road to a 4 Lane Highway with separate SMVT Lane Project	26-Oct-20	404.000
	Loan	Rural Water Sanitation and Hygiene for Human Capital Development Project	18-Feb-21	200.000
	Loan	COVID-19 Emergency Response and Pandemic Preparedness Project	19-Feb-21	100.000
	Loan	COVID-19 Emergency and Crisis Response Facility Project	26-Feb-21	300.000
Total				1174.000

Source Flow of External Resources into Bangladesh, 2021, Detailed Commitments by Development Partners (July 2020–June 2021)

In 1976, Sino-Bangladesh associations began with trade deals, and this continued well into the first decade of the twenty-first century. The Sino-Bangladesh relationship underwent two contrasting phases prior to and following the commencement of the BRI. In the wake of 2010, the bilateral association transformed into strategic cooperation when the two nations signed several trade, transit and defense acquisition agreements. The two nations are striving to alleviate massive trade deficits through the establishment of free trade zones. The Chinese are working to try and become dependable friends of Bangladesh through the formation of diplomatic, defense and economic bonds. They are injecting enormous money into Bangladesh and trying to take the relationship to a higher level. Despite the apparent portrayal of the Chinese as vindictive agents trying to trap Bangladesh in the "payday loan diplomacy," the opposing narrative describes that Chinese soft debts decrease the pressure that Western donors may put for economic and political improvements.

10.5 Debates Over the BRI's Debt in Bangladesh

Bangladesh is one of the most significant South Asian recipients of Chinese loans under the BRI scheme, with a debt profile so large that it falls only behind Pakistan's. Recently, China has stepped up its massive infrastructure investments in Bangladesh, which are not well worth 10 billion USD. Nine projects are running under the BRI in Bangladesh, which include the mega project of the Padma Bridge Rail Link, the

Bangabandhu tunnel under the Karnaphuli River, and the Dasher Kandi Sewerage treatment plant. Rahman claims that the success of BRI projects in Bangladesh is highly dependent on two issues: sustainable financing and the economic viability of the projects.[32]

While sustainable financing of BRI projects has been an important concern for participating countries and borrowers, Bangladesh has been a cautious borrower, and one must be a cautious critic when comparing the nation to examples such as Sri Lanka and Djibouti. Rahman studied other BRI partner nations that are at risk of falling into the "debt trap" and found that a comparative analysis of the external debt ratio shows that Bangladesh is not yet in a similar situation.[33] The foreign debt stock of Bangladesh amounted to approximately 78.04 billion USD in FY 2020–21, which is approximately 22% of the nation's GDP. Whereas for Sri Lanka, the debt ratio to nominal GDP stood at 104% and for Pakistan at approximately 41%. Hence, it is safe to say that Bangladesh is adeptly monitoring its debt and reducing its risk of falling prey to the Chinese "debt trap".

Datta discusses that while Sri Lanka's plunge into the 'debt trap' has strongly resonated with the other nations of the region, several Bangladeshi specialists and think tanks acknowledge that the BRI will "promote higher financial assimilation and expedite more Chinese ventures into the Bangladesh Stock market."[34] Experts are hoping that BRI will pave the way for Bangladesh to enter China's equity (worldwide 2nd biggest) and their bond market (worldwide 3rd biggest). Chinese loans and investments are positively welcomed by the Bangladeshis in general, with interest rates for earlier projects reported to be 2% and repayment periods of 20 years. Few articles suggest that while BRI debts possess large commercial rates, there are no official data to back this because credible information regarding the terms and conditions of the project loans are seldom shared by both nations.

To accelerate economic growth, Bangladesh has also been considering foreign assistance, such as official development assistance (ODA). Bangladesh's total public investment target was set at 8.4% of the GDP for FY2022, and the government's budget deficit was planned to be financed by a foreign aid of 2.0% of GDP. To meet Bangladesh's investment needs in the social front for sectors such as health, transportation, infrastructure, electricity and education, the ERD has been surveying for foreign assistance. Rahman's analysis also shows that on the one hand, in the last five fiscal years, i.e., from 2017–18 to 2021–22, it has received commitments of amounts up to 52.33 billion USD, which is an average of 10.46 billion USD per FY.[35] On the other hand, Bangladesh has received disbursements of foreign assistance up to 38.69 billion USD in the same period, which amounts to an average of 7.74 billion USD per FY.

Figure 10.1 shows that Bangladesh's total external debt in the FY 2019–20 fiscal year is 38% from the WB, 24.5% from the Asian Development Bank (ADB), 17%

---

[32] Rahman (2021).

[33] Ibid.

[34] Datta (2021).

[35] Rahman (2019).

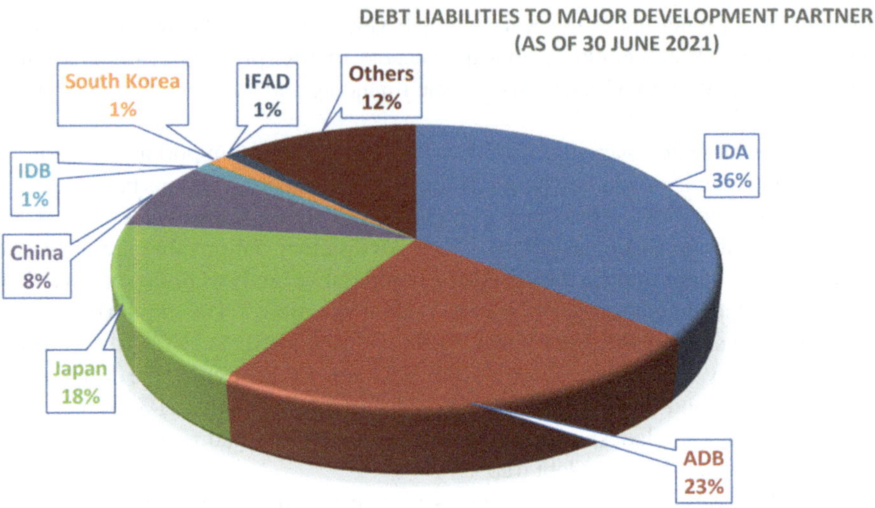

Fig. 10.1 Bangladesh's total external debt in the FY 2019–20 fiscal year. *Source* FABA and ICT wing, ERD

from the Japan International Cooperation Agency (JICA), 6.81% from China, 6.14% from Russia, and 1.3% from India. These data show that Bangladesh has been on the right trajectory. However, Table 10.4, indicating the debt liabilities of major development partners of Bangladesh as of June 2021, shows the rising debt of China.

As government borrowing remains on the rise, there is also an expected rise in foreign debt servicing liabilities in the near future. Where the external debt servicing on MLT loans was 1.92 billion USD and 2.01 billion USD in FY2020–21 and FY2021–22, respectively, ERD projections indicate that this will rise to 4.02 billion USD in FY2024–25 and further to 5.15 billion USD in FY2029–30. Consequently, one can outline from these projected figures some of the hard term loans such as those from Russia, China and India, for which the grace period will end in a couple of years and principal amounts along with their interest would have to start to be repaid.

Eventually, Bangladesh needs to be careful both in accepting and rejecting Chinese loans because funding options are very limited for Bangladesh most of the time due to concerns and claims presented by foreign investors on the governance and policy reforms of the country. If loans are not optimally utilized and if repayments are not done on time, the burden of debt starts to accumulate. However, we have seen that Bangladesh has shown effective management of its debt thus far with all its lenders. There is not an instance yet where Bangladesh has accepted all the requirements and signed a financial agreement blindfolded. It can be inferred that the macroeconomic practice that Bangladesh is currently exercising is vigilant and able to avoid China's "debt trap", should there be one.

Table 10.4 Total External Debt Composition of Bangladesh as of June 2021 (million USD)

Component	Public sector	Private sector	Total
1. Long—term Debt as at end of Jun'22	67,016.63	8195.24	75,211.87
1.1 Multilateral	34,347.05	2044.55	36,391.60
1.2 Bilateral	24,499.15	1064.69	25,563.84
1.3 Supplier's Credit	0.00	135.97	135.97
1.4 IMF loan	3024.07	0.00	3024.06
1.5 Commercial Borrowing	3707.51	4572.88	8280.39
1.6 Others	1438.85	377.15	1816.01
2. Short-term debt as at end of Jun'22	2890.31	17,755.68	20,645.99
Total external debt as at end of Jun'22 (1 + 2)	69,906.94	25,950.92	95,857.86
Total external debt as at end of Mar'22	68,251.48	24,981.49	93,232.97
% Changes Jun'22 over Mar'22	2.43	3.88	2.82

Source BB

It is also important to assess Bangladesh's current economic advantages or lack thereof in other aspects as well, such as the scopes and risks associated with debt repayment. Currency depreciation has rather significant implications for debt repayment strategies, especially in light of the rise in external debts incurred by the country's private sector, which further increases the pressure of foreign exchange for loan repayment. This is especially pertinent for projects where financial assistance is received in foreign currencies but repayments are to be made from the generated income in the local currency. This is a rather pressing concern as well given Bangladesh's recent experiences with currency depreciation of approximately 12% within a period of a few months.

10.6 Bangladesh's Caution as a Borrower

It is important to note that thus far, Bangladesh has also canceled five proposed projects, which amount to 3.6 billion USD. China has also recently conveyed its hesitation in considering projects that contribute to high pollution and demand high energy consumption, such as coal mining and coal-fired power stations.

Bangladesh also canceled the Sonadia deep-sea port project in 2020 and rejected loans to construct a highway in 2018. The quotation was inflated, and there were claims of corruption, which the Bangladeshi government took into notice. This shows that the authority is well aware of the risks that Chinese loans present. The state is looking into other means to finance its projects as well, with solutions such as public–private association models. The government is further cautious about connectedness to ease the transport of goods from China to Bangladesh, which will ultimately influence the trade equilibrium.

This is also an opportunity for Bangladesh to demand increased transparency and public disclosure of BRI projects, debts, terms and agreements so that appropriate strategies can be suggested and designed for effective project completion and debt repayment. In the long run, this could contribute to measures that seek better accountability against corruption and increased monitoring and reporting in the country.

Another geopolitical tension to take into consideration for Bangladesh is India's disinterest in the BRI. The BCIM Economic Corridor begins at Kunming, passes through Myanmar, enters India in its northeast territories, and ends in Kolkata through Bangladesh. However, there are doubts about the effective implementation of the corridor because India has not joined the scheme, and the corridor was also not mentioned in the postsecond BRI Summit. This is a concern for Bangladesh, as relations with India carry great importance for the country, and a large stake of Bangladesh's membership in the BRI is based on this Economic Corridor, which is dependent on India. Bangladesh is also involved in Indo-Pacific strategic initiatives. Both the United Nations Economic and Social Commission for Asia and the Pacific (UNESCAP), with its Asian Highway Network, and BRI are motivated to create better connectivity between Asia and Europe, and the BRI project seems to raise many questions.

It is unlikely for the BCIM land corridor to be completed fruitfully, given India's nonparticipation in BRI. Therefore, China is proceeding with its bilateral infrastructural development plans within the boundaries of Bangladesh.[36] Since India and China are both important to Bangladesh, the country is trying to navigate these relations very delicately so that it is not seen as taking sides. The BRI's success in Bangladesh and in South Asia cannot be guaranteed without the collaborative efforts of all the states in the region to resolve existing regional problems.[37] As pointed out by Touhid Hossain, Former Foreign Secretary of Bangladesh, "BRI is not going to immediately bring substantial change for Bangladesh as the effectiveness of this strategy depends on the combined effort of the partners in the region".[38] PM Sheikh Hasina had also previously urged India to join the project and assured that the China-led BRI would pose no worrying challenges. However, the fact remains that India is not participating in the BRI, and Bangladesh must proceed with strategic caution. The transportation network of Bangladesh can find success if it is able to efficiently integrate with the regional transport network, especially with India. For now, Bangladesh has successfully managed its partnership with China and India, but the future cannot be of certain.[39] Nonetheless, while features of Sino-Bangladesh

[36] Liu and Dixon (2020).

[37] Plagemann (2022).

[38] Belt and Road Initiative (2019).

[39] Anwar (2022).

ties, together with their defense association, influence India, China is also keeping a close eye on the Indo-Bangladesh association. Therefore, Bangladesh is acting deftly with both parties to amplify its national interest.

10.7 Positioning Bangladesh and Way Forward

The Economic Relations Division or ERD of Bangladesh engages in routine activities to make an approximation for prospective debt servicing liabilities, which offers a perspective regarding the amount to be paid for underwriting overseas loans. The estimations are established on account of the expiration of the grace period of certain loans, interest rates and additional conditions of accepting loans. Several new loans from countries such as Russia, China, and India are halfway or not completely concessional because service rates are added to these loans. Moreover, recurrent setbacks in project execution tend to increase the costs approximated at the beginning of the project. It can be observed that, thanks to the changing income status of Bangladesh, in the future, the existing upward trend of nonconcessional loans may also become steeper. Therefore, Bangladesh should assess the reality of the debt situation, evaluate sincere predictions, and measure foreseeable hazards before making commitments on debt reimbursement.

- **Ensuring good governance in PIP implementation**

The Public Infrastructure Projects in Bangladesh have been backed by enormous amounts of loaned investments where ensuring good governance is utterly significant. Many large-scale projects of the nation have gone through critical and routine investigations. Nonetheless, these projects entail large sums of loaned finance, and the more and more time is spent on them, the greater becomes the expenditure, which is a serious issue to consider. These issues can be resolved by establishing a sincere governing organization. The governing organization can refer to the OECD principles for good administration, which provides guidelines for properly executing infrastructural ventures. The declaration from the government to offer zero-tolerance with regard to any wrongdoings in the management of the feasibility study, estimating the cost, acquisition and implementing the activities of the PIPs, must prevail. We can take away a message from Sri Lanka that to accomplish great value for financing in PIPs from loaned credit, the greatest principles of ethics should be applied for selecting, procuring, managing, and implementing PIP.

- **Factor-in exchange rate movement**

Currency depreciation is another risk that Bangladesh should consider when forecasting returns from overseas loan-induced investment, especially when projects are primarily made for the domestic market and the revenue is earned in local currency. Many of the mega-scale projects in the country, such as roadways, transportation, and power sectors, have PIPs, which are executed with foreign funding. However, these projects will bring revenue to Bangladeshi Taka. Hence, when the revenue collected is compared with the borrowed financing in these projects, it is imperative that the foreign exchange market be considered and added into the evaluations; a possible way of tackling the drawbacks of exchange rate fluctuations could be currency hedging.

- **Be mindful of dual graduation**

Since Bangladesh hopes to graduate from LDCs in 2026, it is crucial to bear in mind that after this transition, the country will no longer receive international support measures for LDCs such as the LDC-dedicated Climate Fund, which in turn will facilitate more borrowing. In addition, graduation will also impact the decisions of lending nations, as they tend to prioritize LICs and LDCs to extend loans on concessional and soft terms. Hence, it is wise for Bangladesh to make good use of its existing 'gap' and 'blend' position before it graduates to the IRBD status-only state.

- **Look for alternative funding sources**

In Bangladesh's pursuit of achieving the SDGs and Vision 2041 ambitions, a considerable number of resources and funding is understandably needed; hence, humanistic necessities are given utmost priority, and large sums of ODA are devoted to them. This, in turn, puts a strain on the funding needed for development requirements. Under such circumstances, Bangladesh should look for alternate resources to fund its future endeavors, such as blended finance, global climate funding and south-south cooperation.

- **Diversify the sources of development finance**

To have more freedom in using the finances, Bangladesh should procure further loans that are of the budgetary supply category. The New Development Bank (NDB) and AIIB should be ventured further as contemporary areas of financing (Bangladesh has previously taken loans from these banks). The movement of funds from South–South cooperation and blended financing should be further observed; this funding should be used not only for infrastructural development but also for health, education and SMEs. The IMF's Resilience and Sustainable Trust Fund (presently values at 100 billion USD which became effective May 2022. The initial idea was for 300 billion USD), which provides financing to build durability in facing outside blows and could be a model for Bangladesh to try and delve into other prototypes of funding. The potential of swapping currency is being explored by some developing countries in hopes to lessen the burden on foreign exchange by reducing the demands on dollar-dominant forex reserves. This has been unsuccessful until now due to institutional provisions being absent. Henceforth, Bangladesh should take cognizance of the lessons learned from other developing states, and the Bangladesh Bank should reflect on forthcoming needs and explore other avenues.

- **Estimate reliable forex reserve figure**

The forex reserve is utilized in underwriting imports, service loans and other liabilities. Hence, it becomes imperative to have an accurate idea regarding the forex reserves. Recently, there was a dispute between Bangladesh Bank and the IMF regarding the real amount of forex reserves. According to the IMF's estimation, the actual forex reserve that could be utilized for underwriting several expenses and liabilities was 7.0 billion USD less than what Bangladesh Bank claimed.

- **Keep private sector borrowings under vigilance**

The volume of private sector loans obtained from offshore parties is increasing at a higher rate. Although regarding the repaying of private loans, no absolute warranty is provided, the complete accrued foreign loans, both public and private (approximately 93.2 billion USD until March 2022), might put a strain on repaying of debts and the forex. In view of this, to prevent Bangladesh's credit rating from defaulting, the government along with the central bank must oversee private sector borrowings diligently to keep their usage and debt service records credible.

As mentioned in the country's 8th Five Year Plan presented by the National Development Strategy, Bangladesh needs to prioritize timely completion of all transport infrastructure projects, which consist of intercity bridges, highways, tunnels, and sea ports. Acknowledging that these transformational projects require high and intensive inputs of capital, must be implemented over several years, and require strong supervision and good governance to avoid excess costs and delays, Bangladesh can avoid falling into any trap and, after all, attain its desired development results. If there are any lessons to be learned from the case of Sri Lanka, it is the need for debt repayment strategies that assess and enforce high standards in the efficient completion of these developmental projects, such that projects that have higher possibilities of timely completion and faster income generation are prioritized. This must take into account the problems of corruption in delays and budget exceedance.

Bangladesh's government must also take into account exchange rate movements in making debt repayment strategies, especially to justify the investments made in projects that are expected to generate income and return debts. The risks of currency depreciation must be taken into account, and currency hedging could be one possible strategy to prevent the adverse effects of fluctuations in exchange rates. While Bangladesh has been exercising caution in debt management and the selection of sustainable projects, it must also be wary in this regard of the fast pace at which private sector borrowing is incurred because the repayments of such loans have increased burdens on foreign exchange movements. Bangladesh must also be proactive in diversifying its sources of development finance and searching for alternative funding sources. According to Rahman, some examples of such sources could be blended finance, global climate finance, finance available under south–south cooperation, etc.[40]

[40] Rahman (2019).

10.8 Conclusion

In conclusion, Bangladesh needs enormous amounts of capital for its economic and infrastructural development. In spite of all the risks associated with loans, China is an easy lending partner, as the chances for Bangladesh to borrow from others are slim. Our analysis shows that Bangladesh is well vigilant of its debt liabilities and has exercised caution thus far in staying well below suggested thresholds of foreign borrowings. However, foreign loans have been on the significant rise, while older, cheaper sources of loans and grants have swiftly been on the decline in synchrony with their economic graduations. However, the country also needs to exercise further caution in various aspects, such as governance, foreign exchange movements, strategizing of debt repayment, efficient project implementation, risks of corruption, transparency, etc., to avoid falling into risks of a debt trap. Hence, the country needs to ensure careful selection of projects, maintain strong leadership in the implementation of the projects and ensure timely repayment of the debts to China.

References

Anu Anwar, China-Bangladesh Relations: The Way Balancing Between China, India, and the US in Jacob Gunter & Helen Legarda eds., *Beyond Block: Global Views on China and US-China Relations,* MERICS, 2022, pp.15–25.

Anna Gelpern, Sebastian Horn, Scott Morris, Brad Parks, Christioph Trebesch, "How China lends: A rare look into 100 debt contracts with foreign governments", Peterson Institute for International Economics, May 2021, https://www.piie.com/publications/working-papers/how-china-lends-rare-look-100-debt-contr acts-foreign-governments.

Bappy Rahman, "Belt and Road Initiative: An Opportunity for Bangladesh", *Daily Sun,* November 19, 2019, https://www.daily-sun.com/post/439975/Belt-and-Road-Initiative:-An-Opportunity-for-Bangl adesh.

Brahma Chellaney, "China's debt-trap diplomacy", *The Hill,* 2021, https://thehill.com/opinion/int ernational/551337-chinas-debt-trap-diplomacy.

"Bangladesh-China signs 27 deals", *Bangladesh Awami League*, October 14, 2016, https://albd.org/articles/news/28615/Bangladesh-China-signs-27-deals.

"Belt and Road Initiative: Perspective from Bangladesh", *The Daily Star*, 2019, https://www.thedai lystar.net/round-tables/news/belt-and-road-initiative-perspective-bangladesh-1782928.

Bao [People's Daily], August 26, 2023, http://paper.people.com.cn/rmrbwap/html/2023-08/26/nw.D110000renmrb_20230826_6-03.htm.

"Chinese consortium signs deal to acquire 25 pct stake in Bangladesh's premier bourse", *Xinhua News Agency,* May 14, 2018, http://www.xinhuanet.com/english/2018-05/14/c_137178673.htm.

"China in focus: Lessons and challenges", OECD, 2012, https://www.oecd.org/china/50011051.pdf.

Deborah Brautigam and Meg Rithmire, "The Chinese 'Debt Trap' Is a Myth. There Is No Chinese 'Debt Trap'", *The Atlantic,* February 6, 2021, https://www.theatlantic.com/international/archive/2021/02/China-debt-trap-diplomacy/617953.

Flow of External Resources into Bangladesh, 2020–2021, Golden Jubilee Special Edition. Economics Relations Division, Ministry of Finance, Government of Bangladesh. https://erd.portal.gov.bd/site/page/7f192f96-1442-48b4-a947-2e09ce30ec54/Flow-of-Exter.

Fahmida Khatun and Syed Yusuf Saadat, "How can Bangladesh benefit from the Belt and Road Initiative?", *Dhaka Tribune,* 2020, https://cpd.org.bd/how-can-bangladesh-benefit-from-the-belt-and-road-initiative.

Ganiu Oloruntade, "Why the $475 m Chinese telecom loan deal is causing so much controversy", *Technext,* December 1, 2022, https://technext.ng/2022/12/01/475 m-chinese-telecom-deal-controversy.

Hossain, M, Green Finance in Bangladesh: Policies, Institutions, and challenges, ADBI Working Paper Series no.898, 2018, https://www.adb.org/sites/default/files/publication/467886/adbi-wp892.pdf.

Imogen T Liu and Adam D Dixon, What does the state do in China's state-led infrastructure financialisation?, *Journal of Economic Geography,* Vol.22, No.5, 2020, pp.963–988.

Johannes Plagemann, Small states and competing connectivity strategies: what explains Bangladesh's success in relations with Asia's major powers?, *The Pacific Review*, Vol.35, No.4, 2022, pp.736-764.

Kai Wang, "China: Is it burdening poor countries with unsustainable debt?", *BBC,* 2022, https://www.bbc.com/news/59585507.

Mark Green, "China's Debt Diplomacy-How Belt and Road threatens countries' ability to achieve self-reliance", *Foreign Policy,* April 25, 2019, https://foreignpolicy.com/2019/04/25/chinas-debt-diplomacy.

Mohammad Zonaed Emran, "BRI: Risks and opportunities for Bangladesh", *The Daily Star,* September 22, 2019, https://www.thedailystar.net/letters/news/bri-risks-and-opportunities-ban gladesh-1803673.

Prachi Agarwal, "South Asia: formulating services sector policies for development a policy perspective", Economic and Social Commission for Asian and Pacific, July 1, 2019, https://www.unescap.org/resources/sswa-development-papers-1903-south-asia-formulating-s ervices-sector-policies-development.

Shaikh Abdur Rahman, "The BRI in Bangladesh: 'Win–Win' or a 'Debt Trap'?", *The Diplomat*, November 2021, https://thediplomat.com/2021/11/the-bri-in-bangladesh-win-win-or-a-debt-trap/.

Shazzad Hussain, "Is Bangladesh at risk of falling into the Chinese debt trap?", *The Daily Star,* 2021, https://www.thedailystar.net/views/opinion/news/bangladesh-risk-falling-the-chinese-debt-tra p-2224391.

Sreeradha Datta, "Bangladesh and Belt Road Initiative: Unfolding Possibilities, National Security", *Vivekananda International Foundation,* Vol. 4, No. 3, September 2021, pp. 254–271, https://www.vifindia.org/sites/default/files/national-security-vol-4-issue-3-article-SreeradhaDatta.

Yan Fujing and Chen Weiwei. *Wo Guo Yi Yu 152 Ge Guo Jia, 32 Ge Guo Ji Zu Zhi Qian Shu Gong Jian 'Yi Dai Yi Lu' He Zuo Wen Jian* [China has singed cooperation agreements on jointly building BRI with 152 countries and 32 international organizations], *Ri Min Ri.*

Chapter 11
The Reality and Myth of the BRI's "Debt Trap": Evidence from Nepal

Khadga Kc and Hari Prakash Chand

Abstract The Belt and Road Initiative (BRI) is a global infrastructure development and connectivity tool initiated by China in 2013 to finance investments in over 150 countries and institutions. Nepal joined the BRI on 12 May 2017, but no projects have been initiated under the BRI so far. Nepal has also signed the Millennium Challenge Corporation (MCC) agreement with the US on 14 September 2017. Many analysts view the MCC as a rival to the BRI, while some in Nepal have raised concerns about the BRI's 'debt trap' narrative. This chapter examines the reality and myth of the BRI's debt trap' from a Nepali perspective, using the neoliberal concept as a theoretical framework to evaluate Nepal's financial cooperation with great powers and institutions. The study employs a qualitative method under a descriptive and critical analytical approach. The findings suggest that the 'debt trap' narrative in Nepal is largely a myth rather than a reality, and Nepal should continue BRI projects based on its major priorities and national interests. To do so, Nepali authorities should first seek grants from their Chinese counterparts, and the remaining amount can be obtained through soft loans.

Keywords BRI · Debt trap · Financial investment · Nepal · International cooperation

11.1 Introduction

In the 1980s, under the reform and opening-up policy introduced by Deng Xiaoping, China was silently emerging without interfering in the internal affairs of other countries. After the normalization of relations with the United States (US) after 1971, especially after following Deng's policy in 1978, China proceeded to build the

K. Kc (✉) · H. P. Chand
Department of International Relations, Tribhuvan University, Kathmandu, Nepal
e-mail: khadga.kc@dird.tu.edu.np

H. P. Chand
e-mail: Hari.757738@dird.tu.edu.np

N. Peng and M. Y. Cheng (eds.), *The Reality and Myth of BRI's Debt Trap*, Indo-Pacific Focus, https://doi.org/10.1007/978-981-97-1056-0_11

country through peaceful means and stand up in the world. It tried to make relations with major and all developing countries cordial and harmonious and refrained from aggression toward regional and global powers except in cases of security threats to its sovereignty. China's progress in the economic sector based on the policy of reform and opening up was a milestone in bringing the country to the level of a developed country. The World Bank (WB) report says, "Since China began reforming and opening up her economy in 1978, growth of Gross Domestic Product (GDP) averaged not less than 9% in every year and greater than 800 million people graduated out of poverty.[1] China's GDP grew by 9% in 2008 despite facing a serious financial crisis in 2007–08 by the US. It was the most severe economic crisis since the Great Depression (1929). It affected the whole world economy in the early twenty-first century. In this context, China and Russia led to the formation of a global platform of emerging economies in 2009, which is called Brazil, Russia, India, and China (BRICs).[2] According to Lowe, BRIC (later BRICS) countries emerged as a powerful group in the world economy with the possibility of changing the existing world order. This is not only an example of new global initiatives for bringing change to the existing world order; there are so many developments even after the emergence of BRICS. Paul Kennedy has well articulated the rise and fall of world powers in different eras in his book "The Rise and Fall of the Great Powers". His book remains silent about the post-1990 world order. The China-led Asian Infrastructure Investment Bank, The New Development Bank, and the Global Initiative of the BRI are the major developments in the post-1990 period that have geared up the speed of multipolar world order.

India, an emerging global power, has parallel relations with Russia and the US. India again did not vote on the UN General Assembly's resolution condemning Russia's attack on Ukraine, which began a year ago.[3] India also has good strategic relations with the US and indispensable trade relations with China. The US has tense strategic relations with China, especially in the case of the South China Sea (SCS) and Taiwan issues. The superpower and the rising superpower have been recently competing through the Indo-Pacific Strategy (IPS) and Global Security Initiatives (GSI), which are geopolitical tools of the US and China. The MCC and the BRI are geoeconomic tools of the same countries that are also in competition. China has recently announced the Global Civilization Initiatives (GCI). The US considers these Chinese initiatives threats to the US strategic, economic, and cultural frontiers. Both countries have recently focused on Nepal through the MCC and the BRI. India, as the dominant neighbor of Nepal, has been applying all of its approaches to make India's role stronger in changing Nepali geopolitics.

[1] The world bank in China (2023).

[2] Lowe (2016).

[3] Ukraine war: India abstains from UN vote on Russian invasion (2023).

In these contexts, this chapter is focused on assessing the key roles of major external players via their economic means and method in Nepal. In doing so, Nepal's economic relations with great powers and major global financial institutions are investigated through the lens of foreign direct investment (FDI). Moreover, the chapter has investigated whether the narratives developed about BRI's "debt trap" in Nepal are true or false because some of the intellectuals have been raising the issue of BRI's "debt trap" compared with Sri Lanka. Because of such scientifically unverified narratives, policymakers and political leaders are in a dilemma about whether the BRI is beneficial for Nepal. Mainly due to this problem, China and Nepal are unable to start BRI projects in Nepal in a timely manner and complete them on time for mutual benefits. It is expected that the research findings of this chapter will be a reference for policymakers and political leaders to make the right decisions on this crucial bilateral issue.

11.2 Nepal and International Cooperation

For developing and underdeveloped countries, FDI is an important economic growth and development tool. Nepal is scheduled to graduate into a developing country on 24 November 2026; however, Nepal has to accomplish numerous processes.[4] Nepal needs much foreign aid as a candidate for a developing country not only to strengthen the indicators to graduate but also to materialize the ambition of national prosperity and development. Nepal is also one of the countries in the world that started to receive FDI more visibly at a higher level, especially after 1990 when Nepal entered into the liberal policy model. Nepal has effectively cooperated with the international community since its diplomatic expansion, especially after WW-II. Nepal's international cooperation generally can be observed in political, economic, and diplomatic frontiers, but in this section, Nepal's international cooperation in the economic sector is briefly assessed.

According to the International Development Cooperation Policy-2019 report, international development cooperation has contributed to the overall development efforts of Nepal.[5] This report has accepted international economic cooperation for pursuing sustainable economic growth and achieving the goal of "Prosperous Nepal, Happy Nepali".[6] To achieve this goal, the government of Nepal has actively been participating in all kinds of international fora to gain aid from the international community and to gain their trust. According to another report from the Ministry of Finance, Nepal has listed 15 bilateral International Development Partners: Australia, China, Denmark, Finland, Germany, India, Japan, Korea, Kuwait Fund for Arab Economic Development, Netherlands, Norway, Switzerland, Saudi

[4] https://www.un.org/ldcportal/content/nepal-graduation-status#:~:text=During%20the%20triennial%20review%20held,Developed%20Country%20(LDC)%20category.

[5] International Development Cooperation (2019).

[6] Ibid.

Arab: Saudi Fund for Development, United Kingdom (UK), and US. Similarly, the report has listed 20 Multilateral Development Partners: Asian Development Bank (ADB), European Union (EU), Food and Agriculture Organization, Global Environment Facility, Global Fund, International Fund for Agricultural Development, International Finance Corporation, International Labor Organization, International Monetary Fund, OPEC Fund for International Development, South Asian Association For Regional Cooperation (SAARC) Development Fund, United Nations Children Fund, United Nations Development Programme, United Nations Educational Scientific and Cultural Organization, United Nations Population Fund, United Nations High Commissioner for Refugees, UN Women, United Nations World Food Programme, World Bank, and World Health Organization.[7] Nepal has been cooperating with these major international development partners except for some other partners.

Development cooperation is not a value-free matter from political and strategic fronts. To a great extent, economic cooperation is guided by the political and strategic interests of the actors involved in the cooperation. However, this chapter has focused on Nepal's development cooperation with key international partners from an economic perspective only. Nevertheless, the implications of both sides are always present and cannot be ignored. For example, the US has been implementing the MCC in Nepal, which is a financial grant to Nepal, but Nepal must consider its strategic and political implications as well.

Nepal basically receives funds from its development partners in two ways. One is aid, and the next is loan. First, the trend of foreign aid in the last five years from different bilateral development partners (from 2016/17 to 2020/21) is analyzed in Table 11.1, and the above data are analyzed in Fig. 11.1. As seen from Fig. 11.1, Nepal has received the largest grant from the US, followed by the UK, Japan, and China. According to Fig. 11.2, aid received from China is 15% of total aid received from major countries, and 85% is from other countries. Similarly, the aid received from various multilateral development partners (from 2016/17 to 2020/21) is shown in Table 11.3. According to Fig. 11.3, Nepal received the most aid from the WB, followed by the ADB and the EU, during the last five-year period, as mentioned above. Likewise, the aid received from various multilateral implementing partners (from 2016/17 to 2020/21) is analyzed in Table 11.4. According to Fig. 11.4, Nepal has received the most aid from the United Nations Children's Fund, followed by the World Food Programme and International Fund for Agricultural Development. Nepal's debt receipt trend from bilateral and multilateral international partners for the last five years is shown in Table 11.5. According to Fig. 11.5, Nepal received the largest debt from the International Development Association (WB), followed by the ADB. Debt received from other multilateral development partners is too minimal. According to Fig. 11.6, due to Excel limitations, the debt of China-led institutions seems zero percent, but in fact, it is 0.0015% of Nepal's total international institutional major debt, and other international institutional debt is almost 100%, i.e., 99.998% of Nepal's total major international institutional debt. Nepal has received debt from

[7] Profiles of development partners, Kathmandu: Ministry of Finance of Nepal (2014).

various countries as well. Table 11.7 is related to the data on debt received from some major countries. According to Fig. 11.7, the largest debt received from countries is from Japan, followed by China and India. According to the data, the US has provided only aid but not debt. According to Fig. 11.8, 26% of the total major debt is from China, and 74% is from other countries.

Table 11.1 Aid received from bilateral development partners (2016/17–2020/2021)

No	Bilateral development partners	Amount of disbursement (million USD)	Remarks
1	Australia	73.55	
2	China	380.45	Aid Disbursement (in US$) for Different Projects (Grant, Interest-free loan & Concessional loan)
3	Finland	59.00	
4	Germany	147.3	
5	India	340.8	
6	Japan	399.9	
7	Kuwait	7.60	
8	Norway	105.60	
9	Republic of Korea	38.00	
10	Saudi Arabia	23.00	
11	Switzerland	147.3	
12	The Netherlands	3.77	
13	United Kingdom	548.62	
14	United States	558.9	

Source International economic cooperation coordination division, Ministry of finance

Table 11.2 Aid comparison between China and other countries (2016/17–2020/21)

China	Other Countries
380.45	2173.49

Source from Table 11.1

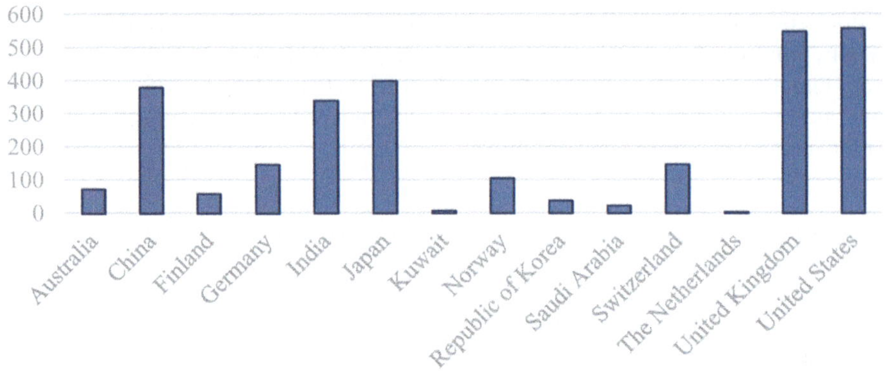

Fig. 11.1 Aid received from bilateral development partners (2016/17–2020/2021) (million USD)

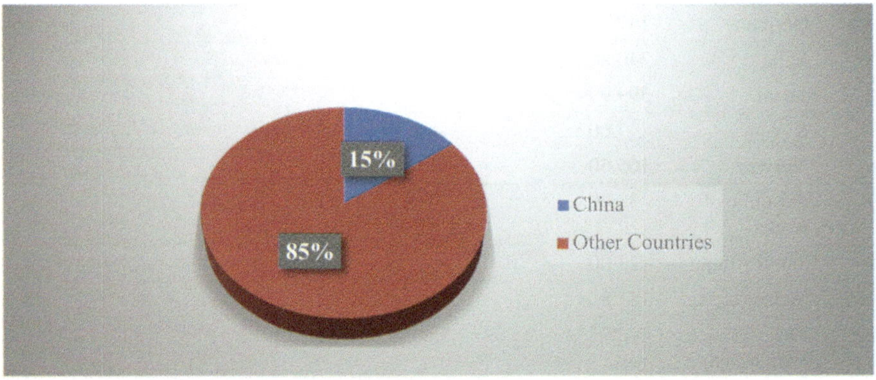

Fig. 11.2 Aid comparison between China and other countries (2016/17–2020/21)

11.3 Nepal-China Economic Engagements

11.3.1 Nepal-China Economic Ties

The Nepal-China economic relations date back to the 1950s. In October 1956, the first agreement on "economic aid" was signed between the two countries. Since the mid-1980s, China has been a promising financial and technical assistance program under the Economic and Technical Cooperation to the Nepal government for Nepal's development.[8] China has been supporting Nepal in three ways: grants, interest-free loans, and concessional loans.[9] As per the website of the Embassy of Nepal in Beijing, fifteen China-supported projects have been completed, and twenty projects are under

[8] Nepal-China Relations (2019).

[9] Ibid.

Table 11.3 Aid received from multilateral development partners (2016/17–2020/2021)

No	Multilateral development partners	Amount of disbursement (million USD)	Remarks
1	Asian development bank	1810.8	
2	Asian Infrastructure Investment Bank (AIIB)	115.2	Including loan
3	European Union	379.1	
4	Global fund to fight AIDS, tuberculosis, and malaria	19.2	
5	OPEC fund for international development	20.85	
6	SAARC development fund	0.57	
7	The global alliance for vaccines and immunization	22.4	
8	The world bank	2675.5	

Source International economic cooperation coordination division, Ministry of finance

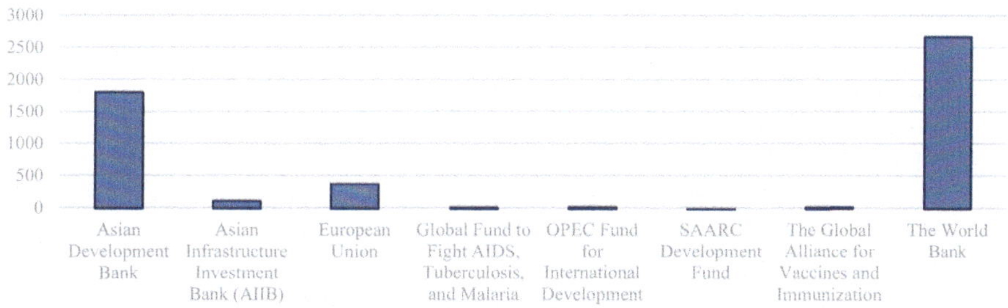

Fig. 11.3 Aid received from multilateral development partners (2016/17–2020/2021) (million USD)

construction.[10] One of the most strategically important projects among them is the construction of the Arniko Highway, which has significantly changed Nepal's foreign affairs since the 1950s. It massively decreased the asymmetric geopolitical and geoeconomic dependency of Nepal on India and has been the most significant diplomatic tool to minimize the Indian influence in Nepal. Under the Nepal-China economic engagement, major projects supported by China are as follows:

(1) Arniko Highway Long–Term Opening Maintenance Project in Nepal, Phase III
(2) Repair and Reinforcement Project for the existing China-aided Projects in Nepal (4 Projects)
(3) Kathmandu Durbar High School (Bhanu Secondary School) Reconstruction project

[10] https://cn.nepalembassy.gov.np/bilateral-relations/.

Table 11.4 Aid received from multilateral implementing partners (2016/17–2020/2021)

No	Multilateral implementing partners	Amount of disbursement (million USD)	Remarks
1	Food and Agriculture Organization	3.85	
2	Global Environment Facility	4	
3	International Fund for Agricultural Development	56.1	
4	International Labor Organization	4.48	
5	United Nations Children's Fund	155.6	
6	United Nations Development Programme	29.59	
7	United Nations Educational, Scientific and Cultural Organization	2.6	
8	United Nations Entity for Gender Equality and the Empowerment of Women	5.2	
9	United nations population fund	23.9	
10	World Food Programme	104.7	
11	World Health Organization	19.9	

Source International economic cooperation coordination division, Ministry of finance

(4) Earthquake Monitoring Network Project
(5) Provision of Medical Equipment
(6) Medical training
(7) Post–Disaster Recovery for the Tatopani Frontier Inspection Station Project
(8) The Amended Project for Kathmandu Ring Road Improvement Project (Phase I)
(9) International Sports Centre Reconstruction Project (Satdobato)
(10) Cross Border Bridge in Tatopani
(11) Cross Border Bridge in Rasuwagadi
(12) Kathmandu Ring Road Improvement Project (Phase I)
(13) Upper Trishuli 3A Hydropower Project (Power Station and Transmission Line Projects (concessional loan $114.7 million-EXIM bank)
(14) Installation of Solar Energy in Singha Durbars (Grant-completed)
(15) Pokhara International Regional Airport (Loan and Grant)[11]

Similarly, the following projects are under implementation as per the website of the Embassy of Nepal, Beijing, which are supported by China:

(1) Syaphrubesi-Rasuwagadi Highway Repair and Improvement Project
(2) Nepal-China Cross-border Railway (Jilong-Kathmandu) Project
(3) Nine–storied Basantapur Tower Restoration Project at Durbar Square, Kathmandu
(4) Capacity Building in Disaster Prevention and Control (Disaster Rescue Centers)

[11] Ibid.

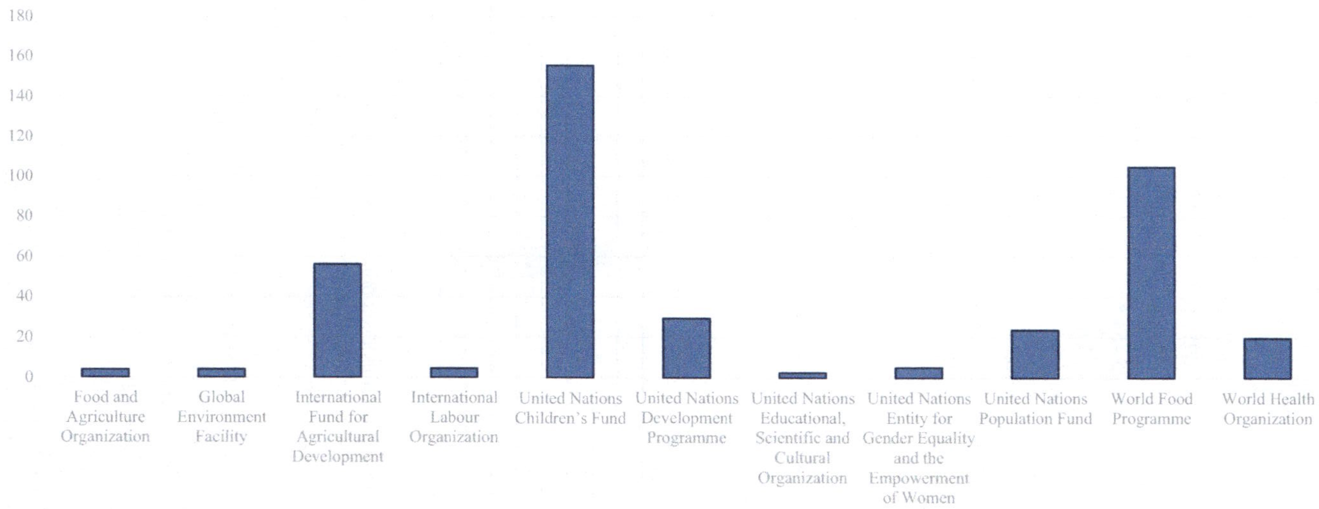

Fig. 11.4 Aid received from multilateral implementing partners (2016/17–2020/2021) (million USD)

Table 11.5 Debt received from multilateral development partners (2016/17–2020/2021)

No	Multilateral institutions	Debt received (million in NRs.)	USD (Million) as per the exchange rate in May 2023
1	ADB	1,127,337.1	8566.39
2	EEC	1399.2	10.63
3	EIB	8917.6	67.76
4	AIIB	33.6	0.255
5	IDA	1,625,463.8	12,351.54
6	IFAD	43,726.9	332.27
7	IMF	65,203.2	495.46
8	NDF	10,940.5	83.13
9	OPEC	32,981.5	250.62

Source Public debt management office, Ministry of finance

Table 11.6 Debt comparison between Chinese led institutions and other institutions

China led institution (million in NRs.)	Other institution (million in NRs.)
33.6	2,915,969.8

Source from Table 11.5

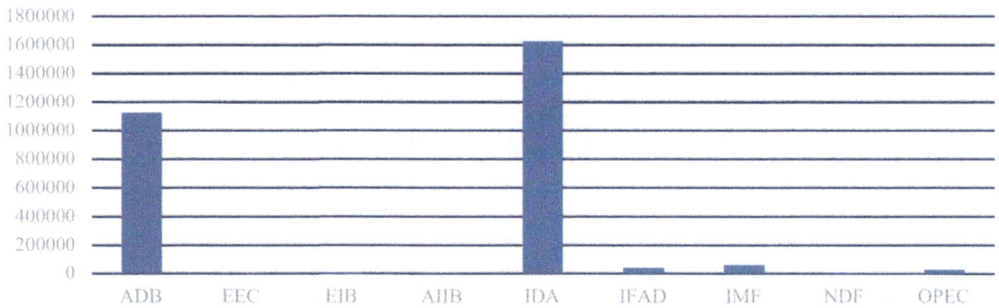

Fig. 11.5 Debt received from multilateral development partners (2016/17–2020/2021) (million in NRs.) (Note: Because of limitations of Excel, debts received from some of the development partners show zero but actual amount is not zero. Too minimal amount seems like zero in the below figure)

(5) Kathmandu Ring Road Improvement Project (Phase II)
(6) Upgrading and Renovation Project of Civil Service Hospital of Nepal
(7) The Public School Recovery Project in Sindhupalchok
(8) The Hospital Recovery Project in Sindhupalchok
(9) The Public-School Recovery Project in Rasuwa
(10) The Public-School Recovery Project in Dolakha
(11) The Hospital Recovery Project in Manang
(12) Repair Project for Nuwakot Durbar Square (Phase I)
(13) Dasarath Rangasala Reconstruction Project

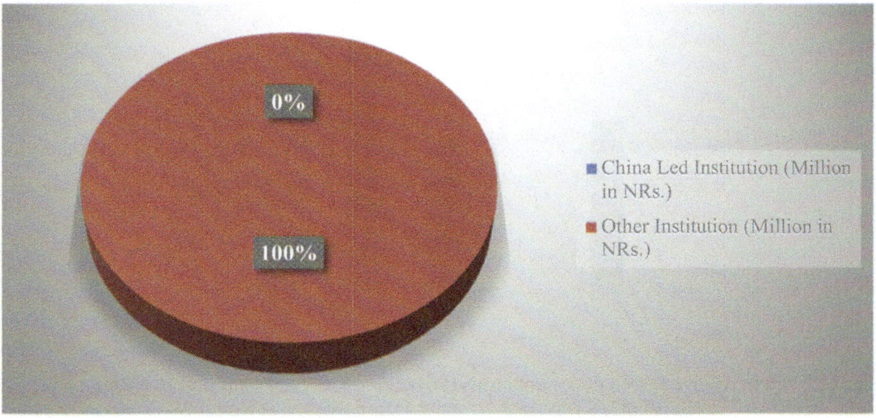

Fig. 11.6 Debt comparison between Chinese led institutions and other institutions

Table 11.7 Debt received from major countries (2016/17–2020/2021)

No	Major countries	Debt received (million in NRs.)	USD (million) as per the exchange rate in May 2023
1	Austria	130.4	0.99
2	Belgium	4012	30.48
3	China	97,833.3	743.41
4	France	1877.4	14.26
5	India	86,299.1	655.76
6	Japan	145,173.0	1103.13
7	South Korea	30,628.8	232.74
8	Kuwait Fund	3271.3	24.85
9	Russia	0	0
10	Saudi Fund	4195.4	31.88

Source Public debt management office, Ministry of finance

Table 11.8 Debt comparison between china and other countries

China (million in NRs.)	Other countries (million in NRs.)
97,833.3	275,587.4

Source from Table 11.7

(14) Renovation of the International Convention Centre Project
(15) Bir Hospital Extension Project in Duwakot
(16) Tokha-Chhahare and Mailung-Syabrubesi Tunnel
(17) Xiarwa River Bridge
(18) Ratmate-Rasuwagadhi-Kerung 400 kV Transmission Line Project
(19) Narayanghat-Butwal Road

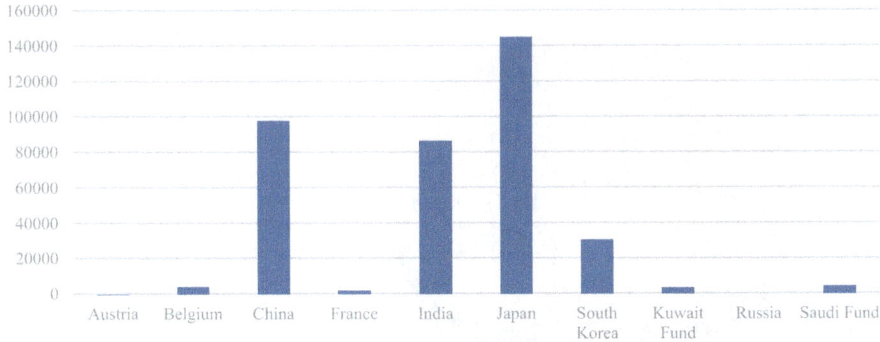

Fig. 11.7 Debt received from major countries (2016/17–2020/2021) (million in NRs.)

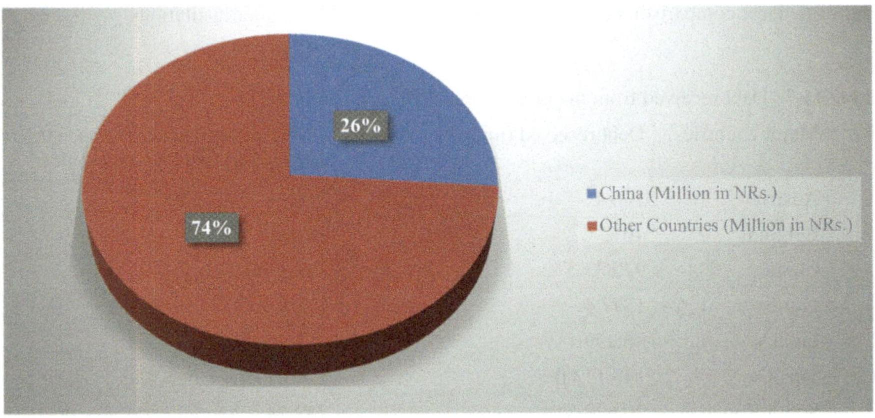

Fig. 11.8 Debt comparison between China and other countries

(20) Timure Frontier Inspection Station Project (Grant).[12]

China's support during Nepal's critical period is significant. During the period of the disastrous earthquake-2015 and inhuman India's embargo in the same period, China supported Nepal in the field of reconstruction of 25 projects worth 3 billion yuan.[13] and provided for needy goods, including fuel. According to the website of the Chinese Embassy in Kathmandu, China has pledged to provide grant aid for 25 reconstruction projects in five areas, including infrastructure, the livelihood of people in mountainous areas, reconstruction of archaeological heritage, disaster preparedness, and health after the devastating earthquake in 2015 shocked Nepal.[14] Similarly, Tiezzi writes that China supplied 1.3 million liters of fuel, which was

[12] Ibid.

[13] Ibid.

[14] China Aid Post-Quake Reconstruction Projects in Nepal (2021)

transported to Nepal from the northern border via 100 tanker trucks.[15] Likewise, *Reuters* writes, "Nepal signs deal with China for supplies as fuel crisis deepens".[16] In this way, China has emerged as a relatively new but strong Partner to help Nepal on its path to prosperity,[17] and the global community is noticed on this China's support to Nepal. Therefore, the Nepal-China economic engagement is deeper, more significant, and more trustworthy for both countries for more reliable future relations and the journey ahead.

11.3.2 BRI's Benefits to Nepal

Despite both countries having signed the Belt and Road Initiative (BRI) on May 12, 2017, Nepal has not benefited much from China's ambitious BRI projects thus far. The BRI implementation plan proposed by China has not yet been approved by Nepal because of the country's political instability, the media's construction of debt-trap narratives, and outside influences operating in the country. Chinese officials appeared that Nepali political figures who have been constantly shifting their allegiances and financing arrangements for the nine BRI projects that are ranked first were also unwilling to collaborate with them. Despite these deviations, if Nepal could move forward with the Belt and Road Initiative (BRI) to build connectivity with China-including the fastest railway line across the Himalayas, improved road connectivity from Nepal's northern provinces to China's Tibet Autonomous Region, and an energy transmission line-it would undoubtedly encourage bilateral trade, increase Chinese foreign direct investment (FDI) in Nepal, and lessen the country's asymmetric dependence on its southern neighbor. Over time, projects funded by the Belt and Road Initiative could boost Nepal's confidence both in local and global arenas. The Belt and Road Initiative (BRI) has facilitated the development of a highly inclusive platform for global development and prosperity by emphasizing development that best serves the interests of all nations. The Belt and Road partnership is a symphony that is played by everyone, not just one person. Through the successful synchronization of development strategies and pragmatic demands among partners, the Belt and Road Initiative (BRI) has assisted partner nations in converting their own advantages into concrete benefits of development.

The BRI creates fresh contributions to people's well-being while shining a light on happiness. A state's people are its foundation. The state will be safe when the foundation is solid. Enhancing people's quality of life has emerged as another unique BRI selling point. The Belt and Road Initiative (BRI) creates new opportunities for shared prosperity and shines hope. The implementation of the US The 2030 Agenda for Sustainable Development is currently facing challenges, and the development gap

[15] Tiezzi (2015).

[16] Nepal signs deal with China for supplies as fuel crisis deepens (2015).

[17] Pandey (2020).

continues to widen. Globally, nations are increasingly striving for growth and collaboration. Many emerging nations have jumped on the BRI's momentum and joined China's development express train. More opportunities for collaboration will arise as we quicken the development of the Silk Roads of innovation, digital health, green, and green infrastructure. This will provide those nations with more opportunities for innovative development, energy transformation, and industrial upgrading.

11.3.3 Challenges of the BRI in Nepal

China wants to implement and be a partner with the BRI in Nepal and in other SAARC members as she is implementing in other continents.[18] Nepal signed an agreement with China for bilateral cooperation under the BRI on 12 May 2017.[19] After signing it, the way has opened for Nepal to diversify its relations with Northeast Asian countries, at least theoretically.[20] However, the projects agreed upon under the BRI are still delayed due to the different perspectives of Nepal and China. One of the Chinese experts (he does not want to be disclosed) says, "The BRI is not for hundred percent aid to other countries, but it is bilateral cooperation. China and partner countries need shared investment for mutual benefits, but Nepal expects a hundred percent aid to implement BRI projects. However, some Nepali leaders say that Nepal cannot afford investment from the national budget in BRI projects due to insufficiency. The major reason behind the delay of BRI projects is both countries' diverse stands and views in this way.

The absence of trade openness and other intangible barriers, the dearth of opportunities for profitable infrastructure development, and a well-thought-out program for road maintenance present challenges. This restricts economic opportunities among the participating countries; these will be more fully realized in the upcoming phase, which runs through 2020. However, the goal of the Belt and Road Initiative (BRI) is to use infrastructure connectivity, increased trade, investment, and learning from existing regional cooperation programs in Asia to put Asia and the Middle East, Europe, and Africa on a new trajectory of higher growth and human development. It makes the case for regional cooperation and shared approaches to infrastructure development by supranational organizations, especially the development banks and advocates for the Belt and Road initiative, to be more widely multilateralized. Against this background, China's Belt and Road initiative has gained tremendous interest as a strategic vision for intensifying trade and investment flows and lends new dynamism to the development trajectories of countries from Asia to Europe and beyond. Potential benefits are expected by intensifying regional supply networks to sustain competitiveness, lower tariffs and nontariff barriers (NTBs) to trade, thereby decreasing the

[18] Chand (2021a, b).

[19] Nepal, China sign bilateral cooperation agreement under Belt and Road Initiative (2017).

[20] Chand (2021a, b).

cost of importing inputs and favoring participation in value chains. The implementation of the Belt and Road Initiative (BRI) will present several significant challenges for Nepal, including the potential for market cultivation of Nepali goods in China, geopolitical and geoeconomic fallout from its neighbors and beyond, funding concerns for the BRI projects and successful completion of the proposed projects.

Nepal had submitted 35 projects to China under the BRI, but as its Chinese counterpart requested, Nepal had downsized it into a single digit, which means nine.[21] During the visit of Chinese Foreign Minister Wang Yi in March 2022, nine projects were signed between Nepal and China, which are listed below.

(1) Economic and technical cooperation
(2) Technical assistance scheme for the China-aided feasibility study of the China-Nepal cross-border project
(3) A cooperation agreement on the feasibility study of China-Nepal power grid interconnections
(4) Protocol for the safety and health conditions of haylage exports from Nepal to China
(5) Letter of exchange on duty-free treatment for 98% of imported goods in China
(6) Handover certificate of the Araniko Highway Maintenance Project (Phase III)
(7) Minutes of the 7th meeting, held in January 2022, on enhancing cooperation in the railway sector
(8) Delivery and acceptance certificates of the China-aided Covid vaccine
(9) Protocol for sending a Chinese medical team to work in Nepal[22]

However, these projects are still not being implemented. Giri writes, during bilateral negotiations, the Nepali side emphasized a grant. However, if such a grant is not possible, either it should be a "soft or concessional loan", while Beijing offers loans at higher interest rates with shorter repayment periods.[23] Therefore, it is verified on the basis of Nepali and Chinese officials/experts that the delay of implementing these projects under the BRI is mainly due to the dilemma of investment modality.

In fact, the "debt trap" discourse created by the West to block China's BRI is also a hot debate in Nepal. Some Nepali intellectuals also started arguing that China wanted to put Nepal under her "debt trap" via BRI projects. Some Nepali media houses published a number of news and opinion; for instance, Bhattarai said that critics of the BRI say it is a "debt trap" that lacks transparency and that it "damages the investment climate" and contributes to cross-border corruption.[24] Similarly, Jha asked whether Xi Jinping promotes "debt-trap diplomacy" in the name of safeguarding small and poor nations such as Sri Lanka and Nepal by luring these countries with cheap China-funded projects.[25] Increased trade flows and the development of infrastructure are two ways that the Belt and Road initiative is predicted to boost growth in Asia and around

[21] Giri (2022).
[22] Ibid.
[23] Ibid.
[24] Bhattarai (2023).
[25] Jha (2022).

the world. With the founding of the ASEAN Economic Community (AEC) at the end of 2015, the Association of Southeast Asian Nations (ASEAN) is already functioning as a Free Trade Area, demonstrating the relative advance of trade integration in some parts of Asia. Although it is lagging behind, South Asia is making an effort to take advantage of the opportunities presented by increased trade and investment connectivity. There will be investments soon. Although the ambitious plans for the Belt and Road Initiative (BRI) to increase infrastructure and industrial investments in Nepal may offer a promising outlook for the country's economic growth as well as that of South Asia and beyond, it is important to remember that economic growth in the twenty-first century must take on a new kind. While implementing BRI projects, Nepal would benefit from the following policies and plans as well, as haphazard and mega projects undertaken solely for political gain would equally justify the debt-trap narrative. Therefore, strategic project planning on financing infrastructure building in Nepal is also necessary to avoid debt-trap false narratives.

The BRI would gain credibility if it were to gradually become more multilateralized. This would also expand the opportunities for government and private sector involvement, which is essential for increasing investments and placing them within the framework of development goals among the people. For instance, it is crucial that nearby companies take part in investments in cross-border value chains and infrastructure development.

These are few representatives of news of China's "debt trap diplomacy" in Nepal. However, the findings of this research are not similar. The research shows that China has been supporting Nepal since diplomatic relations were established in 1955. China's support received during the 2015 Delhi blockade and after the devasted earthquake was not guided by such a debt trap mentality. Three billion yuan of Chinese support for 25 reconstructions in Nepal was the aid. Many Chinese experts told us that they are trying to support Nepal for its economic development and prosperity but not for expanding its GDP. Fifteen accomplished projects and twenty ongoing projects supported by China are also not part of China's "debt trap" tool in Nepal. Nobody has proven that these projects have pushed Nepal into the Chinese "debt trap".

The most important fact is that China is far behind Western countries and other countries in providing debt to Nepal. Based on the data analyzed from FY 2016/17 to FY 2020/21, China has supported 380.45 (15%) million USD, whereas thirteen other countries, including India, Japan, the US, and the UK, have supported Nepal 2173.49 million (85%) USD. Similarly, the China-led multilateral institution-AIIB has provided debt to Nepal only 33.6 million Nepali rupees, which is 0.0015%, but the other eight multilateral institutions' debt to Nepal is 2915969.8 million Nepali rupees, which is almost 100% (99.998%). As far as country-wide debt is concerned, China's debt in Nepal is 97833.3 million Nepali rupees (26%). However, the other major nine countries' debt to Nepal is 275587.4 million Nepali rupees (74%). These are all the facts and figures that prove the discourse of China's debt under the BRI is only a myth but not a reality. Therefore, all the arguments about China's "debt trap diplomacy" in Nepal have been proven wrong from these research findings. Thus, the research has proven that the debate about China's "debt trap diplomacy" in Nepal is the effect of global strategic and political competition and confrontation. Therefore, the research recommends that the Nepal government dealing with China start implementing BRI projects in Chinese aid first, and the deficit budget can be fulfilled from soft loans.

Even in the case of Nepal, which has not received a single penny from the PRC under the BRI since it entered the program in 2017, there is no logic to the false debt narratives. Such narratives would ipso (?) facto nullify for Nepal unless it initiates any BRI projects. Additionally, the debt-trap argument will not apply to Nepal unless China has not influenced domestic politics by funding BRI projects there. However, until recently, China refrained from pursuing geopolitical objectives through the acquisition of strategic assets in Nepal to satisfy debt repayment. Certain indicators, such as China's reactive diplomacy toward US-sponsored MCC projects in Nepal, raised doubts about her long-standing noninterference and Panchasheel-based foreign policy toward a nation such as Nepal. However, given that the BRI is marketed as a win–win collaboration and that neither China nor Nepal have yet participated in debt-based BRI initiatives, the notion that Nepal is in a financial bind and "debt-trapped" is a false one, perpetuated by funded thinkers and the media.

11.4 Conclusion

It will be necessary to develop suitable supranational governance regimes by learning from the experiences of current regional cooperation initiatives. The development banks in particular, who are frequently the primary financiers, will need to come up with fresh ideas to transition from a national strategy as opposed to a regional strategy for financing and planning. They are summoned to create novel strategies for both the introduction and growth of capital markets of fresh tools for boosting private investment in infrastructure projects. To accomplish this goal, to create shared strategies, they will need to work together creation of new investment initiatives, and they must cooperate with each other to develop banking families to take advantages that are unique to them. When Nepal signed an MOU with China in 2017, all of the country's political parties supported the agreement, demonstrating the overwhelming acceptance of China's Belt and Road Initiative projects in that country. Nepali stakeholders were adamant that the BRI would revolutionize Nepal's socioeconomic development and alter the country's geopolitical and geoeconomic paths.

In this context, Nepal's frequent changes in government have made the implementation of the BRI too slow and nonfunctional. A few failed stories of Sri Lanka in the airport, etc., rumored to be a debt trap, have further stalled the BRI, and some political leadership in Nepal has even retracted from their previous commitment to implement the nine prioritized projects. However, Nepal is already a member of the BRI, and to further connectivity for trade and tourism-which ultimately serves to advance Nepal's national interests-she does require modern infrastructure.

References

Bilateral relations. Embassy of Nepal in Beijing, Embassy of Nepal in Beijing, May 2022, https://cn.nepalembassy.gov.np/bilateral-relations/.

Bhattarai, K. D., "Understanding BRI in Nepal", *The Annapurna Express*, March 24, 2023, https://theannapurnaexpress.com/news/understanding-bri-in-nepal-40041.

China Aid Post-Quake Reconstruction Projects in Nepal, The Embassy of China, October 23, 2021, http://np.China-embassy.gov.cn/eng/78085/chinaaid/202004/t20200416_1998209.html#:~:text=After%20the%20devastating%20earthquake%20shocked,renovation%2C%20disaster%20preparedness%20and%20health.

Chand, H. P., Trilateral engagement in Nepalese geopolitics: Soft, 2021, p.149.

Chand, H. P., Trilateral engagement in Nepalese geopolitics: Soft, 2021, p. 144.

Giri, A., "Wang visit: Nepal, China sign nine agreements, none on BRI", *The Kathmandu Post*,. March 27, 2022, https://kathmandupost.com/national/2022/03/27/wang-visit-nepal-China-sign-nine-agreements-none-on-bri.

International Development Cooperation, Ministry of Finance of Nepal, 2019, p. 1.

Jha, S., "Has Nepal Fallen Prey To China's Debt-trap Diplomacy Under BRI Projects Akin To Sri Lanka?", *Republicworld.com*, 2022, https://www.republicworld.com/world-news/China/has-nepal-fallen-prey-to-chinas-debt-trap-diplomacy-underbri-projects-akin-to-sri-lanka-articleshow.html.

Lowe, P., (2016) The rise of the BRICS in the global economy, *Teaching Geography*, Vol.41, No.2, 2016, pp.50-53.

Nepal graduation status, United Nations, https://www.un.org/ldcportal/content/nepal-graduation-status#:~:text=During%20the%20triennial%20review%20held,Developed%20Country%20(LDC)%20category.

Nepal-China Relations, Ministry of Foreign Affairs of Nepal, February 2019, https://mofa.gov.np/nepal-China-relations/.

"Nepal signs deal with China for supplies as fuel crisis deepens", *Reuters*, October 28, 2015, https://www.reuters.com/article/nepal-China-fuel-idUKKCN0SM23X20151028.

"Nepal, China sign bilateral cooperation agreement under Belt and Road Initiative", *Xinhua News*, May 12, 2017, http://www.xinhuanet.com/english/2017-05/12/c_136276949.htm.

Profiles of development partners, Kathmandu: Ministry of Finance of Nepal, 2014, https://mof.gov.np/uploads/document/file/20140820115245.pdf.

Pandey, A., "Economics and Influence: Chinese Investment in Nepal", Stimson, November 12, 2020, https://www.stimson.org/2020/economics-and-influence-chinese-investment-in-nepal/.

The world bank in China, The World Bank, April 20, 2023, https://www.worldbank.org/en/country/China/overview#:~:text=Results-,Since%20China%20began%20to%20open%20up%20and%20reform%20its%20economy, services%20over%20the%20same%20period.

Tiezzi, S., "China Steps In After Indian Fuel Stops Flowing to Nepal", *The Diplomat,* October 27, 2015, https://thediplomat.com/2015/10/China-steps-in-after-indian-fuel-stops-flowing-to-nepal/#:~:text=China%20will%20provide%201.3%20million,India%20continue%20to%20be%20disrupted.&text=China%20will%20supply%20gasoline%20to, disrupted%20supply%20lines%20with%20India.

"Ukraine war: India abstains from UN vote on Russian invasion", BBC, February 24, 2023, https://www.bbc.com/news/world-asia-india-64753820.

Chapter 12
China Came, China Built: The Economic Implications of SGR Development in Africa Within the Context of BRI

Michael Mitchell Omoruyi Ehizuelen

Abstract This chapter contributes to the ongoing debate on China's investments in the Belt and Road Initiative (BRI) on the continent of Africa by examining the potential economic benefits and challenges of the BRI in the development of railway projects with an emphasis on Abuja-Kaduna and Lagos-Ibadan Standard Gauge Railway (SGR). Other issues deliberated in this chapter include the emergence of a debt burden in the continent of Africa and how Africa and China would engage in the future to bolster Africa–China relations in BRI projects, especially transport infrastructure. With specific reference to the SGR in Nigeria, this article relies on secondary data from accessible published literature on railway transport infrastructure in Africa. This chapter's results reveal that (i) the Chinese-built SGR will bring about the socioeconomic development of Nigeria, (ii) from the levy levied on containerized conveyance, the SGR will contribute revenue to the Nigerian government, and (iii) through better rail connectivity, the SGR will help bolster trade and regional integration. The author recommends that to make BRI projects more transparent, it is necessary not only to have more stakeholder involvement in these projects but also to review the funding mechanism to make borrowing more affordable.

Keywords Africa · China · BRI · Nigeria · SGR

12.1 Introduction

Since the reform and opening-up period, China has developed a vibrant economy and opened up its foreign policy to the outside world.[1] Successful Chinese economic reforms have brought about formidable changes, placing China as a leading global economy. After four decades of economic reform, China has also shifted from internal

[1] Alexander (2016), Breuer (2017), Lauren (2019).

M. M. O. Ehizuelen (✉)
Institute of African Studies, Zhejiang Normal University, Jinhua, China
e-mail: mmacroe@yahoo.com

N. Peng and M. Y. Cheng (eds.), *The Reality and Myth of BRI's Debt Trap*, Indo-Pacific Focus, https://doi.org/10.1007/978-981-97-1056-0_12

reforms to a global strategy involving the BRI.[2] The BRI is the next step in China's global strategy after the reform and opening-up period, and it is important for job creation, infrastructural development, trade, investment, and other related developments for landlocked least developing nations in Africa. The BRI that was launched by Chinese President Xi Jinping in September 2013 is considered a novel worldwide development model. This is because within ten years after its launch in 2013, the BRI has grown from a concept to a key platform that has proven to be politically and economically effective.

Politically, by 2023, China has signed over 200 BRI cooperation pacts with 152 nations and 32 worldwide organizations, making China's BRI circle of friends not only growing but also making the initiative probably the grandest investment drive put forward by a single nation. As a result, some commentators think that the total spending of BRI will eventually, by 2027, reach 1.2–1.3 trillion USD, while others think, by 2049, it will fall within the range of 4 trillion USD and 8 trillion USD. The 147 pacts make up approximately half of all diplomatic pacts signed by China since 2012.

According to a recent report from the National Development and Reform Commission (NDRC) of China, economically, in 2021, China's trade in goods with BRI nations amounted to 11.6 trillion yuan, a novel increase over the previous eight years and a year-on-year surge of 23.6%, accounting for 29.7% of China's total foreign trade. The report further stated that in the same year, China's direct investment in the BRI nations totaled 138.45 billion yuan, up 7.9% year-on-year, accounting for 14.8% of the total outbound investment. The report added that the direct investment from the BRI nations in China reached 11.25 billion USD; this surpassed the 10 billion USD record for the first time.

Additionally, as an initiative that is making headway internationally, from 2013 to December 2021, China's involvement in the BRI via numerous construction contracts (frequently funded via China's financial institutions) and investments amounted to approximately 890 billion USD in nations of BRI. Apart from this, the business turnover of Chinese firms of the contracted projects in the various BRI nations registered 578.57 billion yuan, accounting for 57.9% of the total contracted abroad projects with more than 500 billion USD worth of Engineering Procurement and Construction (EPC) contracts signed.[3] Notably, as of 2021, 79 zones for trade and economic collaboration in twenty-four BRI nations have been constructed, with China investing 43 billion USD and generating 346,000 employment opportunities for local dwellers in the host economies.[4] Today, such a grandiose initiative that is unprecedented in the worldwide economy has turned out to be the most vital, far-reaching project the Chinese government has ever embarked on, making it one of the most discussed subjects about China's evolving role in the global economy.[5]

---

[2] Breuer (2017), Renwick et al. (2018).

[3] Deloitte (2018).

[4] Xiang (2019).

[5] Valare and van Putten (2015).

On the continent of Africa, the BRI provides the continent with the opportunity to reverse its anti-industrialization process due to the continent's failed adjustment guided by the West's "structural reforms" in the 1980s. Therefore, being part of the BRI enables the continent to reverse that and, in turn, actualize Aspiration 2 of the African Union Agenda 2063, the African Union vision to create more infrastructure links on the continent. These are also some of the reasons why out of 54 nations reviewed, 52 African nations, as well as the African Union Commission, have already signed agreements on cooperation under the initiative seeking to complement the continent's infrastructural gaps, increase foreign investment, expand trade, and ultimately reduce poverty. Among the first African nations to sign the MoU were Cameroon, Somalia, and South Africa as early as 2015. The most successful accession year was 2018, when 28 African nations entered the BRI.

During the first year of the COVID-19 pandemic, no new MoUs were signed, but in 2021, Botswana, the Democratic Republic of Congo, Eritrea, the Central African Republic, Guinea-Bissau, Sao Tome and Principe, and Burkina Faso revived the BRI's expansion. Malawi signed the latest MoU in March 2022. As of April 2022, only Eswatini and Mauritius have not signed the MoU.[6] In other words, approximately 96% of all African nations have already signed an MoU. Since Mauritius signed a Free Trade Agreement (FTA) with China in 2019, a future BRI MoU is likely. Thus, not having signed the MoU does not exclude bilateral trade agreements. While several studies have been performed on the impacts of the BRI in Asia and Europe, few exist on the continent of Africa. With reference to some existing studies, it is not clear what the gains and challenges of BRI projects are likely to be in the continent of Africa.

Therefore, this chapter aims to investigate the potential economic gains that the development of railway transport projects may bring to Africa by focusing on Nigeria. This will add to the continuing discussion on whether investment from China concerning its BRI infrastructure projects on the continent of Africa is actually mutually beneficial to Africans. The crucial issues deliberated on comprising the economic gains of the SGR in Nigeria, the economic challenges of the SGR given the emergency issues of debt burden in Africa, and how Africa and China would engage in the future to deepen Africa-China relations in BRI projects, especially transport infrastructure. As stated earlier, this chapter depends on secondary data from accessible published literature on railway infrastructure on the continent of Africa with specific reference to SGR in Nigeria.

12.2 China's Infrastructure Involvement in Africa

China's interest in supporting Africa's railway development dates back to the construction of the Tanzania-Zambia (Tanzam) railway, completed and handed over to the Zambian government in 1976. The railway is China's largest foreign aid project

[6] Xuewu et al. (2022).

in Africa ever. China financed the Tanzam railway approximately five decades ago, under the leadership of chairperson Mao Zedong and then premier Zhou Enlai, at a time when China was facing financial difficulties and just emerging from the tumultuous years of the Cultural Revolution. The Tanzam railway was built between 1970 and 1975, at the cost of a billion yuan (billions of US dollars at today's rates) in interest-free loans, with 50,000 Chinese workers helping to build the 1860 km of tracks, stretching from the Zambia copper Port on the Indian Ocean. Ian Taylor affirms that during the Cold War, such infrastructure projects that had the potential to inscribe China's vision of China–Africa cooperation permanently across a broad East African landscape under Mao Zedong were distinctly more ideological in purpose.[7] Nevertheless, the railway was intended to provide a transport corridor to African nations that circumvented the need to enter imperialist Apartheid, South Africa.

China's current infrastructure involvement in the continent of Africa, while more commercial in nature, is linked to the popular proverb originating in the planned-economy era that states 'to become rich, build a road first'-a principle that has also helped orchestrate the Chinese booming and increasingly urban-based economy. The Chinese proverb seems to also hold true for African nations. This is because according to the African Development Bank (AfDB) sponsored Program for Infrastructure Development in Africa (PIDA) study, which recognized priority projects for immediate implementation estimates, the average annual growth rate of 53 African economies will be 6.2% between 2010 and 2040. In addition, thirty-seven of these economies are anticipated to exhibit an average yearly growth rate higher than 5% during 2008–2040.[8] Although Africa has enormous potential for growth, the continent is yet to climb the value chain in mineral processing manufacturing, which would assist Africa in unlocking its complete potential for natural resources. The continent of Africa has great potential to "leapfrog" development stages, but one of the key factors hindering African nations from accelerating development in all spheres and reaching the global value chain is the deficit in the infrastructure sector.

China is aware of the above-mentioned infrastructure implications within the context of China–Africa cooperation. Therefore, China's activities on the continent of Africa that have been largely uncoordinated and mutually less supportive are increasingly integrated into the ambitious Chinese BRI. Presently, the continent's infrastructure is largely financed by traditional Official Development Assistance (ODA), Organization for Economic Cooperation and Development (OECD) investors and non-OECD actors comprising India, Gulf States, and China, with China being far the largest financier.[9] Reports from Deloitte and Zhang affirm that China has participated in over 200 African infrastructure projects to date. Chinese firms have completed and are building projects in various African nations that will assist in adding and upgrading approximately 30,000 km of highways and 2000 km of

[7] Taylor (1998).

[8] "Closing the Infrastructure Gap Vital for Africa's Transformation", Programme for Infrastructure Development in Africa (PIDA), African Development Bank (AfDB) (2010).

[9] Foster et al. (2009).

railways.[10] The Deloitte report added that although African governments continue to finance the largest share of projects, particularly in the transport sector, the Chinese influence on the continent is snowballing, with close to one in every five projects financed by China.[11] As a result, China is presently seen as the single largest financier of infrastructure on the continent of Africa, having surpassed the African Development Bank, the European Commission, the European Investment Bank, the International Finance Corporation, the World Bank, and the Group of Seven (G7) nations combined.

As a single financier of the continent of Africa's infrastructure, the money for financing infrastructure usually comes from the Export–Import Bank of China (EIBC). As an export credit agency offering loans on a bilateral basis, it is worth noting that before the bank gives out loans, it must first evaluate the level of concession by considering the nature of the project. Part of the bank's attractiveness is that the loans are offered at subsidized and relatively low-interest rates and with a maturity period of 15 years or more. In November 2013, the EIBC announced that by 2025, China will have provided the continent of Africa with 1 trillion USD in funding, including direct investment, soft loans, and commercial loans. The bank's competitive edge is that it permits borrowing nations that do not have enough financial guarantees to use their natural resources as collateral for infrastructure development. This funding model is known as the "Angola model" or "resource-for-infrastructure agreement" or "swap formula".[12] This funding model has come in for serious criticism; for the researchers at Brookings, using resources as collateral tends to reinforce the 'resource curse' of recipient nations.[13] Apart from the EIBC, the Chinese government's commitment also comes through mechanisms such as the South–South Fund, the Asian Infrastructure Investment Bank (AIIB), the New Development Bank (NDB), the Contingency Reverse Agreement (CRA), and the infrastructure fund of the AfDB.

With these Chinese financial commitments through these financing mechanisms stated above, infrastructure collaboration with China under the BRI should be a top priority for the African government. This is because the continent of Africa's participation in the BRI can help African economies "leapfrog" directly into the global economy by building a well-targeted infrastructure to support competitive firms and sectors in industrial parks and export-processing zones linked to worldwide markets. Using the continent's limited resources for infrastructure more wisely for novel investments and maintenance will help all African economies leverage these zones to attract light manufacturing from more advanced economies, as "Asian Tigers" did in the 1990s and China in the 1980s. By attracting foreign investment and companies, even the poorest African economies can advance their trade logistics,

[10] Deloitte (2018), Zhang (2018).

[11] Deloitte (2018).

[12] Ehizuelen (2020).

[13] China's Aid to Africa: Monster or Messiah (2018).

surge the knowledge and skills of local entrepreneurs, gain the confidence of national buyers, and increasingly make local companies competitive.[14]

Of strategic importance to Nigeria is the construction of railway lines connecting the hinterland of the region to coastal ports. This is one major area of the Chinese strategic relationship with Nigeria, the building of rail infrastructure, which is gradually positioning Nigeria as a modern economy globally. China Civil Engineering Construction Company (CCECC), a subsidiary of China Railway Construction Company, is involved in the building of these multiple infrastructure projects across the nation, an enormous economic value that has been added to Nigeria's development narrative.[15] Major projects include the Abuja-Kaduna SGR line linking the nation's capital Abuja to Kaduna, a trade and transportation hub in northwestern Nigeria, and the Lagos/Ibadan SGR, which is the first double-track standard gauge modern railway in West Africa linking Lagos, Nigeria's former economic capital to Ibadan, the former administrative capital of southwestern Nigeria, and the Lagos/Kano railway, which is an ambitious project linking the two most populous cities in southern and northern Nigeria. The project is part of Nigeria's greater project to champion the extension of rail lines from land-locked nations to coastal states of the Benin Republic, Togo, Ghana, and other African nations as part of the effort to sufficiently benefit from the opportunities presented by the African Continental Free Trade Agreement (AfCFTA).

12.3 Chinese Investment in the SGR in Nigeria

This section aims to contribute to the literature on the impact of Chinese infrastructure investments through the construction of SGRs in Africa with an emphasis on the Abuja-Kaduna Rail Line and Lagos-Ibadan Rail Line in Nigeria by exploring the projects' benefits and challenges.

In Nigeria, rail transport can be traced back to the colonial administration. During this period, the colonial administration took over with the intention of connecting the northern and southern parts of Nigeria. They started the connection in 1898 by constructing a 32 km railway that goes through Iddo in Lagos State to Otta in Ogun State. In 1901, it was expanded to Ibadan, the capital city of Oyo State constituting a 193 km rail network. In 1912, the construction of the rail line was expanded to Ilorin, the capital city of Kwara State, and finally extended to Kano in the same year; this was the first rail line constructed in Nigeria. After the completion of the first rail line, the construction of the second rail line started in 1913. This rail line ran from Port Harcourt, the capital city of Rivers State, passing through Aba, Enugu, Jos, Kafanchan, and ended at Kaduna in 1923.

[14] Jobs for Youth in Africa: Improve the Quality of Life for the People of Africa (2018).

[15] Chen (2018).

Apart from constructing the rail line to go through these states, in 1958, it was later extended to pass from Kanfanchan through Bauchi and finally ended at Maid-uguri.[16] These various single-track narrow-gauge rail lines were basically used to convey cash crops such as cocoa from the west and palm oil from the east to the seaports.[17] However, the colonial masters' aim for constructing these rail lines was for easy exportation of Nigeria's mineral resources and agricultural resources such as groundnuts, cocoa, cotton, and palm produce for the development of Great Britain.[18] This is one of the reasons the West developed a large amount of infrastructure leading out of the continent; however, China has done the reverse by leading infrastructure inside inland Africa. Notably, during the colonial period, the transport sector was known for substandard railways, so it was not adequate for a competent and rewarding economic activity within Nigeria.

Today, the above-mentioned existing railway network inherited from the British colonial era is outdated and inadequate to handle modern freight and passenger volume. The deteriorating railway has decreased transportation efficiency, resulting in increased transport costs and travel delays, contributing to hindered economic growth. This necessitated the modernization of railway transport in Nigeria by constructing the SGR. This mega infrastructure project is a case of a strategic government-to-government project with major implications for Nigeria's economy. Moreover, the Nigerian government has not adequately maintained the existing rail system. As a result, in 2002, after decades of neglect, the government under President Olusegun Obasanjo commissioned a twenty-five-year strategic vision to modernize the railway network; this vision was amended and ratified again in 2012. The railway modernization initiative plan aimed to rehabilitate and transition existing rail routes while permitting high-speed train operations on the railway network toward higher-capacity standard-gauge tracks and to connect all thirty-six major states and economic hubs by new railway networks; hence, the 8.3 billion USD project awarded to CCECC in 2006 marked the start of the initiative.[19]

However, the project could not be implemented due to funding problems. This is because, since the fall in the price of oil in the international market, it has been difficult for the nation to finance its rail transport infrastructure because the Nigerian economy is to some extent a mono-economy that depends only on one source of foreign exchange earnings-petroleum. Therefore, faced with the phasing out of the Highly Indebted Poor Countries initiative and a decline in official development assistance, Nigeria has seized the opportunity provided by China's healthier balance sheets and continued economic growth to explore new sources of funding. It is in this context that China turns out to be vital because through the BRI, China has come at the right time when Nigeria is in critical need of infrastructure development and improved global trade opportunities. China, leading the group of emerging economies called BRICS (Brazil, Russia, China, and South Africa), has been investing heavily

[16] Chukwurah et al. (2022).

[17] Ochei and Mamudu (2020).

[18] Chidi (2022).

[19] Chen (2018).

in infrastructure. The nation's ambitious, infrastructure-motivated BRI has made infrastructure financing a key source of Nigeria–China debt.

Given the current financial situation in Nigeria, sovereign debt funding is inevitable given that Nigeria's budgetary resources are not enough to facilitate the development agenda of Nigeria. As such, if China is willing to provide support, it should be a welcomed move. As a way of the Nigerian government welcoming China's financial backing, the railway modernization initiative plan was later rescoped into different stand-alone segments, and the existing 1.124 km Lagos-Kano rail line was rehabilitated. Hence, in 2012, the Nigerian government signed a construction contract with CCECC, a Chinese state-owned enterprise to build the Lagos/Ibadan SGR, which is currently the first double track standard gauge modern railway in the West African region. This railway connects Nigeria's former economic capital to Ibadan, the former administrative capital of southwestern Nigeria. The 156-km Lagos/Ibadan SGR was funded by a 1.3 billion USD concessional loan from EIBC and approximately 182 million USD from the Nigerian government. The Lagos-Ibadan SGR became fully operational on 15 June 2021.

For the Abuja-Kaduna SGR, the construction contract was signed in 2006, and it has survived three administrations. Initially, it was conceived by the Olusegun Obasanjo administration in 2006, commenced by the Goodluck Jonathan administration in 2011, completed in 2014, and commissioned by the Buhari-led government in 2016. The 187 km Abuja-Kaduna SGR track that links the nation's capital Abuja to Kaduna, a trade and transportation hub in northwestern Nigeria, was inaugurated on July 26, 2016, and was partly financed by Chinese credit lines for an estimated cost of 874 million USD. The EIBC provided 500 million USD as a concessional loan for the railway project, and the remainder was provided by Nigeria's federal government.[20] Both SGRs are among the most important projects for Nigeria's economy, as they link commercial capital to the rest of the nation.

While both Abuja-Kaduna and Lagos/Ibadan SGRs offered services to over 1.5 million passengers and closed numerous decades-old chapters of reliance on colonial infrastructure, both SGRs are also a critical section of the broader 11.1 billion USD Lagos-Kano standard-gauge north–south railway (2733 km) being constructed by CCECC. The other standard gauge line projects in the pipeline consist of Lagos-Benin city (300 km), Benin-Abakiliki (500 km), Benin Obudu Cattle Ranch (673 km), Lagos-Abuja high-speed (615 km), Zaria-Birnin Koni (520 km), Eganyi-Otukpo (533 km), and Eganyi-Abuja. Other projects scheduled are the Portharcourt-Maiduguri line (1657 km), Ogoja-Maiduguri, Kano-Gamboru Ngala, Kano-Jibia, and Ilela-Minna rail lines. The Lagos-Ibadan/Abuja-Kaduna Railways share several key characteristics and policy goals with the Addis Ababa-Djibouti line in East Africa; the Nigerian government plans to streamline logistics by connecting the two railways to major industrial cities and hence encourages exports from different industries. However, unlike the Addis Ababa-Djibouti Railway, the Lagos-Ibadan Railway is poorly connected with existing inland industrial bases, raising concerns

[20] Chen (2018), Ehizuelen (2020).

over logistics efficiency and, ultimately, the potential for the Lagos-Ibadan Railway to replicate the modest economic gains attributed to the Addis Ababa-Djibouti line.

All these abovementioned SGRs are significant steps in the Nigerian goal of a modernized rail network. Therefore, the Chinese government's investment modernized the corridor that offers Nigeria a port for foreign trade, which has the potential to add to Nigeria's industrialization and help the Nigerian government promote the diversification of the Nigerian economy. Speaking of China, the commitment displayed by the Chinese government in delivering these two projects on time despite the refusal of other foreign actors to finance the project is often pointed to by the Chinese as a symbol of their friendship and commitment to Nigeria. The construction of the railway served as a blueprint for future large-scale Chinese projects in Nigeria. The Chinese government's investment in rail line modernization has helped the Nigerian government reduce the travel time between Abuja, Nigeria's capital, and Kaduna, the nation's commercial hub, and since the Lagos/Ibadan SGR connects Lagos, Ogun, and Oyo, the three major states in southwest Nigeria, and uses trains with potential speeds of up to 150 km/h; it has also reduced the travel time for these cities and environs. Passengers can now travel from one city to the other in one hour and cargo in one and a half hours. These two mega infrastructure projects are specifically vital because it was Nigeria's personal idea, unlike the prior railways that were built by the British during the nineteenth century. The scale and cost of the two railway projects were designed to improve logistical efficiency, increase capacity to transport passengers and freight, and generate comprehensive benefits for local economies along the railways.

12.4 Economic Benefits and Challenges Linked with Investment in SGR

12.4.1 Economic Benefits Linked with Investment in SGR

The absence of railway transport in the transportation system of many African nations, including Nigeria, has heavily impacted other modes of transportation, such as roads and waterways, in these African nations. As a result, railway development has been featured in China's wider BRI across the continent of Africa and specifically in Nigeria. Nevertheless, it is worth saying that at the onset, Nigeria's primary purpose for the construction of railways was partly for administrative purposes: to provide a connection between the northern and southern parts of the nation. On the other hand, the construction of the railway was partly for economic reasons: that is, to convey both mineral resources and agricultural products from the hinterland to seaports for onward shipment to Europe.[21]

---

[21] Adewale et al. (2020).

However, in recent times, contrary to this primary reason mentioned, the Chinese government has stressed the contribution of BRI peace and poverty reduction by promoting the progress and prosperity that emanate from economic connectivity. Railways are an integral part of this formula. The intrinsic advantages of railways over road networks lie in their economies of scale: railways need less frequent maintenance and have higher speed and efficiency over long-distance routes, making them a highly advantageous low-cost option for freight traffic and offering enormous potential for trade promotion. Furthermore, the new railway hubs could help to attract investment and migration to previously underdeveloped hinterlands and provide enormous benefits for Nigerian producers by linking Nigeria's underdeveloped but resource-rich inland regions with wealthier coastal consumer markets and port cities. Lowering inland transport costs-an enormous problem for agriculture and manufacturing industries-would improve the competitiveness of Nigerian firms against imports and potentially promote the export and trade of Nigerian products.

Equally, rail transportation has significant positive spillover effects for complementary industries in upstream manufacturing supply chains, such as steel and construction materials, and creates demand for retail and services, all of which promote employment opportunities. In addition, the central trunk corridor would be useful in opening up the mining and agricultural industries in the northern part of Nigeria, especially in middle-belt and plateau states. This is one of the reasons the northern cattle and leather industries that are at present disadvantaged against cheap imports due to high transport costs would benefit from the Abuja-Kaduna SGR. Furthermore, the Abuja-Kaduna SGR has positively impacted local economies by supporting domestic enterprises and generating novel opportunities for local dwellers. The areas around the SGR stations, along the routes, or towns where the trains stop are set for increased economic activity. This includes sprouting markets, hotels, and a surge in transport and trade that has transformed the living standard of the people close to the SGR.

Some scholars affirm that when entrepreneurs or producers are assured of timely target markets for their produce, processing plants are bound to naturally sprout, creating even more employment opportunities for the host communities.[22] For example, in my interview with Shuaibu Ibrahim, a father of five children who now operates a provision store at the railway station and one of the approximately 100 youths whose source of livelihood is directly tied to the Rigasa station, he said: "In less than a year I have been able to build a house; when I worked for an oil company for years I could not acquire even a plot of land. The train station has not only changed the lives of those of us doing business here but has also brought development to the entire Rigasa community.[23]

In another interview with Musa Usman, a former truck driver, who is another beneficiary of the train service as he now operates a transport business at Rigasa station that boasts one car and two tricycles, all of which he acquired in less than two years he had been at the station-said: "Before the train service was introduced,

[22] Irandu and Owilla (2020).

[23] Ehizuelen (2020).

I used to work for CCECC as a truck driver. When I started here, I did not have my own tricycle. I have now acquired two tricycles and a car. I acquired my first tricycle on a hire-purchase basis; most of us who started like that now fully own the vehicles, having completed the payment".[24] In line with the above statements, macroeconomic studies by Ernest Liang and Thomas Rawski cited from Köll have made convincing arguments that cities and villages along certain railroad lines benefit from increased transportation and communications options that have stimulated the commercialization of agriculture as well as a change in the livelihood of local dwellers.[25] According to their interpretations, lower transaction costs resulted in higher incomes for farmers, facilitated the integration of their products into the national market system, and even linked them to international markets.

For the infrastructure development linked to the Chinese-built Lagos-Ibadan railway corridor, connecting the southwestern cities of Lagos, Nigeria's most populous city, with Ibadan, its third most populated through Abeokuta, the railway is well suited for the movement of large numbers of intercity passengers and high volumes of containerized cargo or bulk freight such as oil, coal, steel, or agricultural produce. The SGR will help to substantially reduce the time and money lost to persistent traffic gridlock at the seaports in Lagos, where roads are regularly clogged with hundreds of trucks and tankers queuing to gain access to the port. Causing a more severe problem to the congestion is the many checkpoints that road haulage must contend with—within the Apapa and TinCan Port axes, there are over thirty checkpoints. All these challenges are some of the reasons why Nigeria is losing approximately NGN140 billion (341 million USD) weekly to traffic gridlock on Apapa ports' access roads.[26]

Based on the above, residents and commuters of the Apapa and TinCan Port axes see the construction of the Lagos-Ibadan SGR as a whole progress that will help solve the existing gridlock problem caused by the craters on the road coupled with the reckless attitude of the tanker and heavy-duty drivers that ply the route to transport fuel and consumer goods from the port. This benefit is substantial since it boosts trade in the South–West corridor with a ripple effect on the national economy. With the construction of the Lagos-Ibadan rail line, the road life span will surge, while the cost of road maintenance will be reduced to the barest minimum, thereby saving the Nigerian government from losing millions of dollars to weekly traffic, as stated above. In addition, with the construction of the SGR, importers operating in the landlocked area that borders Nigeria using Lagos ports will become much more viable.

Furthermore, the Lagos-Ibadan railway creates an end-to-end logistic supply chain with consumer goods and refined petroleum products currently conveyed by the railway directly from the Apapa and TinCan Port quaysides in Lagos to the Inland Container Depot in Ibadan. From there, they can be distributed efficiently to other parts of Nigeria and beyond.[27] Likewise, the two SGRs have improved the efficiency

[24] Ibid.

[25] Köll (2019).

[26] NIGERIA: New Lagos-Ibadan Railway Opens to Freight, Offering Improved Cargo Flows (2021).

[27] Ibid.

of freight transport by shortening the journey time between the cities in which they operate. The economic impact of intraregional road linkages always brings development to the region and upgrades the commercial structure of the economies of the immediate users and impacts the state's economic growth in general. It is evident that when the movement of goods and services is hindered by poor road infrastructure, there will be a direct impact on the local economy of the consumer of these services and goods; as such, a rise in price will be experienced. Furthermore, sustainable public transport gives numerous economic advantages to the nation, moving goods and services to where they can be used more efficiently. The Abuja-Kaduna railway infrastructure that started operation in July 2016 has been efficient in creating this service for its users. It was observed that because of the Abuja-Kaduna railway, the movement of goods and services increased by 35%, and it attracted small-scale commercial activities to the locality.[28]

Beyond providing safety and comfort for travelers, railway lines have improved business and trade between cities in Nigeria. It also contributes to the economic development of the nation. Due to the cumulative number of people purchasing train tickets, 565,385 passengers traveled by railway in the second quarter of 2021 (update to 2023), which is more than the 108,238 passengers recorded in the second quarter of 2020.[29] Due to this increasing number of passengers, the *Premium Times* reported that revenue generated in the second quarter of 2021 by train travel amounted to 1.084 billion naira against 892.467 million naira in the first quarter of the year. The report further stated that in December 2021, at least 300 million naira were generated monthly from the Abuja-Kaduna train service. Making this known publicly, the former Nigerian Minister of Transportation, Chibuike Amaechi, said: "We make 300 million naira per month from the Abuja-Kaduna train. This fund that the Nigerian government generated from the Abuja-Kaduna rail station was used to run the Lagos-Ibadan railway. The minister added that at the end of the day, the railway authority pays back over 100 million naira to the Federal Government".[30] Since 2022, the monthly revenue has increased from 300 million naira to 500 million naira; however, in 2023, the monthly revenue dropped from 500 million naira to 1 million naira due to security challenges linked to knapping.[31] Essentially, when the security situation normalizes and the railway is adequately exploited, the Abuja-Kaduna and Lagos-Ibadan SGRs could add a whopping sum of 7.5 trillion naira every year to the Nigerian economy.[32] Equally, with the 2023 Nigerian budget of 21 trillion naira, the Nigerian transportation sector alone could offer a quarter of the nation's budget. This could serve the Nigerian government as an alternative means of revenue creation and bring relief to a nation that is fiscally stifling.

Additionally, since the traffic pressure in Lagos is high, the Lagos-Ibadan railway will play a vital role in easing the traffic pressure on Lagos, producing a potential

[28] Raji (2020).

[29] Nigeria rail transport generates N1.1 billion in three months (2021).

[30] Ibid.

[31] Monthly revenue from Abuja-Kaduna train service drops from N500 million to 1 million (2023).

[32] Despite Insecurity, High Expectations on Road, Rail Sectors in 2023 (2023).

industrial center in the southern part of Ogun state, which is wealthy in a swath of unexplored land. The railway design has provisions for freight yards at the Apapa and TinCan port axes, Kajola and Ibadan along with the rolling stock factory and depots at Kajola, Omi-Adio and Abeokuta. In addition, the rolling stock factory that is under construction in Kajola will serve as a rail wagon assembly plant. The plant, which will be the first of its kind in Nigeria, is anticipated to create approximately 5000 direct and indirect job opportunities when finished while boosting socioeconomic activities in the environment as well. It is central in the production of spare parts and maintenance of the equipment needed for the railway modernization programme. Equally, it is anticipated to produce some parts of the wagon for the Abuja-Kaduna railway line. Furthermore, the train station could lead to the establishment of economic clusters and special economic zones (SEZs) or industrial parks such as the one in Lekki for logistics and another in Ibadan for manufacturing industries. This is because, for example, along the Lagos-Ibadan rail line, there are several vital manufacturing factories, such as the Nestle production factory, the British-American tobacco processing factory, and the Dangote Cement factory; likewise, there is the Ogun-Guangdong SEZ, which is within a few dozen miles of the railway line.

Likewise, the Abuja-Kaduna train station could lead to the establishment of economic clusters and SEZs or industrial parks such as the Abuja Industrial Park. The Abuja Industrial Park is strategically situated on 250 ha of land at the Idu Industrial Zone close to the Abuja-Kaduna railway station promised to be a development with the grain of boosting the much-needed presence of the private sector driven by entrepreneur activities in the nation's capital city. In addition, when fully established, these SEZs or industrial parks will offer employment opportunities to local communities and promote industrial development. Infrastructure investment coupled with SEZs and industrial park investment are dynamic in several African economies. The investment in SEZs and industrial parks could promote positive spillovers and help to unlock the nation's economic potential in value-added industries across the entire West African region via the complementary nature of trade-facilitating infrastructure that could spur export-oriented industrial zones. The industrial parks model, which has succeeded in China, is anticipated to also help spur industrialization in Nigeria. Apart from spurring industrialization in Nigeria, it will help manufacturers lessen the cost of sourcing inputs, lowering the overall cost of doing business and allowing them not only to remain competitive in the domestic market but also in the regional and international markets. Thus, some studies reveal that the expeditious implementation of the SGR could spur positive advancement for manufacturers and the wider business community.[33]

In terms of local hiring, it is worth mentioning that local hiring refers to the practice of hiring people who originate from investment recipient nations. In this section, local hiring refers to the employment of Nigerians in the Abuja-Kaduna/Lagos-Ibadan Rail Line. According to the World Bank report "Increasing Local Procurement by the Mining Industry in West Africa," the employment of local citizens is a relevant factor when assessing investments, as local hiring exposes local workers to the skills needed

[33] Kithinji (2016), Irandu and Owilla (2020).

to establish their own businesses, which contributes to local enterprise development. Africa is undergoing an unprecedented demographic change that will drastically transform the labor market in the continent and beyond.

Certainly, the recession that hit the worldwide economy and job market since COVID-19 struck African youth the hardest. As a result, based on the African Development Bank data, over 12 million youth enter the labor market yearly, while just 3 million formal employment opportunities are generated. With a median age of 25 years old, the continent of Africa is seen as the continent with the youngest population globally but is most hardly affected by unemployment and underemployment, particularly after the pandemic.[34] Therefore, improving employment opportunities is vital for a continent with the youngest population globally.[35] Based on this, enhancing employment opportunities is currently the main objective of African leaders' and policymakers' development strategies. While Chinese SGR projects have been praised for contributing to job creation in Africa, Chinese firms are also often accused of hiring Chinese workers instead of local workers on contracted projects, especially those related to infrastructure and mining.[36] Therefore, it is important to analyze local hiring to determine whether Chinese-built SGRs have contributed to the creation of jobs in the Abuja-Kaduna and Lagos-Ibadan Rail Lines.

It is worth mentioning that the CCECC in the Abuja-Kaduna and Lagos-Ibadan line offered an employee localization strategy in their investment propositions, which favored the employment of local personnel during and after the construction of the projects. Both the Abuja-Kaduna and Lagos-Ibadan rail lines have already created several job opportunities, in contrast to widespread beliefs that firms from China import their own workers; notably, CCECC's localization strategy mandates a ten-to-one ratio of locals to Chinese employees. The firm estimates that the construction of the Abuja-Kaduna line itself created 4000 local jobs, and currently, approximately five hundred Nigerians are employed in operating the line.[37] According to *Premium Times*, during the construction of the Lagos-Ibadan line, over 20,000 workers were employed in the project, and only 560 of the workers were Chinese. The Lagos-Ibadan SGR is estimated to create 50,000 direct employment opportunities for Nigerian professionals and nonprofessionals and 100,000 indirect employment opportunities during railway construction. Furthermore, the railway construction is estimated to generate over 20,000 permanent jobs for those that will be involved in the operation, maintenance, and management of the railway after construction. Equally, among the 50,000 direct employment opportunities created, the report indicated that 26,000 direct employment opportunities will be for the professional cadre: management staff, engineers, foremen, operators, artisans, etc., and 23,800 for nonprofessionals.[38]

The employment aspect of the two SGR projects follows the local content law inherent in the 1.6 billion USD contract agreement between Nigeria and China.

[34] Jobs for Youth in Africa: Improve the Quality of Life for the People of Africa (2018).

[35] Beegle and Christiaensen (2019).

[36] Dollar (2016).

[37] Chen (2018).

[38] Over 20,000 Nigerians employed for Lagos-Ibadan Rail project-Amaechi (2023).

Notably, the Nigerian government did not seem to have established any regulations for the firm to incentivize local hiring. Studies on Chinese investments in Africa typically claim that Chinese firms bring workers from China instead of employing local people. Nonetheless, the findings in this paper show that the CCECC in Nigeria contributed to job creation during the construction of the project and operations and maintenance. Chinese firms' contributions to local hiring are significant due to Africa's challenge in generating enough jobs for the continent's expanding workforce. It is important to note that although the CCECC hired local personnel for the two SGRs in Nigeria, locals allege that they received unfair wages and treatment from their Chinese managers. These accusations indicate that the companies' localization strategies were focused on providing jobs and not necessarily on the conditions of these jobs, which is an issue that needs further consideration.

As with local hiring, the CCECC in the Abuja-Kaduna and Lagos-Ibadan line specified in their investment proposition their plan to train locals and to transfer the projects' operations and maintenance to local firms upon completion of their contracts. In both cases, the local governments awarded the firms with operations and maintenance contracts after the projects were concluded due to a lack of locally trained staff. As exemplified by the works of Klaver and Trebilcock, these authors present a related argument by observing that the projects carried out by Chinese investors in Africa have few benefits and high costs.[39] Klaver and Trebilcock, along with Adisu and Sharkey, suggest that Chinese investments' transfers of technology, skills, and employment to Africa remain limited.[40] However, the Lagos-Ibadan and Abuja-Kaduna projects prove otherwise, as the firms claim to have followed their investment proposition. They seem to have established diverse programs for local training and had concrete dates for transferring the projects' operations and maintenance to locals. These technology transfers may ultimately contribute to fostering locals' expertise in railways, which can promote the development of local businesses.

Even so, the dearth of local engineering capacity necessitates continued Chinese management and maintenance. The firm has been proactive in running training initiatives and technology transfer hubs for local engineers, including courses on railway maintenance, signals, and communications systems; staff at the Department of Transport also traveled to China for training on railway network management. For instance, 150 Nigerians were trained as engineers in China; in addition, the Chinese have built two training institutions for Nigeria, one in Idu in Abuja and the other, which is the Transportation University in Daura, Kastina State. The two institutions will focus on the research and development of human capital for the nation's transport sector. It is expected to mark a new level of growth and boost economic and educational development in Africa's largest economy. Notably, technology and skills transfer necessitate a long-term systematic investment in local capacity building, which entails the prolonged participation of Chinese firms. In sum, China supporting the

[39] Klaver and Trebilcock (2011).

[40] Adisu and Sharkey (2010).

Nigerian government to build railways such as the Abuja-Kaduna railway is potentially changing the former trade, agriculture, and investment trends laid down by the colonialists, as well as the livelihood of the local dwellers.

12.4.2 Economic Challenges Linked with Investment in the SGR

Rail transportation has long been established in various parts of the world as one of the most important, commonly used, and cost-effective modes of commuting and goods carriage. The various rail projects embarked upon by the Federal Government of Nigeria are therefore highly commendable, as they will contribute significantly to easing the movement of people and goods across the nations and solve the high rate of insecurity, including kidnappings of road passengers. With the construction of the SGR, travelers who traded the activities of bandits, robbers and kidnappers can breathe a sigh of relief. The travelers who practically see the SGR as a good development in the transport sector of Nigeria also felt comfortable with the presence of security personnel on board the train.[41] Nevertheless, although travelers see the SGR as a remarkable development, it is also one of the most scrutinized Chinese mega-projects in Nigeria. As a result of scrutiny, in recent years, Chinese mega-projects such as the Lagos-Ibadan and Abuja-Kaduna SGRs have not been without controversies and allegations that include funding arrangements, opaque contracts, economic viability, costs, debt sustainability and corruption.[42] The speedy expansion of Chinese mega infrastructure projects is supported through debt-based finance, raising questions over African economies' rising debt levels and their sustainability.

Furthermore, the SGR project has bred tensions over the impact of construction on the local community's livelihoods. In particular, there has been tension within local communities regarding employment opportunities. In some cases, the local dwellers demanded that their folks be the only people employed in the various construction projects taking place in their communities. Additionally, during the construction of any project, tensions usually developed over land ownership, especially compensation payments, which galvanized local dwellers, putting them against both Chinese contractors and local authorities. Disputes over wages, land compensation, supply contracts and environmental impacts have also been sources of disagreement within and between local communities, the local authorities, and the Chinese contractors. For the environmental aspect, the CCECC did not seem to have had an investment proposition in terms of the environment for the two SGRs used in this paper. Although the Nigerian government's Environmental Impact Assessment Decree requires all projects to conduct environmental impact assessments along with feasibility studies

[41] Abuja-Kaduna train: Weighing the cost of insecurity (2022).

[42] Wissenbach and Wang (2017).

before projects are awarded to contractors, the construction of the two SGRs was "permitted to proceed without a feasibility study being conducted".[43] This claim indicates that the Nigerian government did not establish specific environmental standards for the construction of the project. Although neither the CCECC nor the Nigerian government set environmental requirements for the construction of the two SGRs, Tovar's study indicates that there were no complaints regarding the CCECC's environmental practices during the project.[44]

While the negative environmental impact that the two SGRs may have had remains unclear, the project has the potential to positively contribute to the environment. The development of a rail line from Abuja to Kaduna and from Lagos to Ibadan has reduced traffic in the cities, as the line provides an alternative to automobile transportation powered by electricity. This makes the rail line more energy efficient and a sustainable mode of transportation. As a result, the rail line has contributed to the decline of the pollution generated by vehicle traffic in both cities.[45] Hence, the Abuja-Kaduna SGR and the Lagos-Ibadan SGR offer an environmentally friendly transportation system for cargo and passengers. In terms of the use of local natural resources, the CCECC did not specify in its investment proposition its materials sourcing plan for the construction of the two SGRs. Therefore, it is not clear whether the CCECC imported building materials or sourced them locally. The rail line needed access to government-owned land between Abuja and Kaduna and between Lagos and Ibadan. According to Chen, the government's ownership of the land used for the project was a key factor in the successful completion of the rail line, as there were no issues with land grabbing and appropriate monetary compensation for locals.[46]

12.4.3 *Role of the SGR in Bolstering Africa–China Cooperation*

Following the "Ten Major Cooperation Programs" and the "Eight Major Initiatives" jointly formulated and implemented within the framework of the Forum on China–Africa Cooperation in 2018, investments in infrastructure, manufacturing, mining, agribusiness, industrial parks, and other areas have started gaining momentum. Additionally, in the 8th Ministerial Conference of the Forum on China–Africa Cooperation (FOCAC) held in Dakar, Senegal from 29 to 30 November 2021, China and Africa jointly prepared the China–Africa Cooperation Vision 2035. In the first three years of the Vision, China intends to work closely with Africa to implement nine programs in line with the "Ten Major Cooperation Programs" and the "Eight Major Initiatives" initiated in 2018 that include healthcare, poverty reduction and agriculture, trade

---

[43] The Second Data Collection Survey on Mass Rapid Transit in the Federal Republic of Nigeria (2014).

[44] Tovar (2019).

[45] Ibid.

[46] Chen (2018).

promotion, investment, digital innovation, green development, capacity building, people-to-people exchanges, and peace and security, with the aim of fostering internal growth drivers in African nations. Moreover, the action plan will be implemented in tandem with the BRI and in line with the African Union (AU)'s Agenda 2063, Africa's strategic framework for the socioeconomic transformation of the continent and the 2030 Agenda for Sustainable Development Goals (SDGs). China has already started implementing these programs and initiatives in African nations; for instance, in the area of infrastructure, China, through Chinese firms, has supported the Nigerian government in constructing various infrastructure projects, such as deep seaports, airports, rail lines, telecommunication, hydropower, and economic and trade cooperation zones. These projects are energizing and bringing significant changes to the economic and social development of Nigeria.

With the construction of the SGR from Abuja to Kaduna and Lagos to Ibadan, a new era of Nigeria–China cooperation started in earnest. This is because as a strategic nation that serves as a gateway to West Africa and needs investment in infrastructure and China, the fastest growing economy in the world wants to invest in Africa's infrastructure. The construction of the SGR is aimed at opening up a fast-growing and gradually integrating region to China and worldwide trade and investment.[47] Since infrastructure development is seen as one of the most crucial components of Nigeria–China cooperation under the BRI, it is worth saying that through the BRI, the movement of passengers and cargo has been enhanced. Infrastructure development has been recognized by numerous researchers, including the multiplicity of global infrastructure-financing initiatives, such as the BRI, the European Union's (EU), and the Partnership for Global Infrastructure Investment (PGII), announced by the Group of Seven (G7) at the Leaders' Summit, the Nigerian government, in recent years not only as a vital economic growth facilitator in the fight to attain social and economic stability but also as the backbone of economic development activities for many industrialized and emerging economies,[48] with the goal of collectively "mobilizing the sum of 600 billion USD by 2027 in financing infrastructure projects globally." Therefore, as one of the notable infrastructure-financing initiatives, with respect to Nigeria, the BRI aims not only to boost industrialization and support the Nigerian government to solve the dearth of adequate and reliable transport but also to build a community of a shared future.

Therefore, recent SGR project development under the BRI is a unifying factor and instrument for promoting harmony, bolstering interdependence, and minimizing conflict situations, not only for Nigeria but also for the entire continent of Africa.[49] In line with Nigeria's vision of becoming the world's top 10 economies by 2050, the SGR infrastructure is among the flagship megaprojects in the region that centers on strengthening the regional framework for infrastructure and economic expansion. Based on this, it is important to mention that the construction of the SGR and other

47 Irandu (2018).

48 Pradhan and Bagchi (2013), Lakshmanan (2011), Kabiru et al. (2022), Adebukola Daramola (2022).

49 The Transport Situation in Africa (2009), Oluchi (2018).

BRI projects encourages the Nigerian government to coordinate economic policy for broader, deeper, high-standard Sino-Nigeria cooperation.

As a way of deepening Sino-Africa relations, through the BRI, China–Africa cooperation promotes a new type of global shared and inclusive modernization. This new type of cooperation will help China and African nations jointly create an open, inclusive, and balanced economic cooperation architecture that will benefit all and leave no one behind. Specifically, the initiative will build a relationship of trust, help in quick attention to problematic issues, reduce costs considerably, build institutional linkages and breakdown barriers to cooperation between African nations and China. As a way of deepening the relations under the BRI, China and African nations undertake to create synergy between the China–Africa Cooperation Vision 2035, the Long-Range Goals for 2035 of China, the 2030 Agenda for Sustainable Development of the United Nations, and the Agenda 2063 of the African Union, therefore drawing a long-term blueprint for China–Africa practical cooperation.

Such a relationship stated above is vital for both sides because African nations receive China's investments and aid, exemplified by the BRI, while China obtains access to vital resources, export markets, and global support for issues the Chinese regard as sensitive, including the One China policy, human rights violations in Xinjiang, and suppression of democratic institutions in Hong Kong. Nevertheless, the relationship between China and African nations is severely unbalanced in favor of China.[50] *The Economist* report further claims that China has won the hearts of African leaders by being picked as the preferred partner for most infrastructure projects because of the Chinese government's financial capability, the rhetoric of its benign aims and the "noninterference" principle. No wonder this has been exemplified by China's 2021 Africa White Paper document, where the Chinese government stated in the document that its objective is centered on "providing more and taking less, providing before taking, and providing without asking anything in return."[51]

Nevertheless, while those sentiments are admirable in deepening China–Africa relations under the BRI, the BRI continues to draw both praise and criticism from "Sinopessimists," who see China through the lens of BRI as exploitative, which is not only already soaking up Africa's resources to fuel its own rapid industrialization but is also bound to destroy Africa's development potential in the process, with African nations having no chance to extract maximum benefits from such an unbalanced relationship.[52] Apart from the above allegations, others accused China of trapping the continent of Africa into unsustainable debt pacts that have overshadowed the discourse around Sino-Africa relations in Western media due to the extortionate rates that the Chinese government intends to enforce on BRI nations.[53]

---

[50] The Chinese-African relationship is important to both sides but also unbalanced (2020).

[51] Full Text: China and Africa in the New Era: A Partnership of Equals (2021).

[52] Amusan (2022).

[53] Chellaney (2017), Krakowska (2017), Zhang and Miller (2017), Mlambo (2022), Al-Fadhat and Prasetio (2022), Vines et al. (2022).

Deloitte's report shows that with the significant amount flowing from China, the average debt-to-GDP ratio in Africa has risen to 57%; as such, there are concerns.[54] These concerns made the former IMF managing director Christine Lagarde urge China to avert its "Belt and Road" infrastructure plan from driving up debt in the region.[55] Hurley and her coauthors affirm that the most vital concern is that the 8 trillion USD initiative will leave participating nations with debt "overhangs" that will hinder sound public investment and economic expansion.[56] Most nations in East Africa have performed better than other nations in Sub-Saharan Africa (SSA).[57] The IMF, on the other hand, has warned that at least 40% of low-income nations in the region are either in debt distress or at high risk of it. Notably, numerous nations on the continent of Africa, such as Chad, Eritrea, Mozambique, Congo Republic, South Sudan, and Zimbabwe, were considered by the IMF to be in debt distress at the end of 2017, while the IMF claims that Zambia, Ethiopia, and Djibouti have also been deemed at 'high risk of debt distress'.[58]

However, some "Sino-optimists" perceive China through the lens of BRI as the ultimate savior and reliable partner, able and willing to support the development of the continent of Africa under the BRI. They also hold the opinion that the BRI aims at sharing the "Chinese dream" of prosperity with African nations. Furthermore, they argue that BRI proclaims China's "ascendancy on the international stage" through the provision of public goods in the form of capital and technical services to other nations.[59] In addition to the "Sino-optimists" claim that certainly, China's rising FDI in Africa faces increasing risks and challenges. In particular, American analysts see enormous problems obscured by African governments and state-owned enterprises. The China–Africa Research Initiative (CARI) report presented by Johns Hopkins University School of Advanced International Studies (SAIS) reveals that between 2000 and 2019, Chinese financiers signed 1141 loan commitments worth the sum of 153 billion USD with African governments and state-owned enterprises. According to their investigations, some African nations are suspending or scrutinizing contracts with Chinese firms, most of which belong to the BRI, because they are feeling unable to repay their loans.[60] These developments triggered the discussion about the so-called "debt trap" from "Sino-optimists," into which China allegedly lures other nations for political reasons.

Other "Sino-optimists" argue that Chinese loans in Africa are a strategy by the "neocolonialist" to extract concessions on assets.[61] Nevertheless, some scholars think this is not true.[62] Other surveys have revealed little proof of a pattern demonstrating

[54] Deloitte (2018).

[55] OBOR Trouble: IMF Chief Christine Lagarde Sends This Big Warning to China Over BRI (2018).

[56] Hurley et al. (2018).

[57] African Economic Outlook 2018 (2018).

[58] World Economic Outlook, April 2019 Growth Slowdown, Precarious Recovery (2019).

[59] Wang (2016).

[60] Xuewu et al. (2022).

[61] Armel (2021), Alyaa et al. (2021).

[62] Ubi (2019).

that Chinese banks, acting at the government's request, are deliberately overlending or financing loss-making projects to secure strategic advantage for China, which in turn will lead to a "debt trap" among recipient BRI nations or make the Chinese act as "neocolonialists" to extract concession on assets.[63] The SAIS-CARI survey discovered that Chinese loans are not a major contributor to debt distress in Africa, identifying only six nations where China, among many other financiers, is contributing to heavy borrowing.[64] Additionally, Aid Data at the College of William and Mary analyzed the effect of Chinese-funded infrastructure on economic activity, and the outcome demonstrates that the positive economic spillovers of Chinese investment created a more equal distribution of economic activity.[65] Other empirical proofs reveal that Chinese actors were repeatedly needed to renegotiate initial conditions resulting in debt relief. Beijing granted at least 12.1 billion USD in global debt relief to several nations in 2020 and 2021. Among those officially confirmed were a 378 million USD debt cancellation by Kenya and a 110 million debt relief by Zambia.[66]

Regarding the actual situation of African nations, since 2000, the Chinese government has made nine commitments to cancel the debts of borrowing nations. For African nations that have not been able to repay their debts on time, the Chinese government has offered a variety of debt restructuring options to assist them in overcoming their difficulties, rather than using asset seizures and other means to require borrowers to pay off their debts. The SAIS-CARI finds that China restructured or refinanced approximately 15 billion USD of African debt between 2000 and 2019, without the "asset seizures" that nations such as the United States criticized in accusations of "debt traps". While some contractual provisions call for arbitration against the borrowing nations in the event of failure to repay the debt on time, there is no evidence that China has actually resorted to court enforcement of payments or the use of penalty rates.

Following the outbreak of the COVID-19 pandemic, the World Bank and the International Monetary Fund urged the G20 to establish a Debt Service Standstill Initiative (DSSI). Since it entered into force in May 2020, 48 nations eligible for the debt moratorium, most of them in Africa, have participated in the initiative before it expires at the end of December 2021. Generally, DSSI nations have shown a diversity of creditors over the past decades, with borrowing primarily coming from Paris Club official creditors, private banks, multilateral institutions, and China. In 2020, the share of DSSI nations borrowing from China rose from 2 to 18%, the share sold to European private creditors surged from 3 to 11%, and the share of external debt owed to Paris Club creditors decreased from 28% in 2006 to 10% in 2020.[67] It is worth noting that China, with 18% of the total share of external debt, became the most significant debt relief nation in this initiative. It suspended 5.7 billion USD in debt payments, contributing to more than half of the total global debt moratorium.

---

[63] Brautigam (2019).

[64] EOM et al. (2018).

[65] Bluhm et al. (2018).

[66] Xuewu et al. (2022).

[67] Ibid.

Through this action, 45% of debts owned by the poorest nations to China were suspended. In contrast, the United Kingdom (UK) had no suspension of payments on its commercial loans and still recovered 3.2 billion USD in debt from nations that applied for the debt standstill initiative.

To allow Chinese contractors and African nations to continue to enjoy the dividend of infrastructure investment as well as avoid a debt crisis in Africa, the recent FOCAC meeting explored new models of infrastructure development that include private sector participation in the BRI in Africa. In the new model, China will encourage Chinese-funded firms to adopt models such as public–private partnership (PPP) and BOT (build, operate, transfer) models to invest in the African industry for more localized production of African brands. Since China is willing to provide more flexible and innovative infrastructure financing, such as PPPs, BOTs, and swap formulas, especially if African governments request it, then it is worth noting that the PPP model coupled with the Chinese swap formula could solve Africa's financial constraints and cut African nations' dependence on raw materials.[68] The swap formula seems truly innovative since, for the first time, it appears that Africa's resources could be directly converted into development projects. The establishment of the abovementioned innovative initiatives made Xiang claim that debt trap diplomacy has been a Cold War mindset, demonizing China's loans as generating economic dependency on China. Xiang further stated that the BRI is helping lift nations out of a "trap of no development" rather than duping them into a "debt trap".[69]

Some experts who work on China–Africa issues have been quite perplexed by divergent views, particularly by some of the criticisms. It is important to position the BRI in a way that places the initiative on the cooperative rather than the competitive side. This is because China's contribution to several African nations' advancement has become the main aspect of these African nations' development strategies. Most of China's BRI projects in Africa address a desperate need for railways, ports, roads, and energy.[70] As such, it is noteworthy to say that Chinese loans are neither inherently good nor bad-they will be whatever African governments choose to make of the loans. As such, it is worth mentioning that China's involvement with African nations is far beyond building railways, bridges, and roads or providing large loans for African nations that will eventually drive them into risky levels of debt. China's involvement with African nations is about replicating the development model that works in East Asia and currently in China in Africa. Nevertheless, the Chinese development model has already found favor in some East African nations, which have embraced some aspects of the model through sizeable Chinese involvement in the region.

Therefore, with the introduction of Xi Jinping's signature programme, BRI, China intends to accelerate its engagement on the continent and ensure that the initiative has positive net benefits for African nations, but much will hinge on whether the China–Africa relationship can be placed on a more equal footing or not. First and foremost, BRI is a Chinese 'geopolitical project' designed to advance China's grand strategy. As

[68] Ehizuelen (2020), Xie and Qi (2021).

[69] Xiang (2019).

[70] Foster et al. (2009).

such, one of the challenges for African nations is in establishing where the continent of Africa's interest converges with China's interests, where they diverge, and how areas of convergence can enhance China–Africa's 'win–win strategy'. China should support African nations to move away from their global position as a 'commodity periphery'. It is imperative for African nations to work with China bilaterally, regionally, and continentally to establish where the entry points might be to access BRI funding. Taylor also noted that while China has an African policy regarding trade and investments, African nations and the African Union do not have a Chinese policy.[71] This can be seen in the nonexistence of Sino-African trade policies regarding investments in the continent of Africa that weaken the bargaining power of African leaders in their engagement with China. The absence of a clear-cut policy on the commercial relations between Africa and China means that predatory African elites may take advantage of advancing their selfish needs.

12.5 Conclusion

This chapter examines the potential economic benefits and problems of BRI in the development of railway projects with an emphasis on Abuja-Kaduna and Lagos-Ibadan Standard Gauge Railway (SGR). Other issues deliberated in this chapter include the emergence of a debt burden in the continent of Africa and how African countries and China would engage in the future to bolster Africa-China relations in BRI projects, especially transport infrastructure.

It has been established that an enormous infrastructure gap exists in Africa and that BRI investments fill the gap. Therefore, inserting African nations into the BRI route is about increasing the Chinese growing presence in global development on the continent through spending money and building large-scale infrastructure projects. The two SGR projects discussed in the paper are two mega infrastructure projects within the context of large-scale infrastructure projects financed by China in Nigeria under the BRI. Notably, the SGR has contributed to the socioeconomic development of Nigeria and, in the long term, is likely to spur economic growth and promote regional trade within the West African region under the Economic Community of West African States (ECOWAS). The railway projects reveal that China's financing of infrastructure projects has contributed much to addressing crucial impediments to industrial development. For instance, the two SGRs will provide a vital link between Nigeria and neighboring West African nations, thereby opening up an enormous area for trade and investments. However, to maximize these benefits and to avoid pitfalls of dependency, it is recommended that African nations, specifically Nigeria, should take a common position that serves its interests. This is lacking now.

The funding mechanism should also be reviewed. There should be a shift from commercial funding of BRI projects to more concessionary funding at lower interest rates and longer repayment periods. This will enable African nations to borrow to

[71] Taylor (2011).

finance BRI infrastructure projects at affordable costs. The funding of BRI infrastructure should also not be guaranteed through national assets such as ports or rail in case of default but should be guaranteed through government-to-government funding. At the national level, Nigeria should formulate policies that can enhance potential gains and limit the negative effects of BRI projects. This calls for proactive engagement from the Nigerian government side to ensure win–win cooperation. All Chinese firms wishing to invest in any BRI project in Nigeria should comply with national laws and regulations. The Nigerian government should ensure adequate stakeholder engagement in the award of BRI contracts. The Nigerian government should also diversify the nation's trading partners so that any downturn in the growth of the Chinese economy may not impede the economic growth of the nation.

References

"Abuja-Kaduna train: Weighing the cost of insecurity", *The Nation*, 2022, https://thenationonlineng.net/abuja-kaduna-train-weighing-the-cost-of-insecurity/.

"African Economic Outlook 2018", AfDB, 2018, www.afdb.org/en/Knowledge/publications/african-economicoutlook/.

"China's Aid to Africa: Monster or Messiah", *Brookings*, 2018, www.brookings.edu/opinions/chinas-aid-to-africa-monster-or-messiah.

"Closing the Infrastructure Gap Vital for Africa's Transformation", Programme for Infrastructure Development in Africa (PIDA), African Development Bank (AfDB), 2010, https://www.afdb.org/fileadmin/uploads/afdb/Documents/Generic-Documents/PIDA%20brief%20closing%20gap.pdf.

"Despite Insecurity, High Expectations on Road, Rail Sectors in 2023", *The Guardian*, 2023, https://guardian.ng/features/despite-insecurity-high-expectations-on-road-rail-sectors-in-2023/.

"Full Text: China and Africa in the New Era: A Partnership of Equals", *Xinhua News*, November 26, 2021, http://www.news.cn/english/2021-11/26/c_1310333813.htm.

"Jobs for Youth in Africa: Improve the Quality of Life for the People of Africa", African Development Bank, 2018, https://www.afdb.org/fileadmin/uploads/afdb/Documents/Generic-Documents/Brochure_Job_Africa-En.pdf.

"Monthly revenue from Abuja-Kaduna train service drops from N500 million to 1 million", *Daily Trust*, 2023, https://dailytrust.com/monthlyrevenue-from-abuja-kaduna-train-service-drops-from-n500m-to-n1m-nrc/.

"Nigeria rail transport generates N1.1 billion in three months", *Premium Times*, 2021, https://www.premiumtimesng.com/business/business-news/483837-nigeria-rail-transport-generates-n1-1-billion-in-three-months.html.

"NIGERIA: New Lagos-Ibadan Railway Opens to Freight, Offering Improved Cargo Flows", HKTDC Research, 2021, https://research.hktdc.com/en/article/Nzg3MjUzODI4.

"OBOR Trouble: IMF Chief Christine Lagarde Sends This Big Warning to China Over BRI", *Bloomberg*, 2018, http://www.financialexpress.com/world-news/obor-trouble-now-imf-chief-christine-lagarde-sends-this-big-warning-to-China-over-bri/1130440/.

"Over 20,000 Nigerians employed for Lagos-Ibadan Rail project-Amaechi", *Premium Times*, 2023, https://www.premiumtimesng.com/news/top-news/409512-over-20000-nigerians-employed-for-lagos-ibadan-rail-project-amaechi.html?tztc=1.

"The Chinese-African relationship is important to both sides but also unbalanced", *The Economist*, 2020, https://www.economist.com/special-report/2022/05/20/the-chinese-african-relationship-is-important-to-both-sides-but-also-unbalanced.

"The Second Data Collection Survey on Mass Rapid Transit in the Federal Republic of Nigeria", Japan International Cooperation Agency, 2014, https://open_jicareport.jica.go.jp/pdf/12245411.pdf.

"World Economic Outlook, April 2019 Growth Slowdown, Precarious Recovery", IMF, 2019.

Adewale E., Adegoriola, P. S. and Obida G. W., The Impact of Rail Freight and Passengers Volume On Economic Growth In Nigeria (1970–2017), 2020, file:///C:/Users/User%20pc/Downloads/ImpactofRailFreightandPassengersVolumeonEconomicGrowthinNigeria.pdf.

Adisu, K. & Sharkey, T., The Impact of Chinese Investment in Africa, *International Journal of Business and Management*, Vol. 5, No. 9, 2010, pp. 3–9.

Alexander, D., China's Belt and Road initiative&its implications for Africa, WWF Kenya, Nairobi Kenya, 2016.

Al-Fadhat, F. and Prasetio, H., How China's Debt-Trap Diplomacy Works in African Countries: Evidence from Zimbabwe, Cameroon, and Djibouti, *Journal of Asian and African Studies,* 2022.

Alyaa W. el-Shafei and Metawe, M., China drives toward Africa between arguments of neo-colonialism and mutual-beneficial relationship: Egypt as a case study, *Review of Economics and Political Science,* Vol. 7, No. 2, 2021, pp. 2631–3561.

Amusan, T., "What Nigeria Can Teach Us about China's Belt and Road", *The Diplomat*, 2022, https://thediplomat.com/2022/11/what-nigeria-can-teach-us-about-chinas-belt-and-road/.

Armel, K., China's Engagements in Africa: Is China a "Partner" or a "Predator"?, *Chinese Journal of International Review,* Vol. 3, No. 1, 2021.

Beegle, K., & Christiaensen, L., "Accelerating poverty reduction in Africa", The World Bank, 2019.

Bluhm, R., A. Dreher, A. Fuchs, P. Bradley, A. Strange, and M. Tierney, "Connective Financing: Chinese Infrastructure Projects and the Diffusion of Economic Activity in Developing Countries", AIDDATA, 2018, https://www.aiddata.org/publications/connective-finance-chinese-infrastructure-projects.

Brautigam, D., "Misdiagnosing the Chinese Infrastructure Push", *The American Interest*, April 4, 2019, https://www.the-american-interest.com/2019/04/04/.misdiagnosing-the-chinese-infrastructure-push/.

Breuer, J., "Two Belts, One Road?-The role of Africa in China's Belt and Road initiative", 2017, file:///C:/Users/User%20pc/Downloads/2018_MAERZ___OBOR-Afrika_Blickwechsel_JuliaBreuer%20(1).pdf

Chellaney, B., "China's debt-trap diplomacy", *Project Syndicate*, 2017, https://www.project-syndicate.org/commentary/China-one-belt-one-road-loans-debt-by-brahma-chellaney-2017-01?barrier=accesspaylog.

Chen, Y., "China's Role in Nigerian Railway Development and Implications for Security and Development", Special Report, The United States Institute of Peace, 2018.

Chidi, E.A, Emmanuel, E.U, Sambo S.A and Chijioke M.A, Decarbonization of the Transport Sector in Nigeria, *Environmental Health Insights*, Vol. 16, 2022, pp. 1–8.

Chukwurah, G.O., Okeke, F.O., Isimah, M.O., & Igwe, A.E., Assessment of the performance of railway transportation in Nigeria from 1970 to 2010, *Scientific African,* 2022, https://doi.org/10.1016/j.sciaf.2022.e01120.

Adebukola Daramola, "A comparative analysis of road and rail performance in freight transport: an example from Nigeria", *Urban, Planning and Transport Research*, Vol. 10, No. 1, 2022, pp. 58–81.

Deloitte, "If You Want to Prosper, First Build Roads", Africa Construction Trends Report, 2018.

Dollar, D., "China's Engagement with Africa", Brookings, 2016, https://www.brookings.edu/wp-content/uploads/2016/07/Chinas-Engagement-withAfrica-David-Dollar-July2016.pdf.

Ehizuelen M.M.O, Examining the importance of the Sino-Africa swap formula in creating backward and forward linkages, *Asian Journal of Comparative Politics*, 2020, pp. 1–33.

EOM, J., D. Brautigam, and L., Benabdallah, "The Path Ahead: The 7th Forum on China–Africa Cooperation", Briefing Paper, China Africa Research Initiative, John Hopkins University, 2018.

Foster, V. W. Butterfield, C, Chen, N. Pushak., "Building Bridges: China's Growing Role as Infrastructure Financier for Sub-Saharan Africa", The World Bank, 2009, http://siteresources.worldbank.org/INTAFRICA/Resources/BB_Final_Exec_summary_English_July08_Wo-Embg.pdf.

Heydarian, Richard Javad, "China's Silk Road Project: A Trap or an Opportunity?", *Al Jazeera*, 2017, http://www.aljazeera.com/indepth/Opinion/2017/05/China-silk-road-project-trap-opportunity-170514142652061.html.

Heydarian, Richard Javad, "China's Silk Road Project: A Trap or an Opportunity?", *Al Jazeera*, 2017, http://www.aljazeera.com/indepth/Opinion/2017/05/China-silk-road-project-trap-opportunity-170514142652061.html

Hurley, J., Morris, S., and Portelance, G., "Examining the Debt Implications of the Belt and Road Initiative from a Policy Perspective", Center for Global Development Policy Paper 121, 2018.

Irandu, E. M and Owilla, H.H., The Economic Implications of Belt and Road Initiative in the Development of Railway Transport Infrastructure in Africa: The Case of the Standard Gauge Railway in Kenya, *The African Review,* Vol. 47, 2020, pp. 457–480.

Irandu, E. M., The China–Africa Infrastructure Cooperation. The Case of the Standard Gauge Railway, Final Paper for the African Economic Research Consortium (AERC), October, 2018, Nairobi.

Kabiru H. I., Rossanto D. H., Wasiaturrahma W. and Tamat S., Services trade and infrastructure development: Evidence from African countries, Cogent Economics and Finance, Vol. 10, No. 1, 2022.

Kithinji, E., The importance of Standard Gauge Railway (SGR) Project to the East African Region, *International Journal of Current Business and Social Sciences*, Vol. 1, No. 5, 2016, pp. 15–32.

Klaver, M. & Trebilcock, M., Chinese Investment in Africa, *Law and Development Review*, Vol. 4, No. 1, 2011, pp. 168–217.

Köll E., *Railroad and the Transformation of China,* United States: Harvard University Press, 2019.

Krakowska, M., "China's One Belt One Road Initiative-A Push for Influence or Debt?", *New Eastern Europe*, 2017, http://neweasterneurope.eu/2017/09/27/China-s-one-belt-one-road-initiative-a-push-for-influence-or-debt.

Lakshmanan, T. R., The broader economic consequences of transport infrastructure investments, *Journal of Transport Geography*, Vol. 19, No. 1, 2011, pp. 1–12.

Lauren, J. A. (2019). The Belt and Road Initiative: what is in it for China?, *Asia & the Pacific Policy Studies*, Vol. 6, No. 1, pp. 40–58.

Mlambo, Courage, China in Africa: An Examination of the Impact of China's Loans on Growth in Selected African States, *Economies,* Vol. 10, 2022, p. 154.

Ochei M.C, Mamudu Z.U, Analysis of the contribution of the transport sector to economic growth in Nigeria, *IOSR Journal of Economic Finance,* No. 2, 2020, pp. 18–35.

"The Transport Situation in Africa", United Nations Economic and Social Council, 2009

Oluchi, J.N., "The Contribution of the Standard Gauge Railway (SGR) Toward Promoting Harmony in The East African Member States", Master's Degree Thesis, 2018, https://erepo.usiu.ac.ke/bitstream/handle/11732/4584/OLUOCHI%20JANE%20NTHENYA%20MAIR%202019.pdf?sequence=1&isAllowed=y.

Pradhan, R. P., and Bagchi, T. P., Effect of transportation infrastructure on economic growth in India: The VECM Approach, *Research in Transportation Economics*, Vol.38, No. 1, 2013, pp. 139–148.

Raji, M.A., Accessing the Impact of Rail Infrastructural Development in Abuja (Nigeria), *International Journal of Scientific&Engineering Research,* Vol. 11, No. 5, 2020.

Renwick, N., Gu, J. and Gong, S., "The Impact of BRI Investment in Infrastructure on Achieving the Sustainable Development Goals", K4D Emerging Issues Report, Brighton: IDS, 2018.

Taylor, I., China's foreign policy toward African in the 1990's, *The Journal of Modern African Studies*, Vol. 3, No. 36, 1998, p. 444.

Taylor, I., "China's Challenges: Africa", *The Diplomat*, 2011, https://thediplomat.com/2011/02/africa/.

Tovar, A., "Chinese Infrastructure Investments in Africa: A Case Study of the Addis Ababa-Djibouti Railway in Ethiopia and Djibouti and the Abuja-Kaduna Rail Line in Nigeria", Senior Theses. 25, 2019, https://fordham.bepress.com/international_senior/25.

Ubi, N. E., "How Africa Can Benefit from China's Belt and Road Initiative", Financial Nigeria, 2019, https://www.financialnigeria.com/how-africa-can-benefit-from-China-s-belt-and-road-initiative-blog-449.html.

Valare, J. and van, Putten, F.P., "One Belt and One Road: An Opportunity for EU's Security Strategy'", Netherlands Institute of International Relations, 2015.

Vines, A., Creon, B., and Yu J., The Response to Debt Distress in Africa and the Role of China, Research Paper, 2022, https://www.chathamhouse.org/sites/default/files/2022-12/2022-12-15-africa-China-debt-distress-vines-et-al.pdf.

Wang, Y., Offensive for defensive: The Belt and Road initiative and China's new grand strategy, *The Pacific Review*, Vol. 29, No. 3, 2016, pp. 455–463.

Wissenbach, U., & Wang, Y., African politics meets Chinese engineers: The Chinese-built Standard Gauge Railway Project in Kenya and East Africa, Johns Hopkins University, July 31, 2017, https://static1.squarespace.com/static/5652847de4 b033f56d2bdc29/t/594d739f3e00bed37482d4fe/1 498248096443/SGR+v4.pdf.

Xiang, B., "Why Belt and Road Initiative is anything but debt trap", *Xinhua News*, April 13, 2019, https://www.focac.org/eng/zfgx_4/rwjl/t1657677.htm.

Xie J. and Qi X., "Digital, green partnership among highlights in China–Africa cooperation during postpandemic period", *Global Times*, 2021, https://www.Globaltimes.cn/page/202111/1240020.shtml.

Xuewu G., Dinkelbach, C., Heidbrink, C.,Huang, Y., Xiaojun K, Maximilian M,, Hendrik W. O., "China's Engagement in Africa: Activities, Effects and Trends", Center for Global Studies (CGS), 2022, file:///C:/Users/User%20pc/Downloads/CGSChina_Africa_Study2022%20(1).pdf.

Zhang, Shu, and Matthew Miller, "Behind China's Silk Road Vision: Cheap Funds, Heavy Debt, Growing Risk", *Reuters*, 2017, https://www.reuters.com/article/us-China-silkroad-finance/behind-chinas-silk-road-vision-cheap-funds-heavy-debt-growing-risk-idUSKCN18BOYS.

Zhang, H., "The Ten Cooperation Plans between China and Africa Have Been Fully implemented, and China's Accumulative Investment in Africa has Exceeded 6 billion dollars", National Business Daily, September 3, 2018, http://www.nbd.com.cn/articles/2018-09-03/1251687.html.

SPRINGER NATURE

GPSR Compliance

The European Union's (EU) General Product Safety Regulation (GPSR) is a set of rules that requires consumer products to be safe and our obligations to ensure this.

If you have any concerns about our products, you can contact us on ProductSafety@springernature.com

In case Publisher is established outside the EU, the EU authorized representative is:

Springer Nature Customer Service Center GmbH
Europaplatz 3
69115 Heidelberg, Germany

The manufacturer's authorised representative in the EU is Springer Nature Customer Service Centre GmbH, Europaplatz 3, 69115 Heidelberg, Germany. If you have any concerns regarding our products, please contact ProductSafety@springernature.com

Printed and bound by CPI Group (UK) Ltd, Croydon, CR0 4YY
30/09/2026
02225314-0006